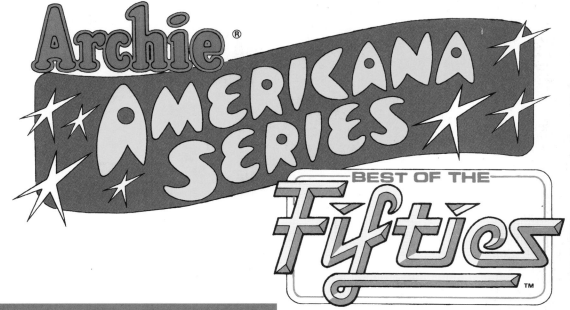

ARCHIE COMIC PUBLICATIONS, INC.

MICHAEL I. SILBERKLEIT
Chairman and Co-Publisher

RICHARD H. GOLDWATER
President and Co-Publisher

VICTOR GORELICK
Vice President / Managing Editor

FRED MAUSSER
Vice President /
Director of Circulation

Archie characters created by
JOHN L. GOLDWATER

The likenesses of the original
Archie characters created by
BOB MONTANA

Americana Series Editor: **PAUL CASTIGLIA**

Americana Series Art Director: **JOSEPH PEPITONE**

Front Cover Illustration: **REX W. LINDSEY**

Archie Americana Series, BEST OF THE FIFTIES, Volume 2, 1992. Third printing June 2001. Printed in CANADA. Published by Archie Comic Publications, Inc., 325 Fayette Avenue, Mamaroneck, New York 10543-23318. The individual characters names and likenesses are the exclusive trademarks of Archie Comic Publications, Inc. All stories previously published and copyrighted by Archie Comic Publications, Inc. (or its predecessors) in magazine form in 1953-1959. This compilation copyright © 1992 Archie Comic Publications, Inc. All rights reserved. Nothing may be reprinted in whole or part without written permission from Archie Comic Publications, Inc.

ISBN 1-879794-01-2

www.archiecomics.com

TABLE OF CONTENTS

4   **INTRODUCTION**
by Victor Gorelick

6   **WINNER LOSE**
This story exemplifies the rivalry between
Archie and Reggie for Veronica's affections.
Originally presented in ARCHIE COMICS #64,
September-October,1953

13   **SAFE AT HOME**
Focusing on a classic motif, this story
examines the relationship between Archie
and Mr. Lodge. Originally presented in
ARCHIE COMICS #64, September-October, 1953

18   **THERE OUGHTA BE A LAW**
A poignant tale exploring the eternal conflicts
between parents and children. Originally presented
in ARCHIE'S PALS & GALS #3, 1954-55 Edition

24   **A GALLERY OF CLASSIC '50s COVER GAGS
BY BOB MONTANA!**

25   **SKIP, HOP AND THUMP!**
In the Fifties, Sock-hop dances were
all the rage! Originally presented in
LAUGH COMICS #75, June, 1956

30   **RHYME NOR REASON!**
Although jingle contests were prevalent during
the heyday of radio in the Thirties and Forties, they
came into their own during Television's Golden
Age, the Fifties! Originally presented in
BETTY & VERONICA #27, November, 1956

34   **GOING, GOING, GOWN**
Even in the Fifties, fashion was a big part of
Betty & Veronica's lives! Originally presented in
LAUGH COMICS #80, April, 1957

40   **CALL TO ARMS!**
One of the funniest stories to appear
during the 1950's! Originally presented in
ARCHIE COMICS #86, May-June, 1957

45   **FAN CLUBBED!**
The Fifties saw the birth of rock 'n' roll--and
even Riverdale had its own would-be Elvis! Originally
presented in ARCHIE'S PALS & GALS #6, 1957-58 Edition

A CLASSIC 1950's ARCHIE AD! 51

THE GOOD OLD DAZE 52
A timely vignette featuring typical Fifties' jargon! Originally presented in BETTY & VERONICA #38, September, 1958

PIPE THE BAG 54
A bonnie good yarn highlighting Archie's Scottish ancestry! Originally presented in LAUGH COMICS #87, May, 1958

AWARD TO THE WISE 59
A hilarious romp that typifies the often slapstick predicaments of Archie and his friends! Originally presented in ARCHIE COMICS #93, July, 1958

WHEELS OF PROGRESS 65
The title of this story couldn't have been more ppropriate--every "with-it" Fifties' teen had rollerskates! Originally presented in LAUGH COMICS #98, May, 1959

A GALLERY OF CLASSIC '50s COVER GAGS BY BOB MONTANA! 71

CIRCLE SALE 72
The Fifties' hula hoop fad found teens across the country swiveling their hips--Archie and pals no exception! Originally presented in ARCHIE COMICS #101, June, 1959

LIKE REAL GONE 78
Dig this crazy, fabulous riff where Archie and Jughead get with the Fifties' "Beatnik" scene--like, it's the most! Originally presented in LAUGH COMICS #104, November, 1959

SPINNER WINNER! 84
Years before stunt skateboarding, teens engaged in the "daredevil" sport of plate-spinning--talk about your thrills, chills and *spills!* Originally presented in ARCHIE COMICS #105, November, 1959

T.N.T. HEE 90
The Cold War was in full swing in the Fifties, and this *explosive* story reflects the attitudes adopted in that Atomic Age. Originally presented in ARCHIE COMICS #106, December, 1959

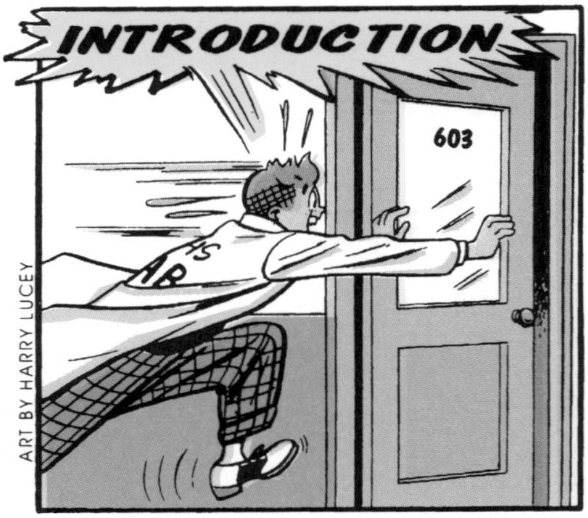
INTRODUCTION
603
ART BY HARRY LUCEY

Room 603. That's where it all started for me over 33 years ago. I had seen that room number many times, hand lettered in bright yellow coupons at the bottom of a page in one of my Archie Comics..."ARCHIE'S MECHANICS #3, ROOM 603, 241 Church St., New York 13, N.Y." This was the home of world famous Archie Comic Publications. When I walked through that door in September, 1958, I had no idea that room number 603 would change the course of my life forever.

My appointment was with Richard Goldwater, who had replaced Harry Shorten as editor one year earlier. I was being interviewed for a job in the art department as a production assistant, to replace Dexter Taylor, who was "going free-lance." He would be assisting Bob Bolling in writing and drawing LITTLE ARCHIE, which at that time was 80 pages and published quarterly. In the Fifties, as well as in the Forties, you would work in the art department as an assistant and learn all you could about comic production. Once you honed your skills, you would go free-lance as a writer, penciller, inker, letterer, colorist or a combination of any of the above. You had the freedom to work at home and mailed or delivered your work in once a week...beautiful.

When you entered room 603, the first thing you saw was a huge oil painting. It portrayed Archie sitting on a stone fence, holding a textbook. The background was the Riverdale High Campus, consisting of the school and a replica of Rodin's "Thinker." The receptionist peeked through her window, asked my name, and called into the art department for someone to usher me in to see Mr. Goldwater. I was brought into the art department and asked to open my portfolio on one of the counters. Richard Goldwater came in and introduced himself, as did Dexter Taylor and the production manager at that time, whose name was Sheldon Brodsky (no relation to Sol).

I can't remember much of what was said at my interview, except that everyone liked my color work. It consisted of animation storyboards, cels, humorous greeting cards and a magazine cover, all of which were art school projects. I had no professional experience. I was told by Richard that they were going to interview a few more applicants and would let me know. One week later, I received a phone call from Sheldon Brodsky to tell me I had the job and could start Monday. To this day, I don't know why they chose me (neither does Richard). I knew most of the other applicants and thought they had a lot more talent than I did. Maybe it was the fact that I said, "I'd even work for free!" My salary was pretty close to that. And so, on October 4, 1958, I began my career at Archie Comics.

Most of the artists working at Archie had started back in the Forties. They were Joe Edwards (Li'l Jinx), Sam Schwartz (Jughead), Harry Lucey (Archie), Bill Vigoda (drew them all) to name a few. But the Fifties brought writers like Frank Doyle, George

Gladir, Sy Reit and Tom Moore (who could also draw). It brought artist/writer Bob Bolling, whose Little Archie stories are still remembered and loved over 30 years later. However, the artists who had the most impact on Archie comics was Dan DeCarlo. His slick style, craftsmanship and dedication to his work is an inspiration to all who've had the privilege to know him, work with him, or see his work...and oh how he can draw those girls!

Working for Archie back in the Fifties, as told to me by the late Bill Vigoda, was tenuous to say the least. The comic book industry was still reeling from the effects of Doctor Wurtham's book, "Seduction of the Innocent," which blamed comics for the increase of crime and juvenile delinquency. Companies were going out of business, artists and writers were out of work. But Archie Comics' policy of producing good, clean, wholesome, family oriented comics kept the company from going under. This policy, by the way, exists even today.

In 1954, the Comics Code Authority was established. This was a self-regulating organization, consisting of comic publishers, distributors, printers and engravers. Comics were reviewed according to a list of guidelines. When approved by the code authority, the comic would receive a seal of approval. This would ensure the public that children would be purchasing good, clean, wholesome comics. My first assignment, as a new art assistant, was to remove cleavages and lift up low cut blouses on Katy Keene (we'll save her story for another book). Hey, someone had to do it.

But the code was no match for Harry Lucey. His sometimes suggestive storytelling, and he was one of the best, almost cost him his job. When his pencilled stories came in, the characters were dressed on page one only. The inker, a woman by the name of Terry Szenics, would have to clothe them on the remaining pages. However, Harry was as dedicated as they come. I remember Harry delivering a job 3 hours late. He came into the art department covered with blood. He had been hit by a car. Though not seriously hurt, he should have gone to a hospital. No way. He had to keep that deadline. He took some white paint, cleaned up the blood from the artwork and went home. Amazing.

Once a year, most of the artists and writers gather for the Archie Christmas party. It's almost like a tribal ritual, where stories of bygone days in the comic book industry are retold. One gets the feeling that some invisible spirit (no pun intended) is watching over them. Interestingly enough, most of these stories took place in the Fifties. After a few drinks, times and incidents become somewhat confused. But that, too, is part of the ritual.

It's funny, but when people think of Archie, they think of the Fifties. Maybe that's because it was a time when families stuck together. School was fun, teachers were goofy and friendships were important. It's the way we'd like it to be. So grab your Hula Hoops, play those Elvis records, dress up in your Poodle skirt, put the top down on your '57 Chevy and go back to the Fifties with Archie.

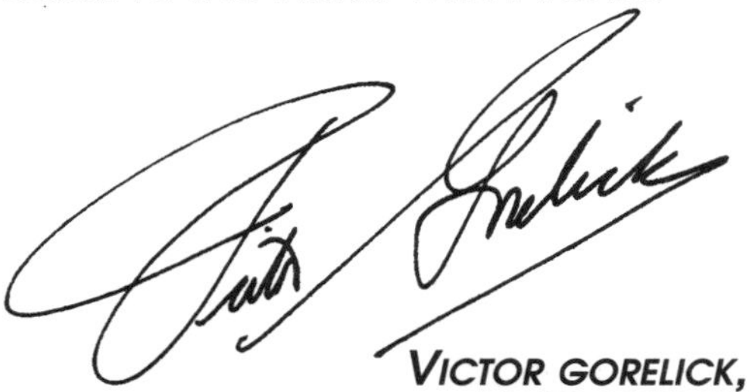

VICTOR GORELICK,
MANAGING EDITOR.

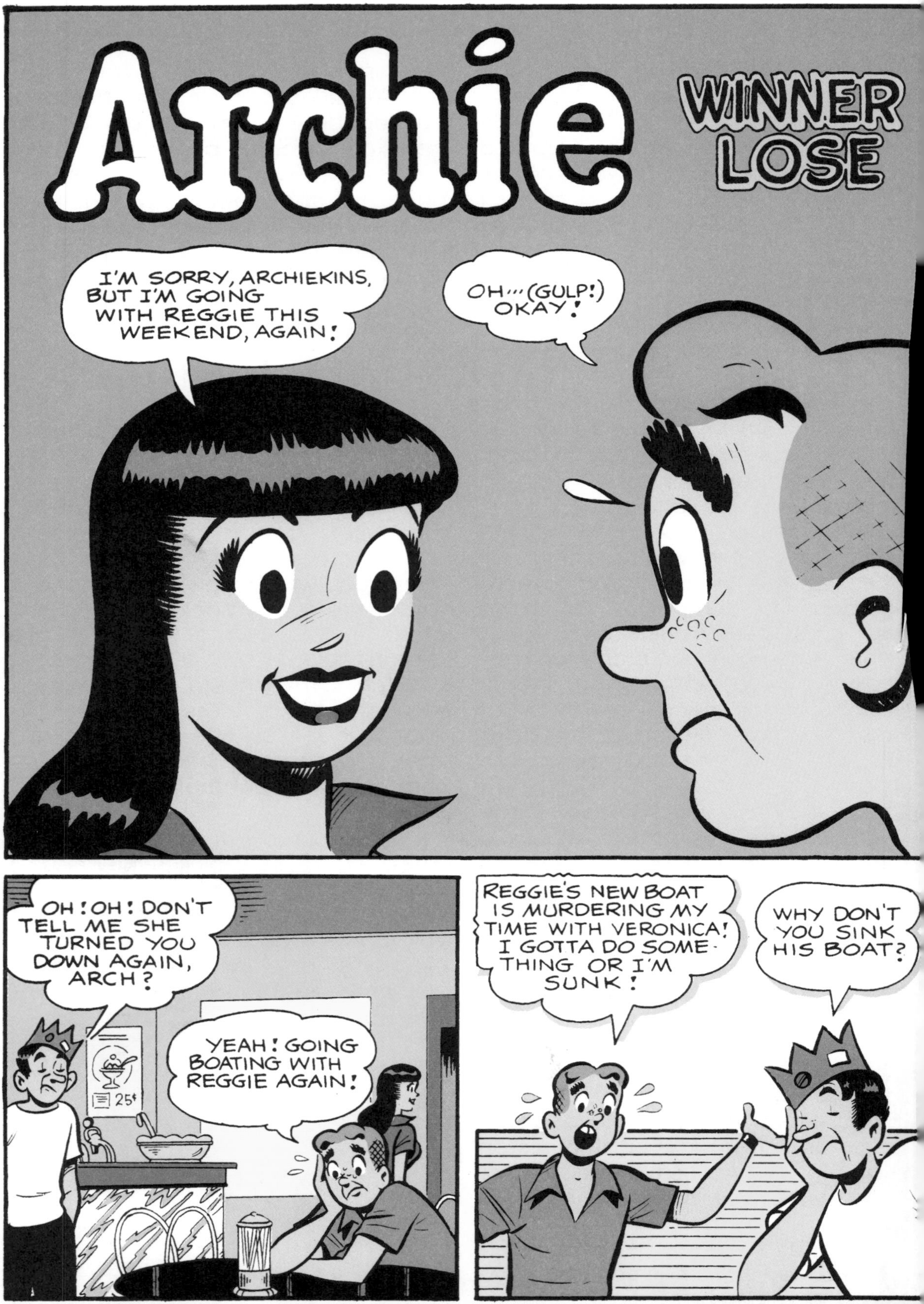
Archie
WINNER
LOSE
I'M SORRY, ARCHIEKINS, BUT I'M GOING WITH REGGIE THIS WEEKEND, AGAIN!
OH... (GULP!) OKAY!
OH! OH! DON'T TELL ME SHE TURNED YOU DOWN AGAIN, ARCH?
YEAH! GOING BOATING WITH REGGIE AGAIN!
25¢
REGGIE'S NEW BOAT IS MURDERING MY TIME WITH VERONICA! I GOTTA DO SOMETHING OR I'M SUNK!
WHY DON'T YOU SINK HIS BOAT?

ORIGINALLY PRESENTED IN **ARCHIE COMICS #64**, SEPTEMBER-OCTOBER, 1953.

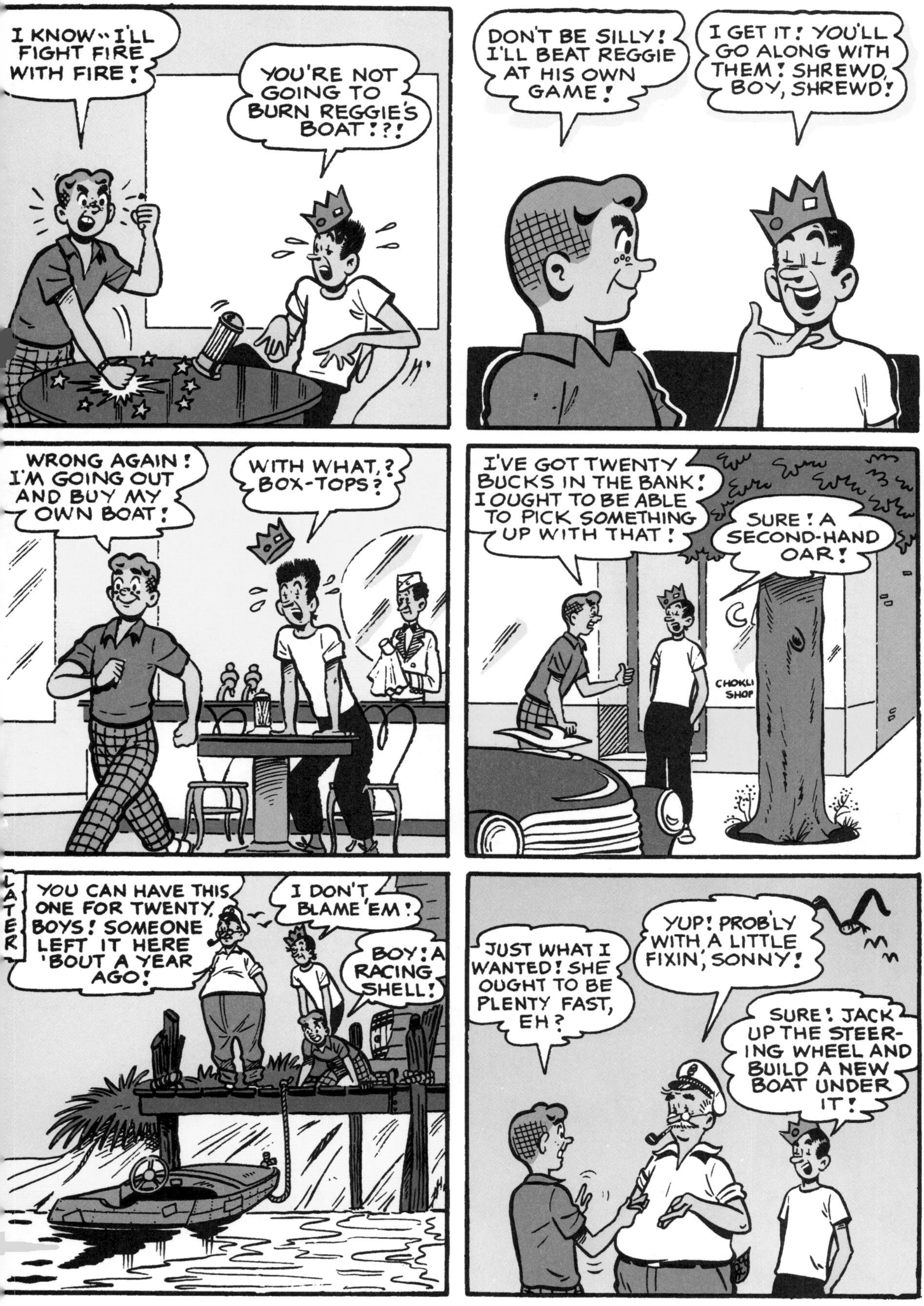
I KNOW -- I'LL FIGHT FIRE WITH FIRE!
YOU'RE NOT GOING TO BURN REGGIE'S BOAT!?!
DON'T BE SILLY! I'LL BEAT REGGIE AT HIS OWN GAME!
I GET IT! YOU'LL GO ALONG WITH THEM! SHREWD, BOY, SHREWD!
WRONG AGAIN! I'M GOING OUT AND BUY MY OWN BOAT!
WITH WHAT,? BOX-TOPS?
I'VE GOT TWENTY BUCKS IN THE BANK! I OUGHT TO BE ABLE TO PICK SOMETHING UP WITH THAT!
SURE! A SECOND-HAND OAR!
CHOKLI SHOP
LATER
YOU CAN HAVE THIS ONE FOR TWENTY, BOYS! SOMEONE LEFT IT HERE 'BOUT A YEAR AGO!
I DON'T BLAME 'EM!
BOY! A RACING SHELL!
JUST WHAT I WANTED! SHE OUGHT TO BE PLENTY FAST, EH?
YUP! PROB'LY WITH A LITTLE FIXIN', SONNY!
SURE! JACK UP THE STEERING WHEEL AND BUILD A NEW BOAT UNDER IT!

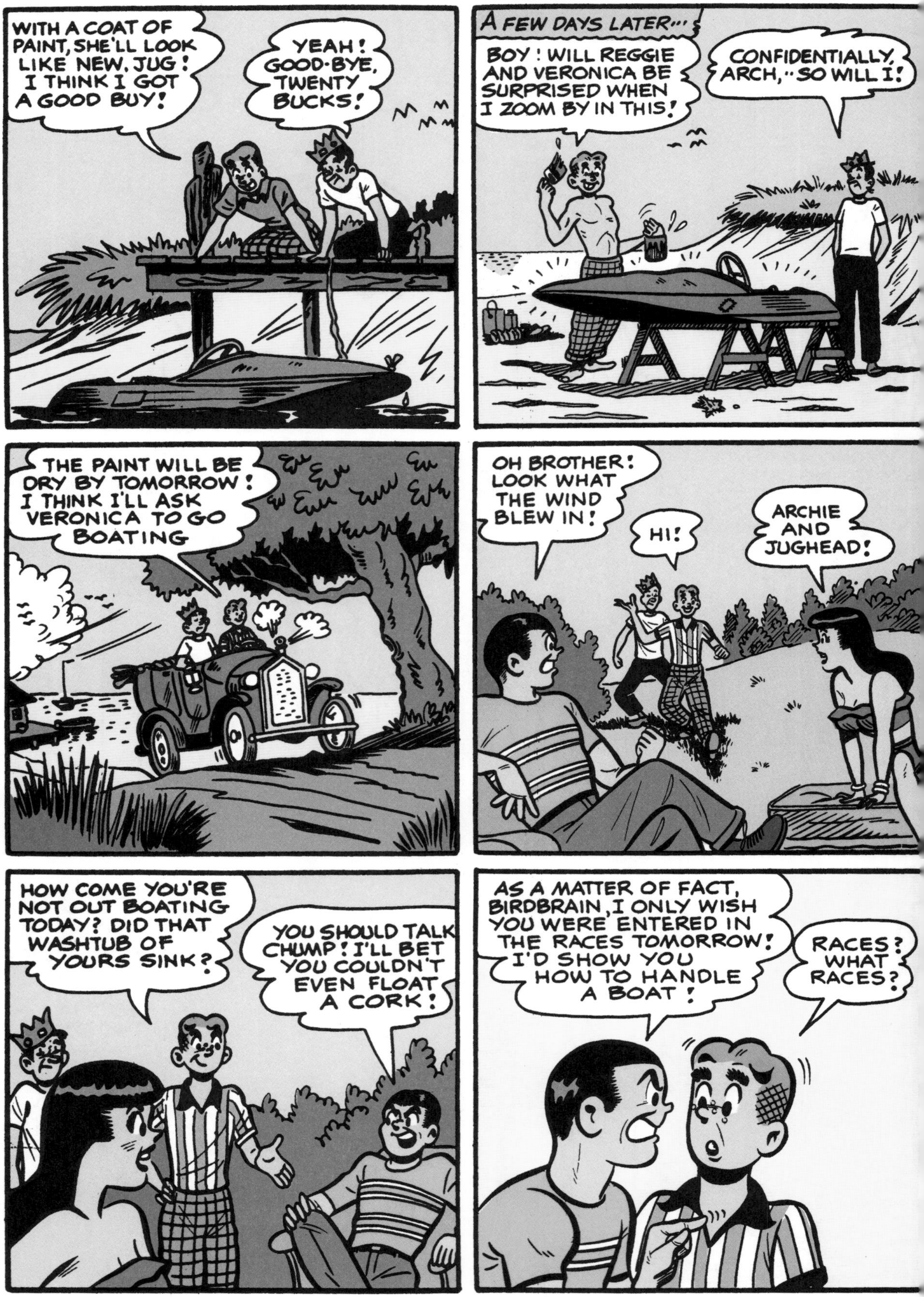
WITH A COAT OF PAINT, SHE'LL LOOK LIKE NEW, JUG! I THINK I GOT A GOOD BUY!
YEAH! GOOD-BYE, TWENTY BUCKS!
A FEW DAYS LATER...
BOY! WILL REGGIE AND VERONICA BE SURPRISED WHEN I ZOOM BY IN THIS!
CONFIDENTIALLY, ARCH,.. SO WILL I!
THE PAINT WILL BE DRY BY TOMORROW! I THINK I'LL ASK VERONICA TO GO BOATING
OH BROTHER! LOOK WHAT THE WIND BLEW IN!
HI!
ARCHIE AND JUGHEAD!
HOW COME YOU'RE NOT OUT BOATING TODAY? DID THAT WASHTUB OF YOURS SINK?
YOU SHOULD TALK CHUMP! I'LL BET YOU COULDN'T EVEN FLOAT A CORK!
AS A MATTER OF FACT, BIRDBRAIN, I ONLY WISH YOU WERE ENTERED IN THE RACES TOMORROW! I'D SHOW YOU HOW TO HANDLE A BOAT!
RACES? WHAT RACES?

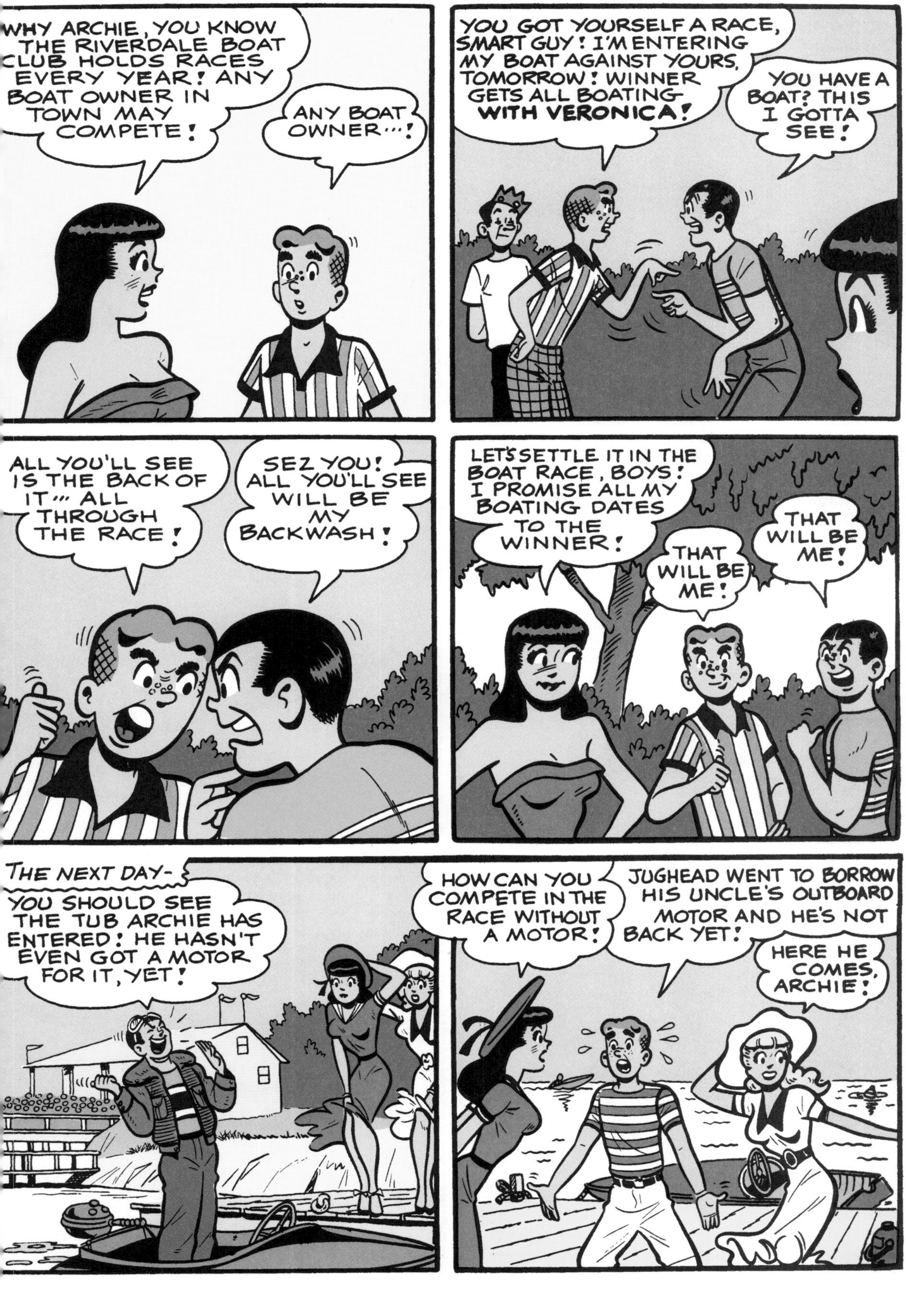
WHY ARCHIE, YOU KNOW THE RIVERDALE BOAT CLUB HOLDS RACES EVERY YEAR! ANY BOAT OWNER IN TOWN MAY COMPETE!
ANY BOAT OWNER...!
YOU GOT YOURSELF A RACE, SMART GUY! I'M ENTERING MY BOAT AGAINST YOURS, TOMORROW! WINNER GETS ALL BOATING WITH VERONICA!
YOU HAVE A BOAT? THIS I GOTTA SEE!
ALL YOU'LL SEE IS THE BACK OF IT... ALL THROUGH THE RACE!
SEZ YOU! ALL YOU'LL SEE WILL BE MY BACKWASH!
LET'S SETTLE IT IN THE BOAT RACE, BOYS! I PROMISE ALL MY BOATING DATES TO THE WINNER!
THAT WILL BE ME!
THAT WILL BE ME!
THE NEXT DAY-
YOU SHOULD SEE THE TUB ARCHIE HAS ENTERED! HE HASN'T EVEN GOT A MOTOR FOR IT, YET!
HOW CAN YOU COMPETE IN THE RACE WITHOUT A MOTOR!
JUGHEAD WENT TO BORROW HIS UNCLE'S OUTBOARD MOTOR AND HE'S NOT BACK YET!
HERE HE COMES, ARCHIE!

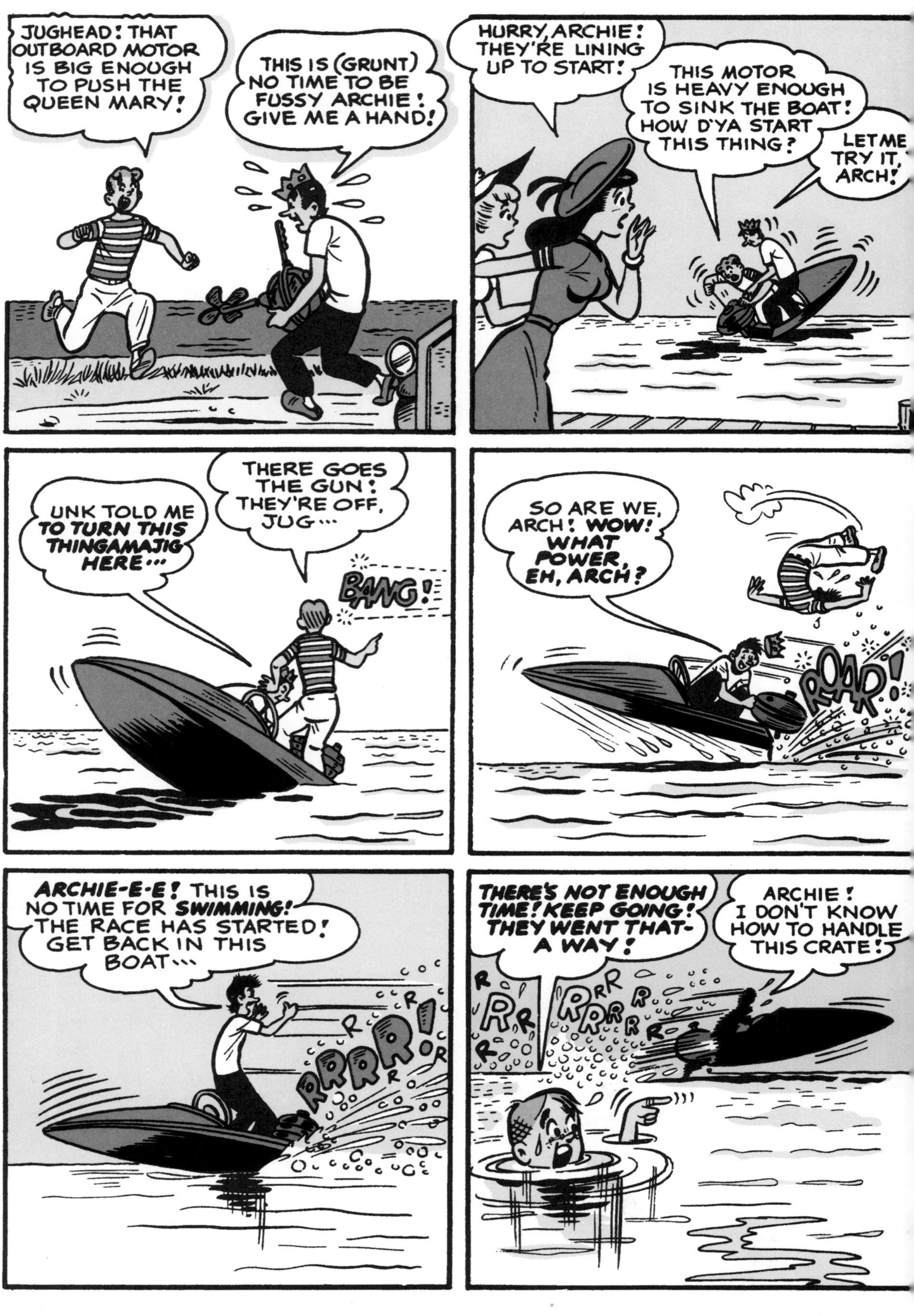

JUGHEAD! THAT OUTBOARD MOTOR IS BIG ENOUGH TO PUSH THE QUEEN MARY!
THIS IS (GRUNT) NO TIME TO BE FUSSY ARCHIE! GIVE ME A HAND!
HURRY, ARCHIE! THEY'RE LINING UP TO START!
THIS MOTOR IS HEAVY ENOUGH TO SINK THE BOAT! HOW D'YA START THIS THING?
LET ME TRY IT, ARCH!
THERE GOES THE GUN! THEY'RE OFF, JUG...
UNK TOLD ME TO TURN THIS THINGAMAJIG HERE...
BANG!
SO ARE WE, ARCH! WOW! WHAT POWER, EH, ARCH?
ROAR!
ARCHIE-E-E! THIS IS NO TIME FOR SWIMMING! THE RACE HAS STARTED! GET BACK IN THIS BOAT...
RRRRR!
THERE'S NOT ENOUGH TIME! KEEP GOING! THEY WENT THAT-A WAY!
ARCHIE! I DON'T KNOW HOW TO HANDLE THIS CRATE!

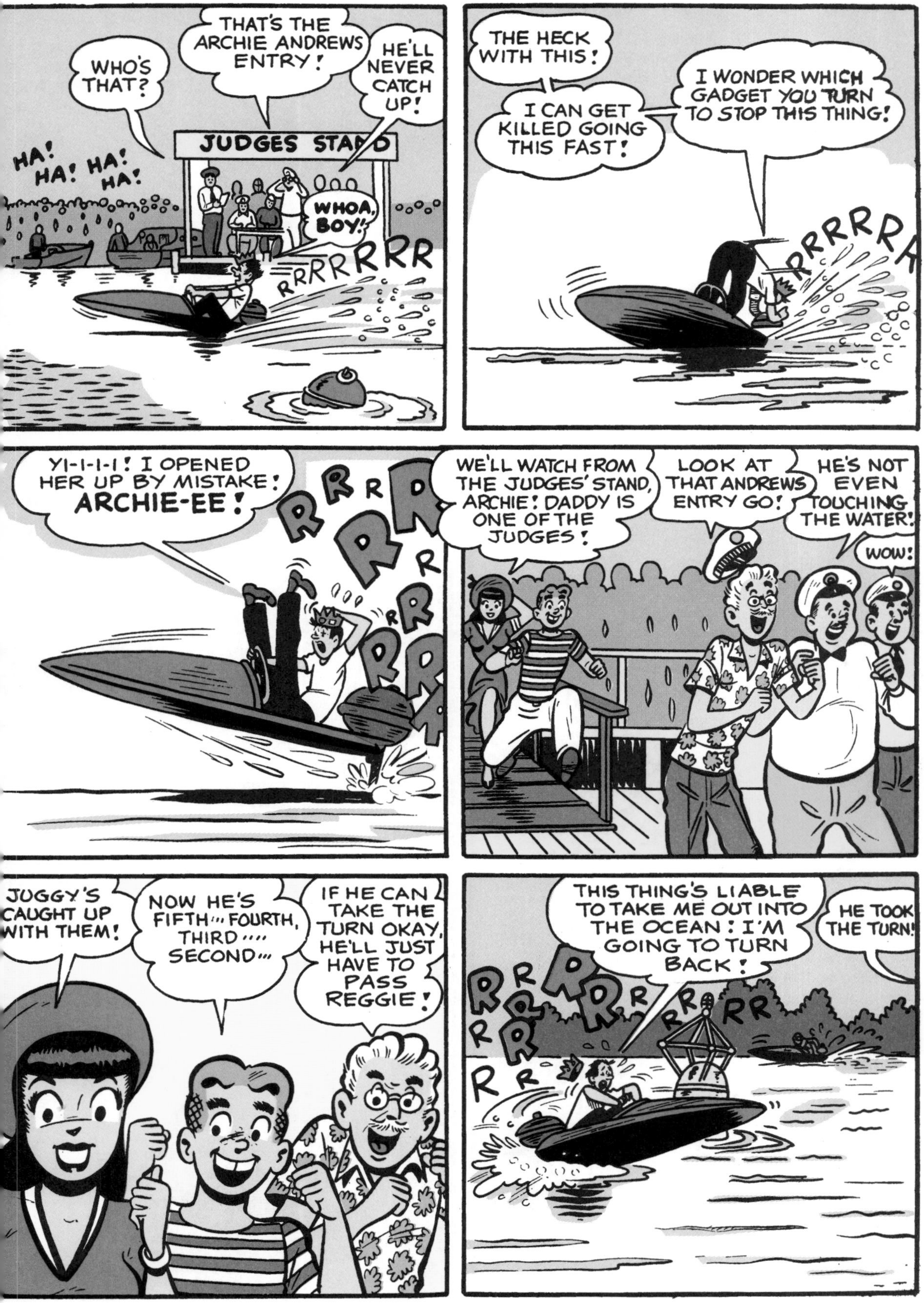
WHO'S THAT?
THAT'S THE ARCHIE ANDREWS ENTRY!
HE'LL NEVER CATCH UP!
JUDGES STAND
HA! HA! HA! HA!
WHOA, BOY!
RRRRRRR
THE HECK WITH THIS!
I CAN GET KILLED GOING THIS FAST!
I WONDER WHICH GADGET YOU TURN TO STOP THIS THING!
RRRRRR
YI-I-I-I! I OPENED HER UP BY MISTAKE! ARCHIE-EE!
WE'LL WATCH FROM THE JUDGES' STAND, ARCHIE! DADDY IS ONE OF THE JUDGES!
LOOK AT THAT ANDREWS ENTRY GO!
HE'S NOT EVEN TOUCHING THE WATER!
WOW!
JUGGY'S CAUGHT UP WITH THEM!
NOW HE'S FIFTH... FOURTH, THIRD.... SECOND...
IF HE CAN TAKE THE TURN OKAY, HE'LL JUST HAVE TO PASS REGGIE!
THIS THING'S LIABLE TO TAKE ME OUT INTO THE OCEAN! I'M GOING TO TURN BACK!
HE TOOK THE TURN!

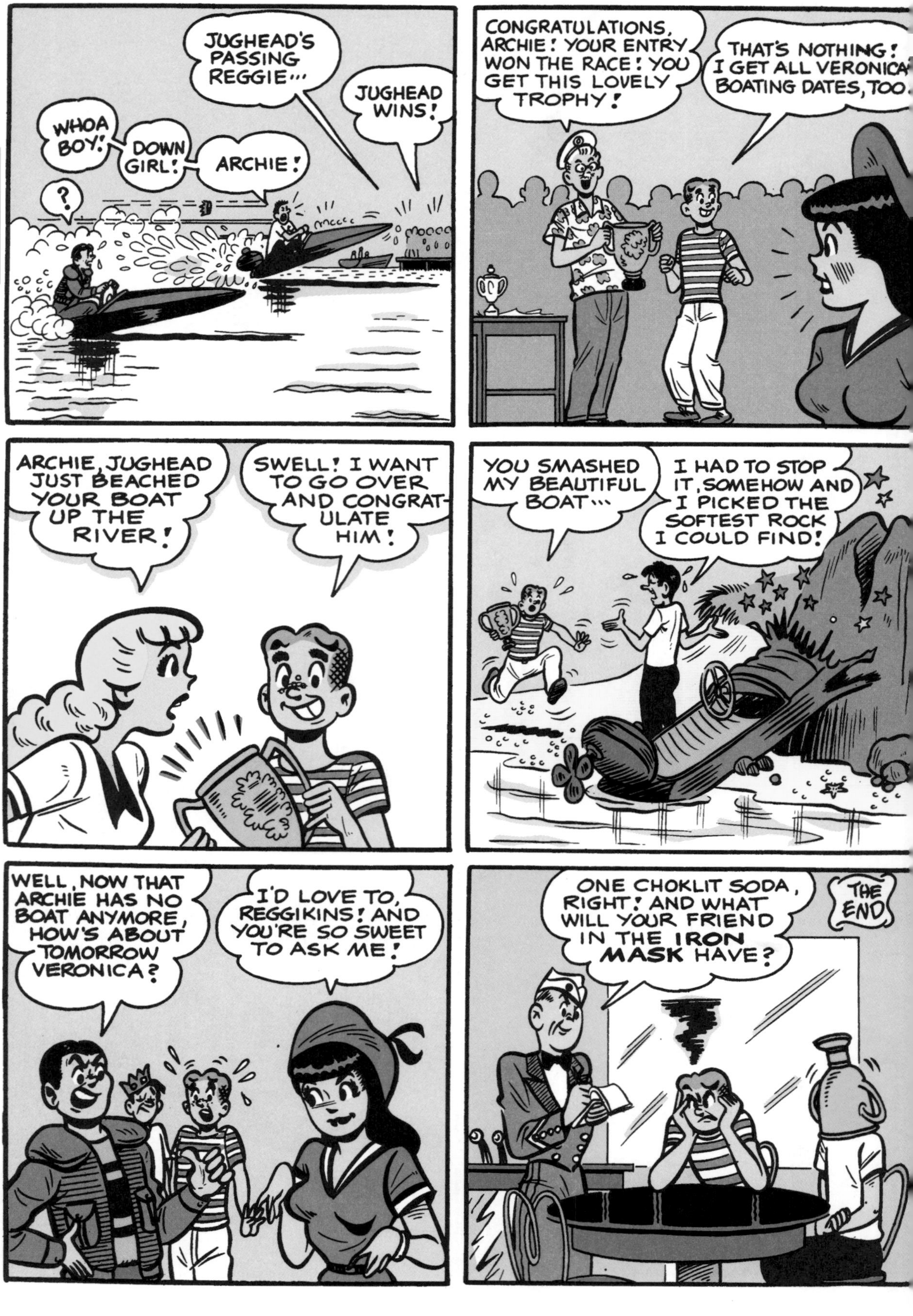
WHOA BOY!
DOWN GIRL!
ARCHIE!
?
JUGHEAD'S PASSING REGGIE...
JUGHEAD WINS!
CONGRATULATIONS, ARCHIE! YOUR ENTRY WON THE RACE! YOU GET THIS LOVELY TROPHY!
THAT'S NOTHING! I GET ALL VERONICA'S BOATING DATES, TOO.
ARCHIE, JUGHEAD JUST BEACHED YOUR BOAT UP THE RIVER!
SWELL! I WANT TO GO OVER AND CONGRATULATE HIM!
YOU SMASHED MY BEAUTIFUL BOAT...
I HAD TO STOP IT, SOMEHOW AND I PICKED THE SOFTEST ROCK I COULD FIND!
WELL, NOW THAT ARCHIE HAS NO BOAT ANYMORE, HOW'S ABOUT TOMORROW VERONICA?
I'D LOVE TO, REGGIKINS! AND YOU'RE SO SWEET TO ASK ME!
ONE CHOKLIT SODA, RIGHT! AND WHAT WILL YOUR FRIEND IN THE IRON MASK HAVE?
THE END

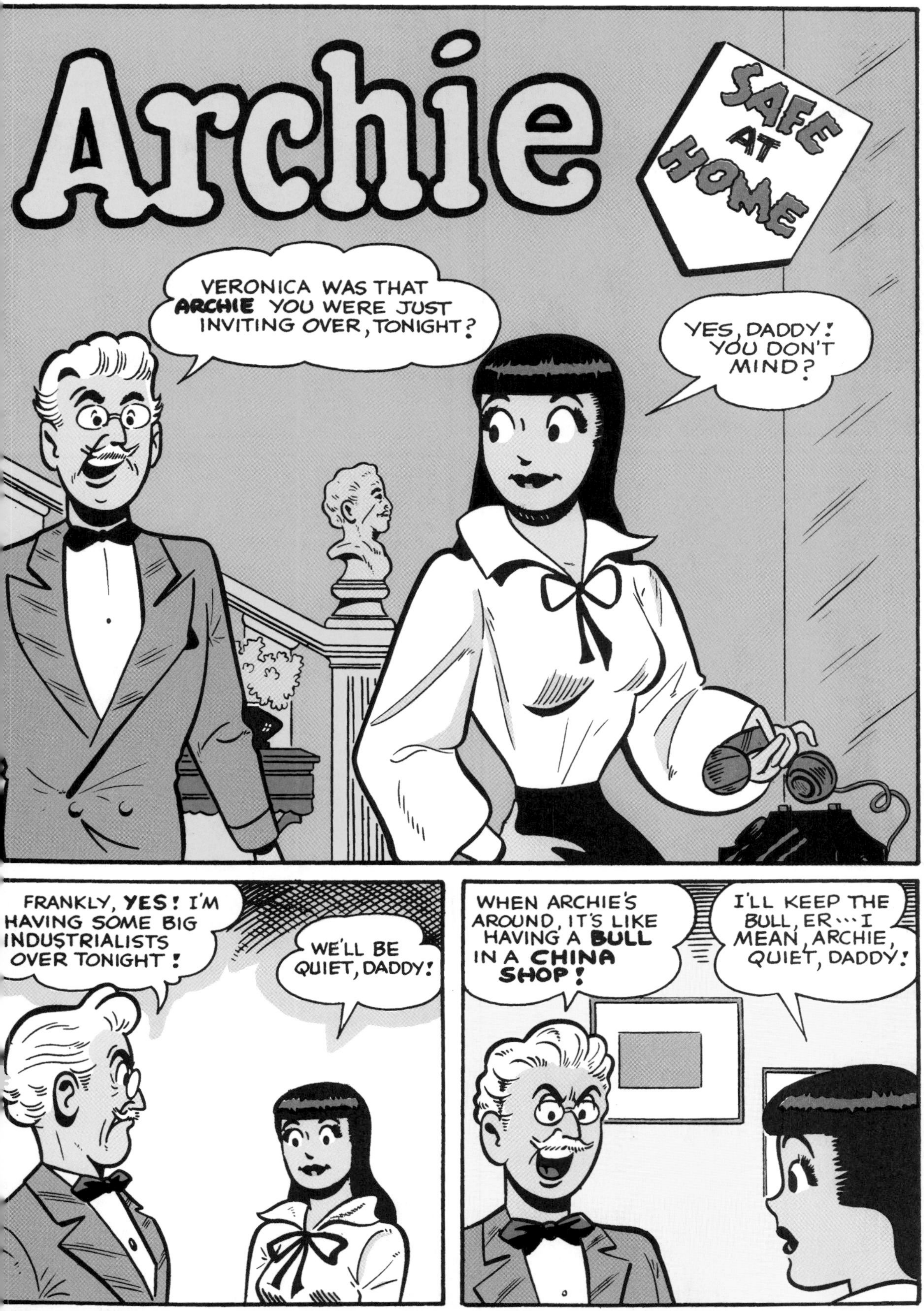
Archie
SAFE AT HOME
VERONICA WAS THAT ARCHIE YOU WERE JUST INVITING OVER, TONIGHT?
YES, DADDY! YOU DON'T MIND?
FRANKLY, YES! I'M HAVING SOME BIG INDUSTRIALISTS OVER TONIGHT!
WE'LL BE QUIET, DADDY!
WHEN ARCHIE'S AROUND, IT'S LIKE HAVING A BULL IN A CHINA SHOP!
I'LL KEEP THE BULL, ER··· I MEAN, ARCHIE, QUIET, DADDY!

ORIGINALLY PRESENTED IN **ARCHIE COMICS #64**, SEPTEMBER-OCTOBER, 1953.

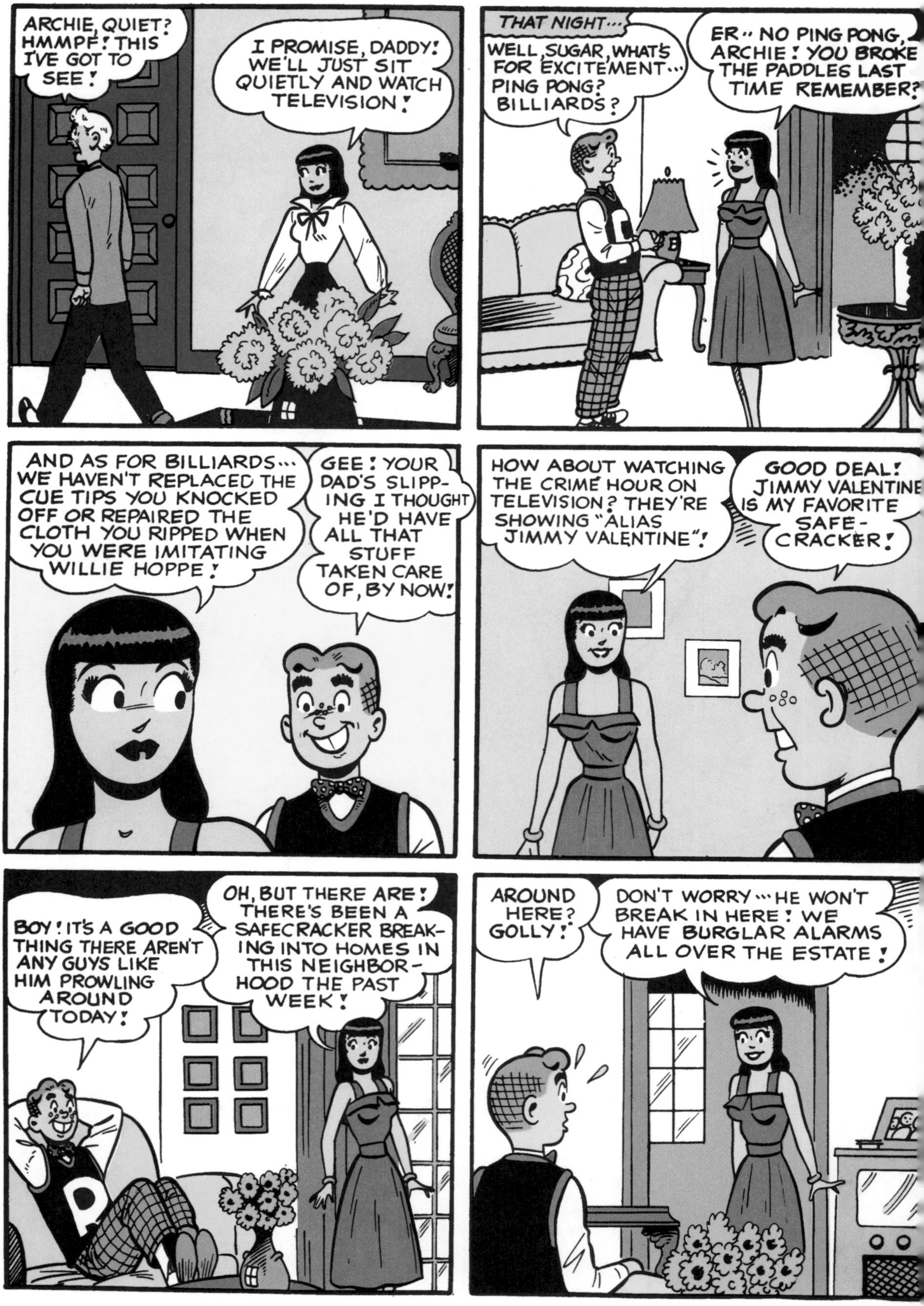
ARCHIE, QUIET? HMMPF! THIS I'VE GOT TO SEE!
I PROMISE, DADDY! WE'LL JUST SIT QUIETLY AND WATCH TELEVISION!
THAT NIGHT...
WELL, SUGAR, WHAT'S FOR EXCITEMENT... PING PONG? BILLIARDS?
ER.. NO PING PONG, ARCHIE! YOU BROKE THE PADDLES LAST TIME REMEMBER?
AND AS FOR BILLIARDS... WE HAVEN'T REPLACED THE CUE TIPS YOU KNOCKED OFF OR REPAIRED THE CLOTH YOU RIPPED WHEN YOU WERE IMITATING WILLIE HOPPE!
GEE! YOUR DAD'S SLIPP-ING I THOUGHT HE'D HAVE ALL THAT STUFF TAKEN CARE OF, BY NOW!
HOW ABOUT WATCHING THE CRIME HOUR ON TELEVISION? THEY'RE SHOWING "ALIAS JIMMY VALENTINE"!
GOOD DEAL! JIMMY VALENTINE IS MY FAVORITE SAFE-CRACKER!
BOY! IT'S A GOOD THING THERE AREN'T ANY GUYS LIKE HIM PROWLING AROUND TODAY!
OH, BUT THERE ARE! THERE'S BEEN A SAFECRACKER BREAK-ING INTO HOMES IN THIS NEIGHBOR-HOOD THE PAST WEEK!
AROUND HERE? GOLLY!
DON'T WORRY... HE WON'T BREAK IN HERE! WE HAVE BURGLAR ALARMS ALL OVER THE ESTATE!

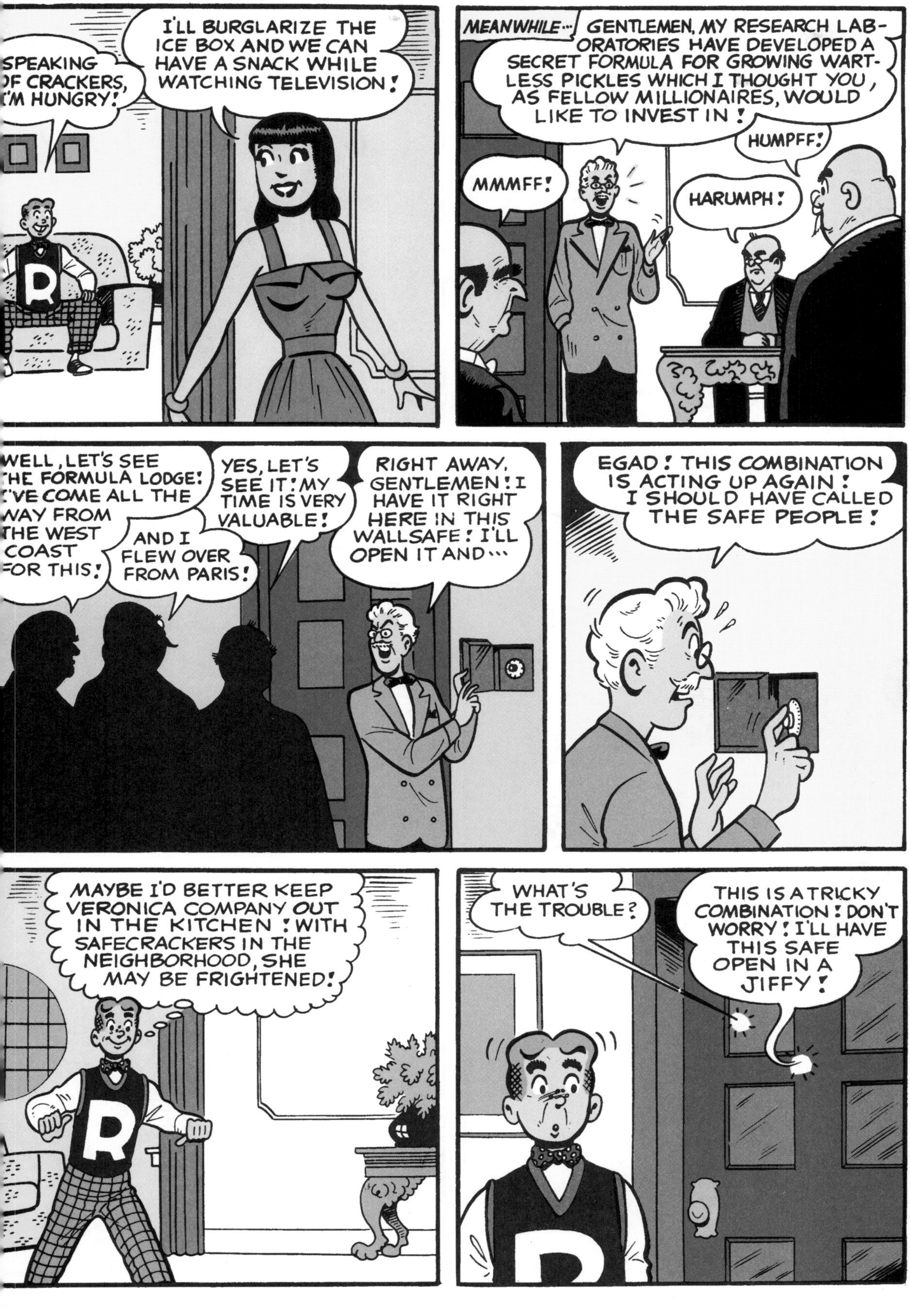
SPEAKING OF CRACKERS, I'M HUNGRY!
I'LL BURGLARIZE THE ICE BOX AND WE CAN HAVE A SNACK WHILE WATCHING TELEVISION!
MEANWHILE...
GENTLEMEN, MY RESEARCH LABORATORIES HAVE DEVELOPED A SECRET FORMULA FOR GROWING WARTLESS PICKLES WHICH I THOUGHT YOU, AS FELLOW MILLIONAIRES, WOULD LIKE TO INVEST IN!
HUMPFF!
MMMFF!
HARUMPH!
WELL, LET'S SEE THE FORMULA LODGE! I'VE COME ALL THE WAY FROM THE WEST COAST FOR THIS!
AND I FLEW OVER FROM PARIS!
YES, LET'S SEE IT! MY TIME IS VERY VALUABLE!
RIGHT AWAY, GENTLEMEN! I HAVE IT RIGHT HERE IN THIS WALLSAFE! I'LL OPEN IT AND...
EGAD! THIS COMBINATION IS ACTING UP AGAIN! I SHOULD HAVE CALLED THE SAFE PEOPLE!
MAYBE I'D BETTER KEEP VERONICA COMPANY OUT IN THE KITCHEN! WITH SAFECRACKERS IN THE NEIGHBORHOOD, SHE MAY BE FRIGHTENED!
WHAT'S THE TROUBLE?
THIS IS A TRICKY COMBINATION! DON'T WORRY! I'LL HAVE THIS SAFE OPEN IN A JIFFY!

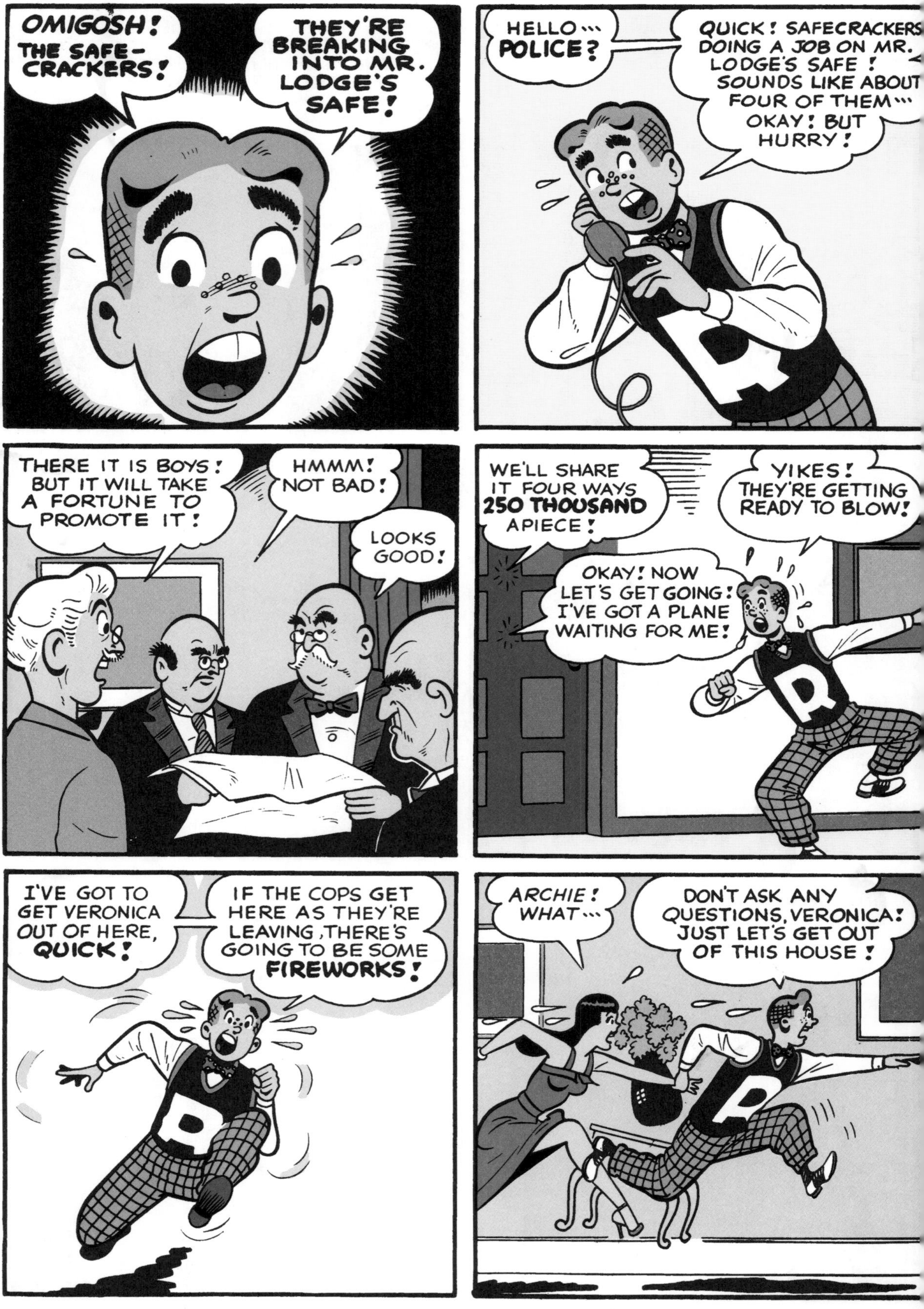
OMIGOSH! THE SAFE-CRACKERS!
THEY'RE BREAKING INTO MR. LODGE'S SAFE!
HELLO... POLICE?
QUICK! SAFECRACKERS DOING A JOB ON MR. LODGE'S SAFE! SOUNDS LIKE ABOUT FOUR OF THEM... OKAY! BUT HURRY!
THERE IT IS BOYS! BUT IT WILL TAKE A FORTUNE TO PROMOTE IT!
HMMM! NOT BAD!
LOOKS GOOD!
WE'LL SHARE IT FOUR WAYS 250 THOUSAND APIECE!
YIKES! THEY'RE GETTING READY TO BLOW!
OKAY! NOW LET'S GET GOING! I'VE GOT A PLANE WAITING FOR ME!
I'VE GOT TO GET VERONICA OUT OF HERE, QUICK!
IF THE COPS GET HERE AS THEY'RE LEAVING, THERE'S GOING TO BE SOME FIREWORKS!
ARCHIE! WHAT...
DON'T ASK ANY QUESTIONS, VERONICA! JUST LET'S GET OUT OF THIS HOUSE!

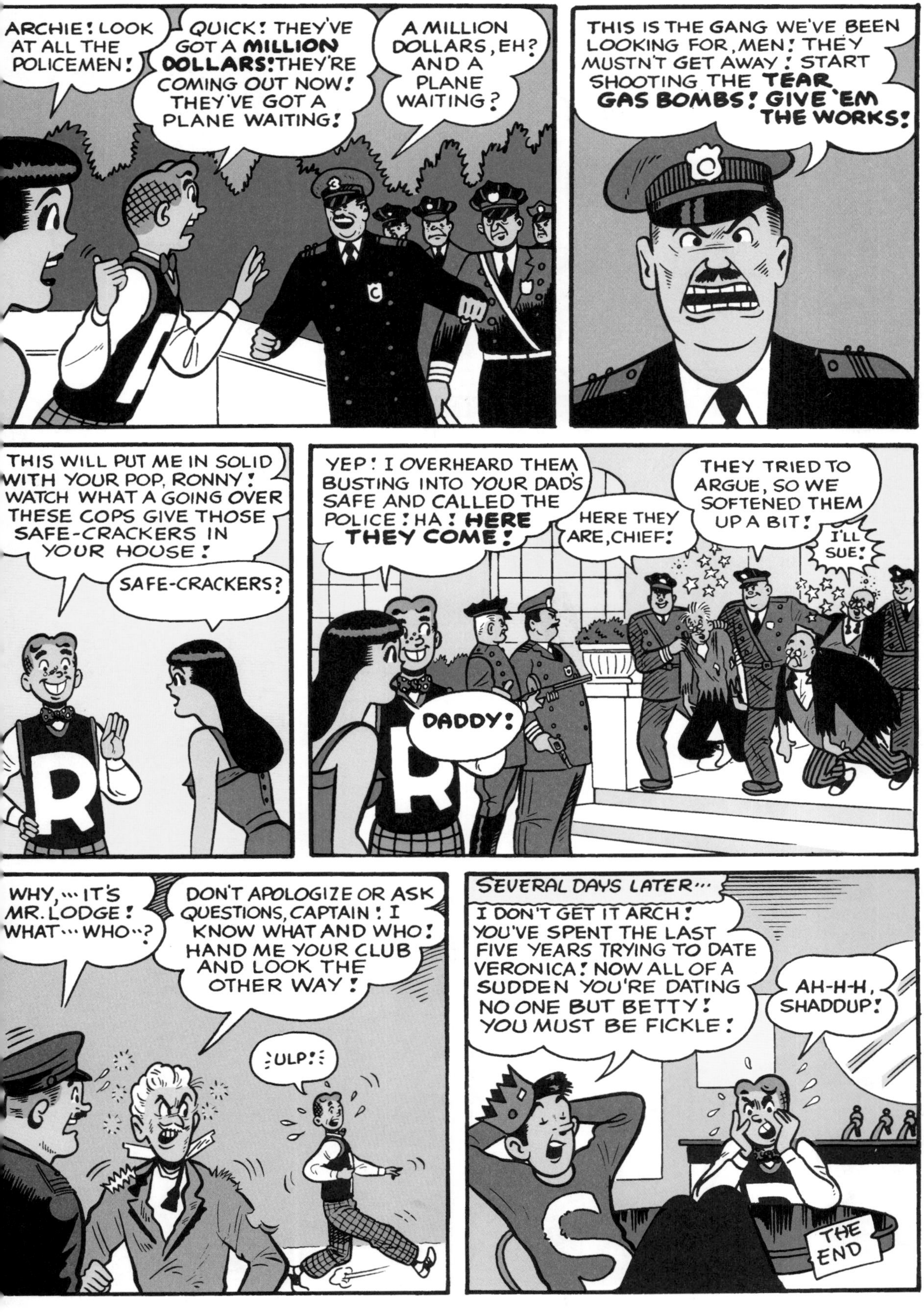
ARCHIE! LOOK AT ALL THE POLICEMEN!
QUICK! THEY'VE GOT A MILLION DOLLARS! THEY'RE COMING OUT NOW! THEY'VE GOT A PLANE WAITING!
A MILLION DOLLARS, EH? AND A PLANE WAITING?
THIS IS THE GANG WE'VE BEEN LOOKING FOR, MEN! THEY MUSTN'T GET AWAY! START SHOOTING THE TEAR GAS BOMBS! GIVE 'EM THE WORKS!
THIS WILL PUT ME IN SOLID WITH YOUR POP, RONNY! WATCH WHAT A GOING OVER THESE COPS GIVE THOSE SAFE-CRACKERS IN YOUR HOUSE!
SAFE-CRACKERS?
YEP! I OVERHEARD THEM BUSTING INTO YOUR DAD'S SAFE AND CALLED THE POLICE! HA! HERE THEY COME!
HERE THEY ARE, CHIEF!
THEY TRIED TO ARGUE, SO WE SOFTENED THEM UP A BIT!
I'LL SUE!
DADDY!
WHY, ... IT'S MR. LODGE! WHAT ... WHO ..?
DON'T APOLOGIZE OR ASK QUESTIONS, CAPTAIN! I KNOW WHAT AND WHO! HAND ME YOUR CLUB AND LOOK THE OTHER WAY!
ULP!
SEVERAL DAYS LATER ...
I DON'T GET IT ARCH! YOU'VE SPENT THE LAST FIVE YEARS TRYING TO DATE VERONICA! NOW ALL OF A SUDDEN YOU'RE DATING NO ONE BUT BETTY! YOU MUST BE FICKLE!
AH-H-H, SHADDUP!
THE END

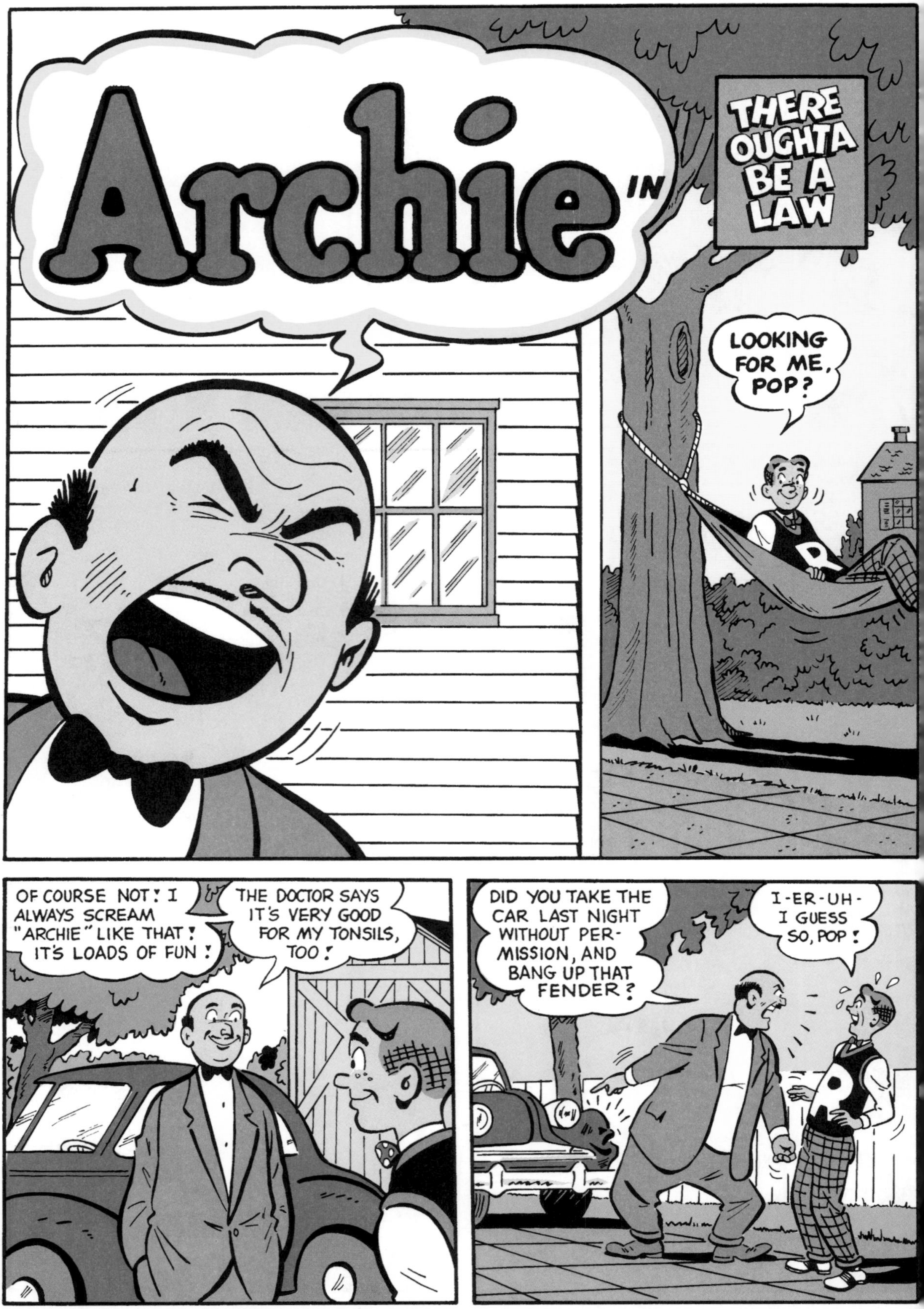
Archie IN
THERE OUGHTA BE A LAW
LOOKING FOR ME, POP?
OF COURSE NOT! I ALWAYS SCREAM "ARCHIE" LIKE THAT! IT'S LOADS OF FUN!
THE DOCTOR SAYS IT'S VERY GOOD FOR MY TONSILS, TOO!
DID YOU TAKE THE CAR LAST NIGHT WITHOUT PER- MISSION, AND BANG UP THAT FENDER?
I-ER-UH- I GUESS SO, POP!

ORIGINALLY PRESENTED IN **ARCHIE'S PALS & GALS #3**, 1954-55 EDITION.

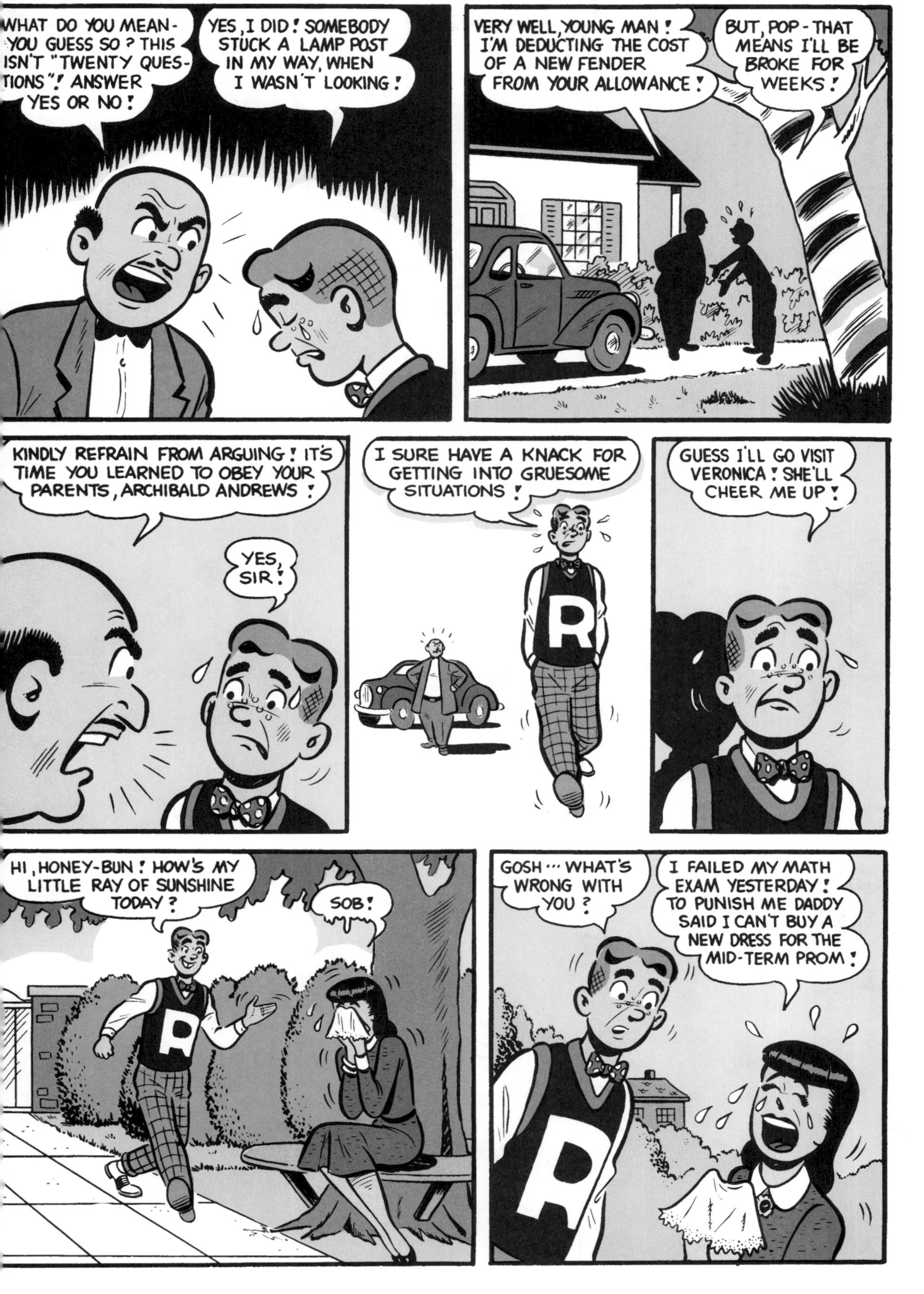
WHAT DO YOU MEAN - YOU GUESS SO ? THIS ISN'T "TWENTY QUESTIONS"! ANSWER YES OR NO!
YES, I DID! SOMEBODY STUCK A LAMP POST IN MY WAY, WHEN I WASN'T LOOKING!
VERY WELL, YOUNG MAN! I'M DEDUCTING THE COST OF A NEW FENDER FROM YOUR ALLOWANCE!
BUT, POP - THAT MEANS I'LL BE BROKE FOR WEEKS!
KINDLY REFRAIN FROM ARGUING! IT'S TIME YOU LEARNED TO OBEY YOUR PARENTS, ARCHIBALD ANDREWS!
YES, SIR!
I SURE HAVE A KNACK FOR GETTING INTO GRUESOME SITUATIONS!
GUESS I'LL GO VISIT VERONICA! SHE'LL CHEER ME UP!
HI, HONEY-BUN! HOW'S MY LITTLE RAY OF SUNSHINE TODAY?
SOB!
GOSH ... WHAT'S WRONG WITH YOU?
I FAILED MY MATH EXAM YESTERDAY! TO PUNISH ME DADDY SAID I CAN'T BUY A NEW DRESS FOR THE MID-TERM PROM!

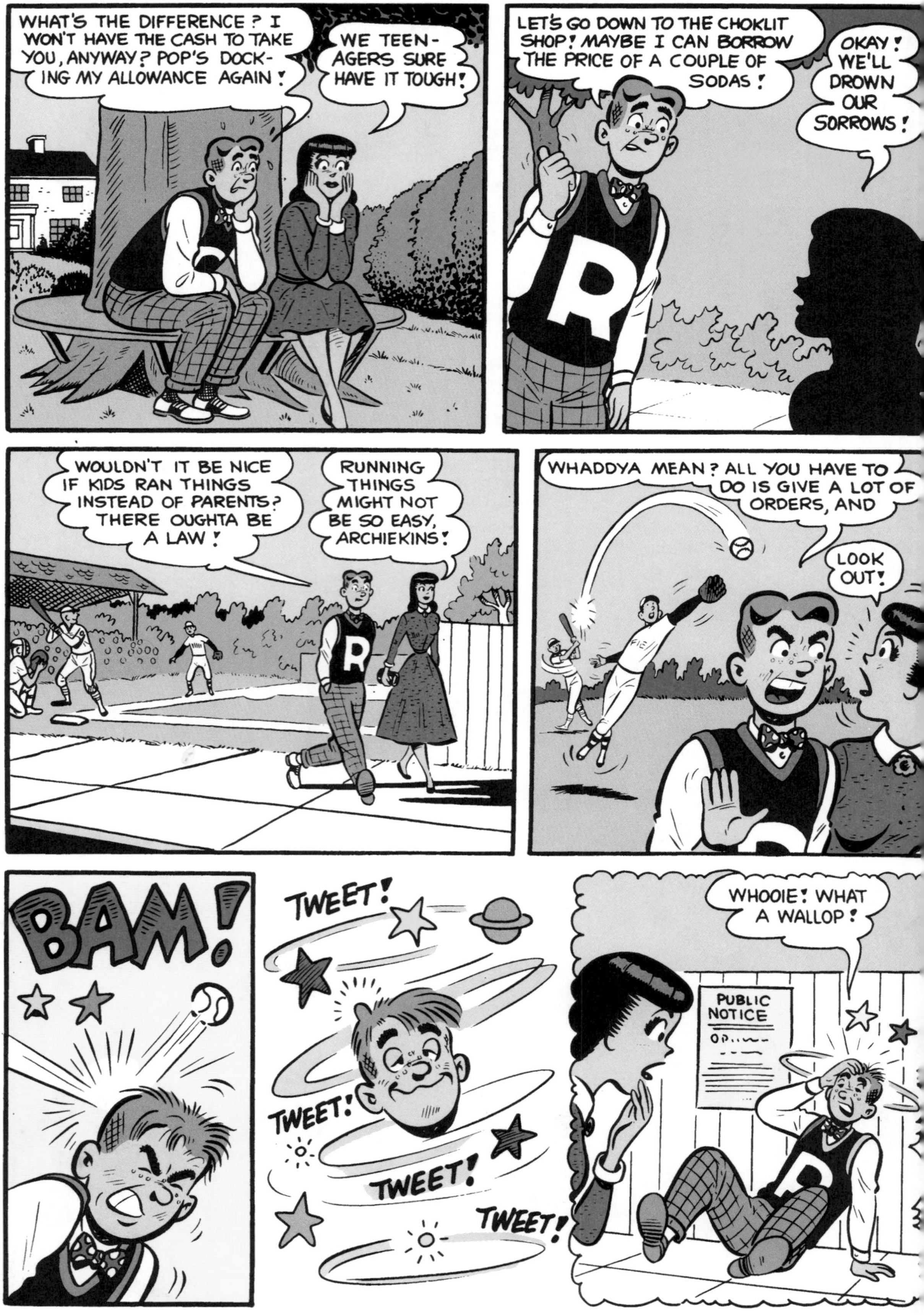
WHAT'S THE DIFFERENCE? I WON'T HAVE THE CASH TO TAKE YOU, ANYWAY? POP'S DOCKING MY ALLOWANCE AGAIN!
WE TEEN-AGERS SURE HAVE IT TOUGH!
LET'S GO DOWN TO THE CHOKLIT SHOP! MAYBE I CAN BORROW THE PRICE OF A COUPLE OF SODAS!
OKAY! WE'LL DROWN OUR SORROWS!
WOULDN'T IT BE NICE IF KIDS RAN THINGS INSTEAD OF PARENTS? THERE OUGHTA BE A LAW!
RUNNING THINGS MIGHT NOT BE SO EASY, ARCHIEKINS!
R
WHADDYA MEAN? ALL YOU HAVE TO DO IS GIVE A LOT OF ORDERS, AND
LOOK OUT!
BAM!
TWEET!
TWEET!
TWEET!
TWEET!
WHOOIE! WHAT A WALLOP!
PUBLIC NOTICE

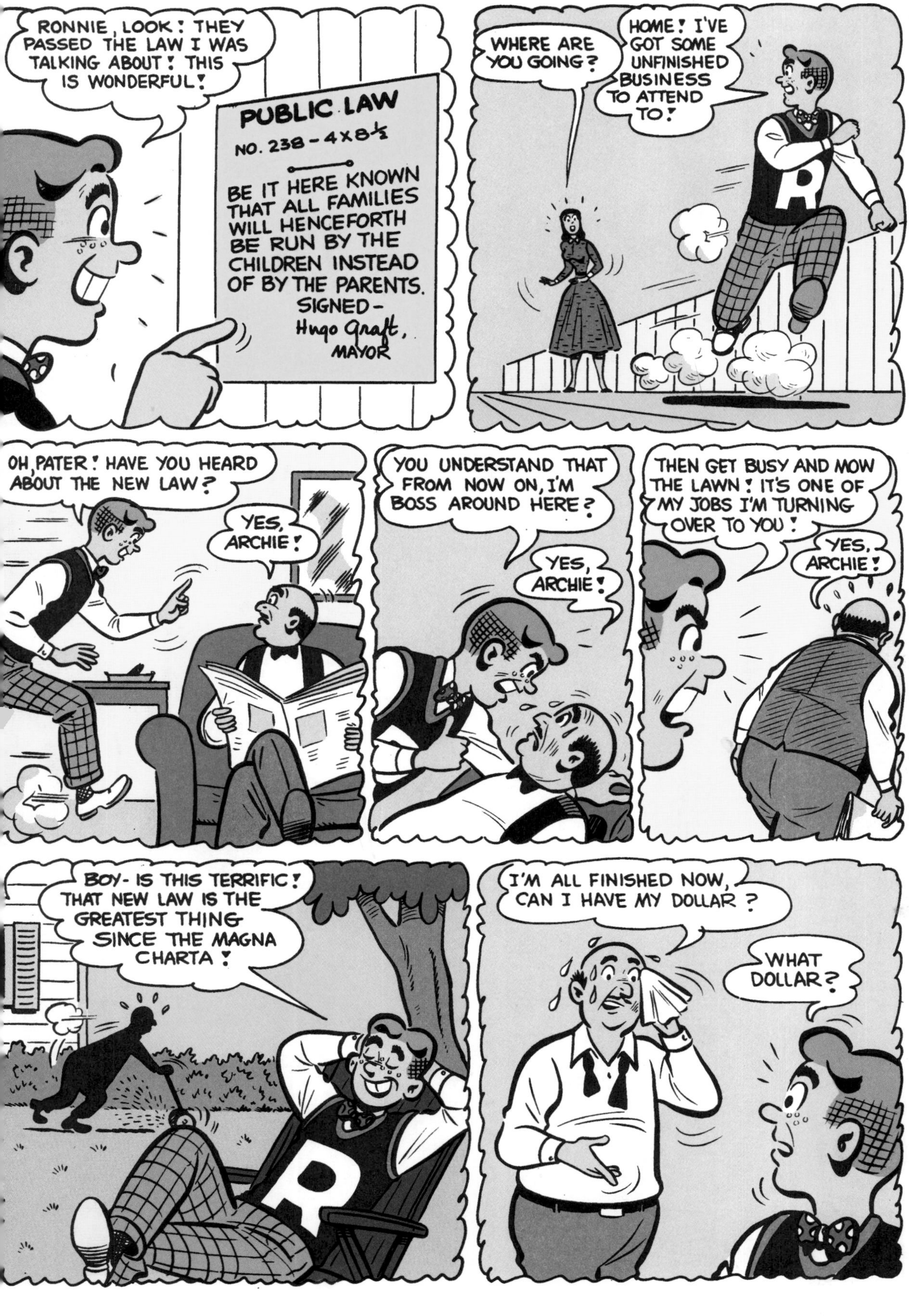
RONNIE, LOOK! THEY PASSED THE LAW I WAS TALKING ABOUT! THIS IS WONDERFUL!
PUBLIC LAW
NO. 238 - 4X8½
BE IT HERE KNOWN THAT ALL FAMILIES WILL HENCEFORTH BE RUN BY THE CHILDREN INSTEAD OF BY THE PARENTS.
SIGNED -
Hugo Graft,
MAYOR
WHERE ARE YOU GOING?
HOME! I'VE GOT SOME UNFINISHED BUSINESS TO ATTEND TO!
OH, PATER! HAVE YOU HEARD ABOUT THE NEW LAW?
YES, ARCHIE!
YOU UNDERSTAND THAT FROM NOW ON, I'M BOSS AROUND HERE?
YES, ARCHIE!
THEN GET BUSY AND MOW THE LAWN! IT'S ONE OF MY JOBS I'M TURNING OVER TO YOU!
YES, ARCHIE!
BOY- IS THIS TERRIFIC! THAT NEW LAW IS THE GREATEST THING SINCE THE MAGNA CHARTA!
I'M ALL FINISHED NOW, CAN I HAVE MY DOLLAR?
WHAT DOLLAR?

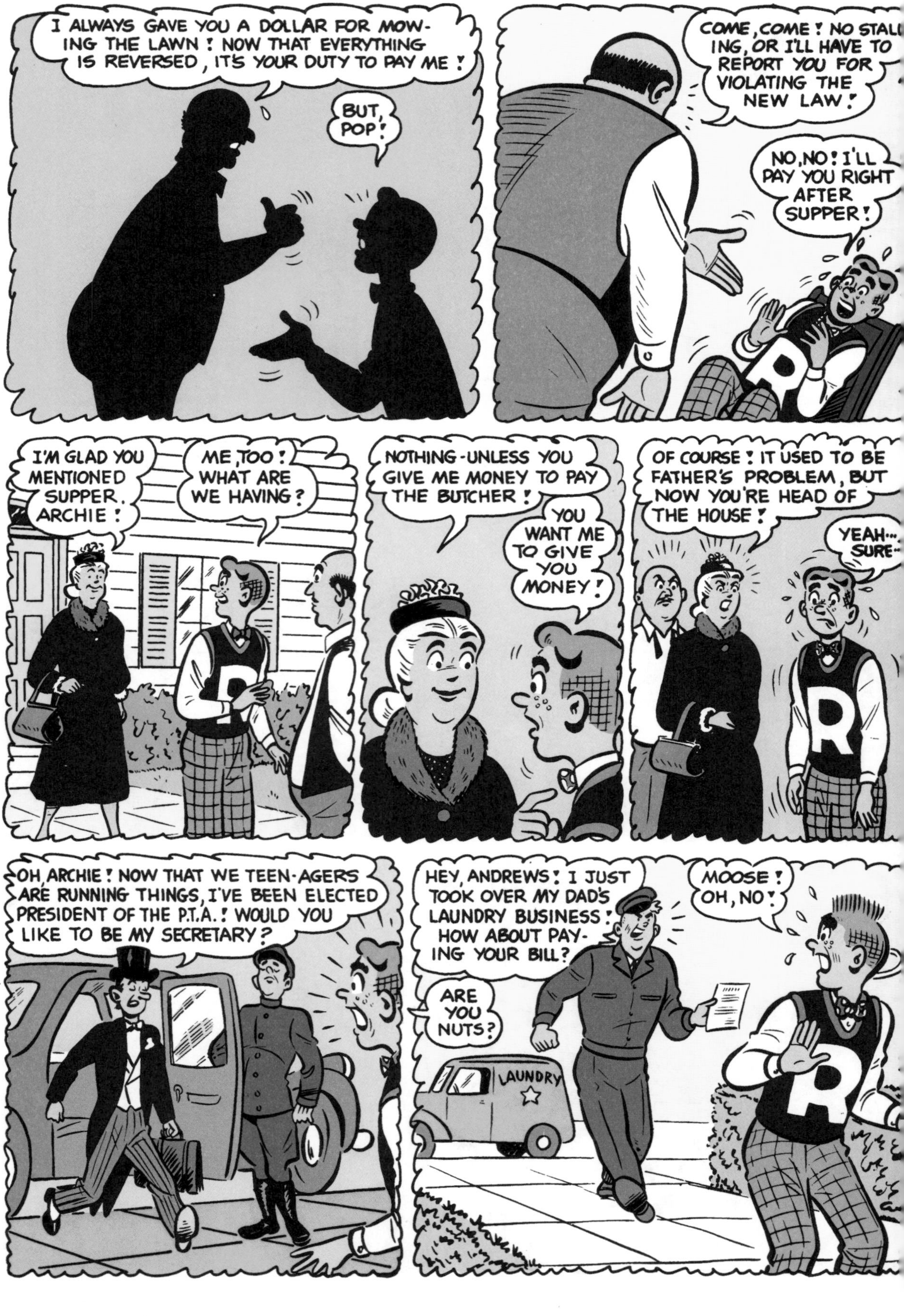
I ALWAYS GAVE YOU A DOLLAR FOR MOWING THE LAWN! NOW THAT EVERYTHING IS REVERSED, IT'S YOUR DUTY TO PAY ME!
BUT, POP!
COME, COME! NO STALLING, OR I'LL HAVE TO REPORT YOU FOR VIOLATING THE NEW LAW!
NO, NO! I'LL PAY YOU RIGHT AFTER SUPPER!
I'M GLAD YOU MENTIONED SUPPER, ARCHIE!
ME, TOO! WHAT ARE WE HAVING?
NOTHING - UNLESS YOU GIVE ME MONEY TO PAY THE BUTCHER!
YOU WANT ME TO GIVE YOU MONEY!
OF COURSE! IT USED TO BE FATHER'S PROBLEM, BUT NOW YOU'RE HEAD OF THE HOUSE!
YEAH... SURE...
OH, ARCHIE! NOW THAT WE TEEN-AGERS ARE RUNNING THINGS, I'VE BEEN ELECTED PRESIDENT OF THE P.T.A.! WOULD YOU LIKE TO BE MY SECRETARY?
HEY, ANDREWS! I JUST TOOK OVER MY DAD'S LAUNDRY BUSINESS! HOW ABOUT PAYING YOUR BILL?
MOOSE! OH, NO!
ARE YOU NUTS?
LAUNDRY

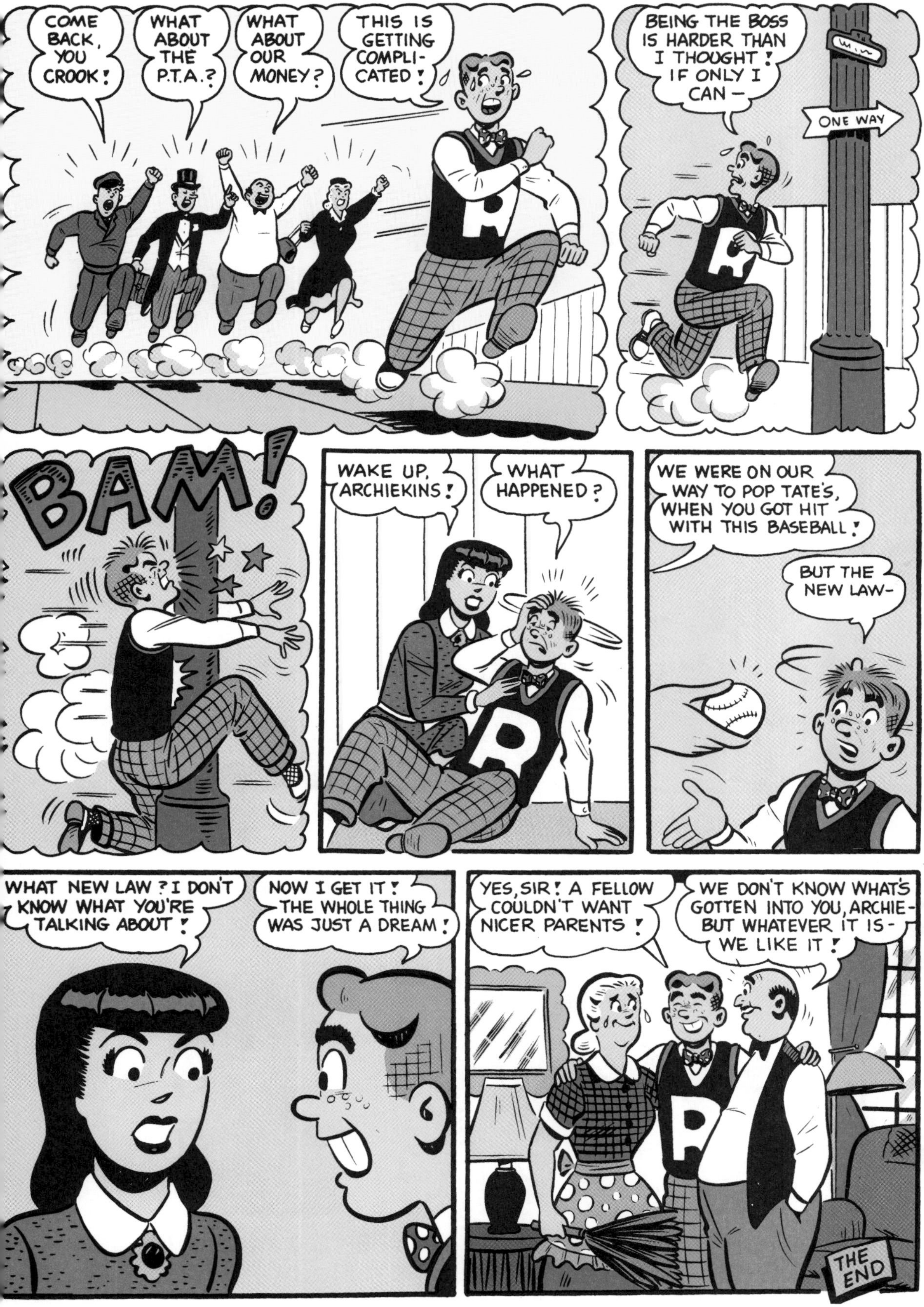
COME BACK, YOU CROOK!
WHAT ABOUT THE P.T.A.?
WHAT ABOUT OUR MONEY?
THIS IS GETTING COMPLICATED!
BEING THE BOSS IS HARDER THAN I THOUGHT! IF ONLY I CAN—
ONE WAY
BAM!
WAKE UP, ARCHIEKINS!
WHAT HAPPENED?
WE WERE ON OUR WAY TO POP TATE'S, WHEN YOU GOT HIT WITH THIS BASEBALL!
BUT THE NEW LAW-
WHAT NEW LAW? I DON'T KNOW WHAT YOU'RE TALKING ABOUT!
NOW I GET IT! THE WHOLE THING WAS JUST A DREAM!
YES, SIR! A FELLOW COULDN'T WANT NICER PARENTS!
WE DON'T KNOW WHAT'S GOTTEN INTO YOU, ARCHIE- BUT WHATEVER IT IS- WE LIKE IT!
THE END

A GALLERY OF CLASSIC 50'S COVER GAGS BY BOB MONTANA

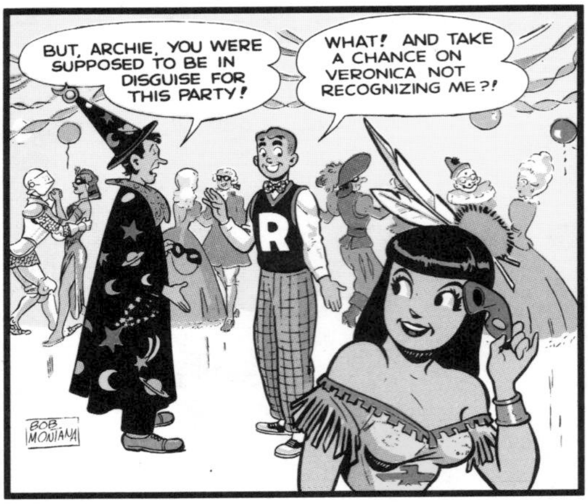

BUT, ARCHIE, YOU WERE SUPPOSED TO BE IN DISGUISE FOR THIS PARTY!
WHAT! AND TAKE A CHANCE ON VERONICA NOT RECOGNIZING ME?!
BOB MONTANA

PEP COMICS #79,
May, 1950.

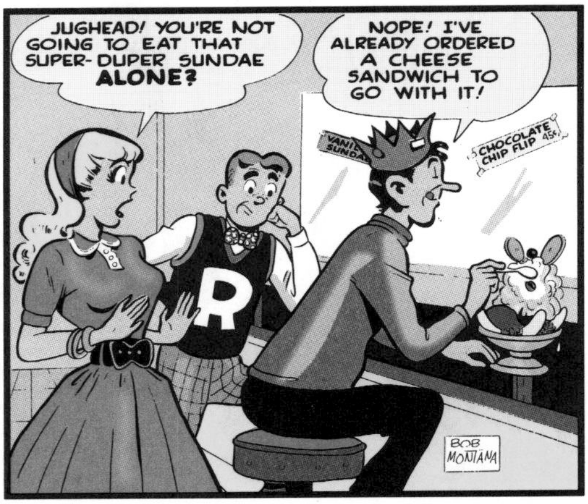

JUGHEAD! YOU'RE NOT GOING TO EAT THAT SUPER-DUPER SUNDAE **ALONE?**
NOPE! I'VE ALREADY ORDERED A CHEESE SANDWICH TO GO WITH IT!
CHOCOLATE CHIP FLIP
BOB MONTANA

JUGHEAD COMICS #16,
February, 1953.

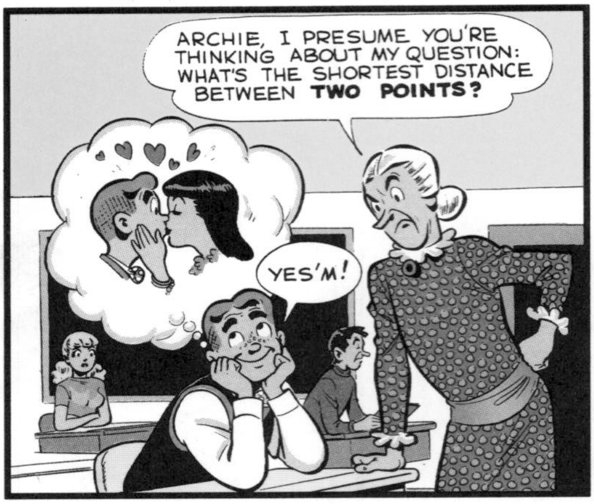

ARCHIE, I PRESUME YOU'RE THINKING ABOUT MY QUESTION: WHAT'S THE SHORTEST DISTANCE BETWEEN **TWO POINTS?**
YES'M!

PEP COMICS #82,
November, 1950.

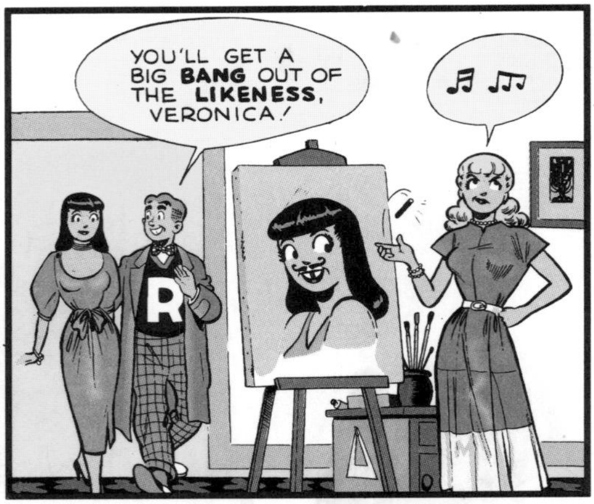

YOU'LL GET A BIG **BANG** OUT OF THE **LIKENESS**, VERONICA!

LAUGH COMICS #42,
December, 1950.

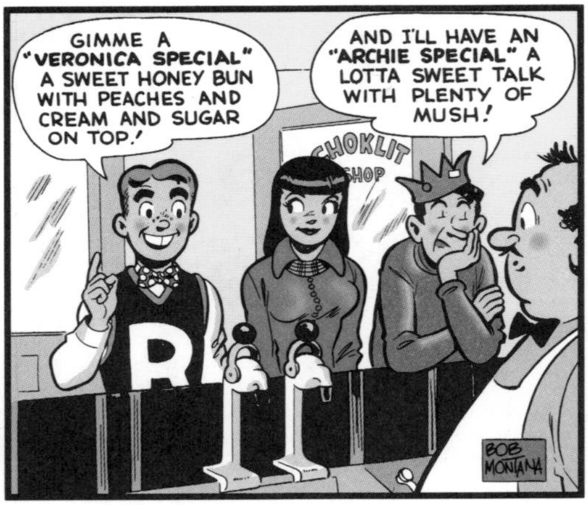

GIMME A **"VERONICA SPECIAL"** A SWEET HONEY BUN WITH PEACHES AND CREAM AND SUGAR ON TOP!
AND I'LL HAVE AN **"ARCHIE SPECIAL"** A LOTTA SWEET TALK WITH PLENTY OF MUSH!
CHOKLIT SHOP
BOB MONTANA

LAUGH COMICS #44,
April, 1951.

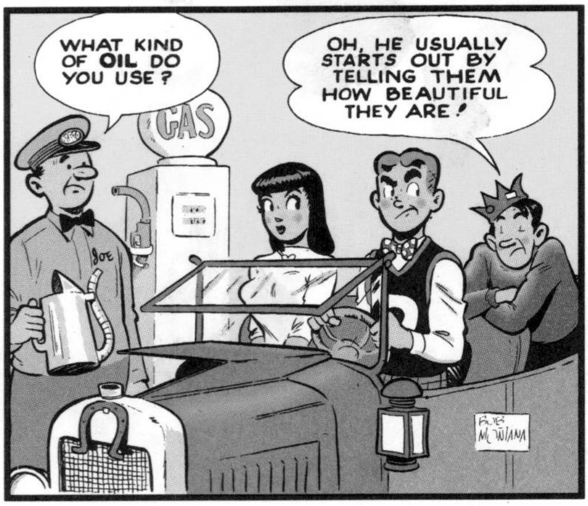

WHAT KIND OF **OIL** DO YOU USE?
OH, HE USUALLY STARTS OUT BY TELLING THEM HOW BEAUTIFUL THEY ARE!
GAS
JOE
BOB MONTANA

PEP COMICS #90,
March, 1952.

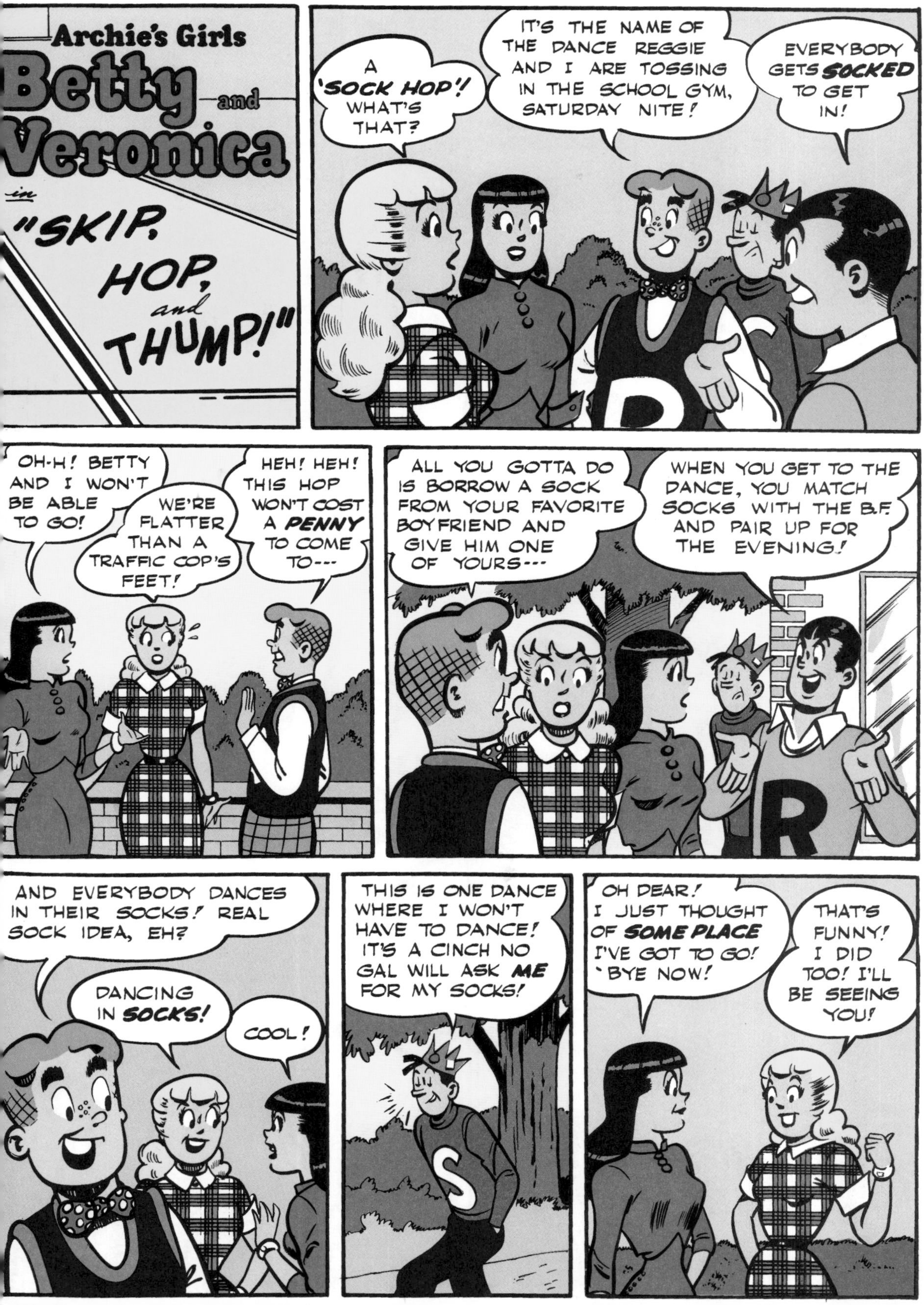
Archie's Girls
Betty and Veronica
in
"SKIP, HOP, and THUMP!"
A 'SOCK HOP'! WHAT'S THAT?
IT'S THE NAME OF THE DANCE REGGIE AND I ARE TOSSING IN THE SCHOOL GYM, SATURDAY NITE!
EVERYBODY GETS SOCKED TO GET IN!
OH-H! BETTY AND I WON'T BE ABLE TO GO!
WE'RE FLATTER THAN A TRAFFIC COP'S FEET!
HEH! HEH! THIS HOP WON'T COST A PENNY TO COME TO---
ALL YOU GOTTA DO IS BORROW A SOCK FROM YOUR FAVORITE BOYFRIEND AND GIVE HIM ONE OF YOURS---
WHEN YOU GET TO THE DANCE, YOU MATCH SOCKS WITH THE B.F. AND PAIR UP FOR THE EVENING!
AND EVERYBODY DANCES IN THEIR SOCKS! REAL SOCK IDEA, EH?
DANCING IN SOCKS!
COOL!
THIS IS ONE DANCE WHERE I WON'T HAVE TO DANCE! IT'S A CINCH NO GAL WILL ASK ME FOR MY SOCKS!
OH DEAR! I JUST THOUGHT OF SOME PLACE I'VE GOT TO GO! 'BYE NOW!
THAT'S FUNNY! I DID TOO! I'LL BE SEEING YOU!

ORIGINALLY PRESENTED IN **LAUGH COMICS #75**, JUNE, 1956.

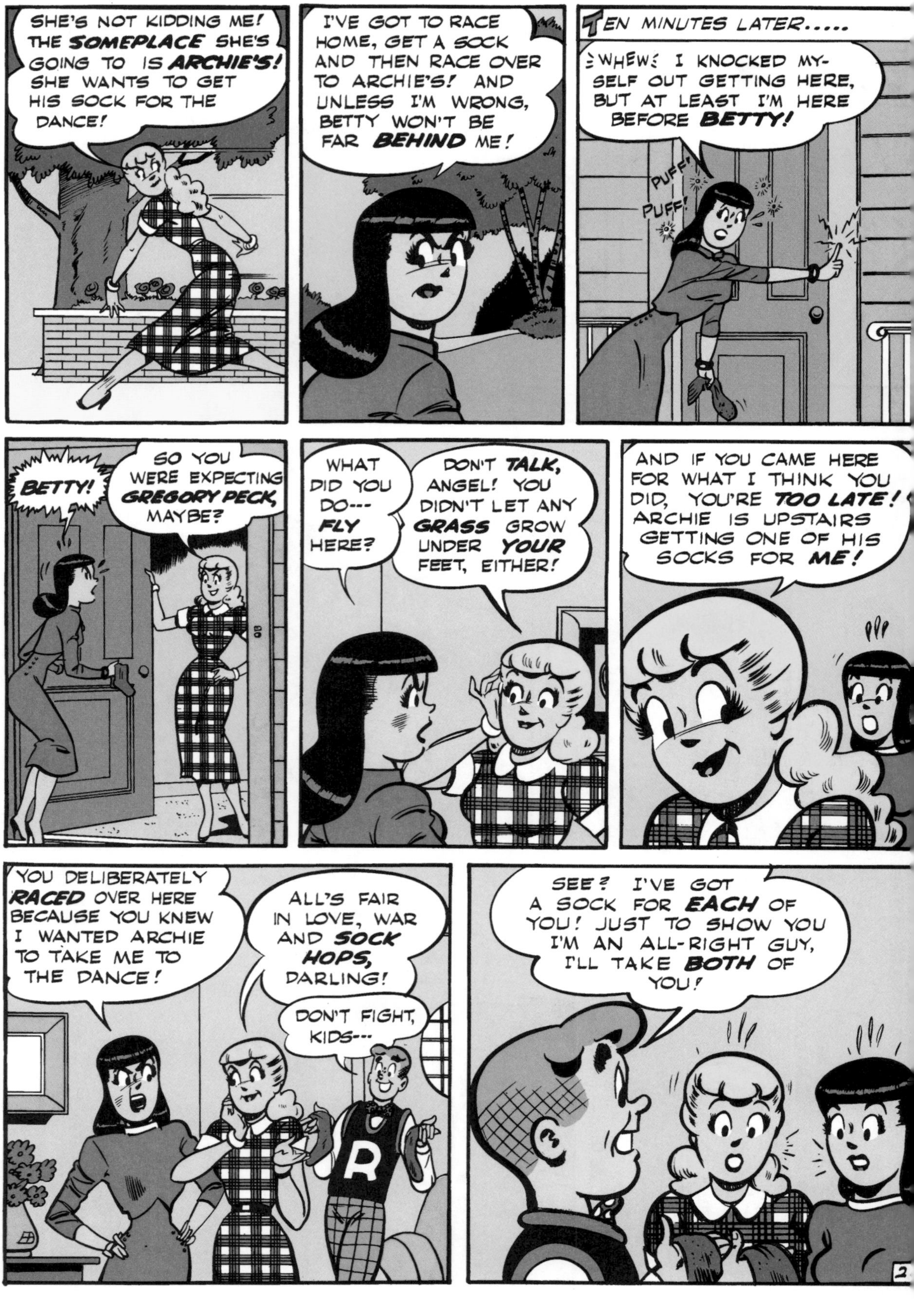
SHE'S NOT KIDDING ME! THE SOMEPLACE SHE'S GOING TO IS ARCHIE'S! SHE WANTS TO GET HIS SOCK FOR THE DANCE!
I'VE GOT TO RACE HOME, GET A SOCK AND THEN RACE OVER TO ARCHIE'S! AND UNLESS I'M WRONG, BETTY WON'T BE FAR BEHIND ME!
TEN MINUTES LATER.....
WHEW! I KNOCKED MYSELF OUT GETTING HERE, BUT AT LEAST I'M HERE BEFORE BETTY!
PUFF! PUFF!
BETTY!
SO YOU WERE EXPECTING GREGORY PECK, MAYBE?
WHAT DID YOU DO--- FLY HERE?
DON'T TALK, ANGEL! YOU DIDN'T LET ANY GRASS GROW UNDER YOUR FEET, EITHER!
AND IF YOU CAME HERE FOR WHAT I THINK YOU DID, YOU'RE TOO LATE! ARCHIE IS UPSTAIRS GETTING ONE OF HIS SOCKS FOR ME!
YOU DELIBERATELY RACED OVER HERE BECAUSE YOU KNEW I WANTED ARCHIE TO TAKE ME TO THE DANCE!
ALL'S FAIR IN LOVE, WAR AND SOCK HOPS, DARLING!
DON'T FIGHT, KIDS---
SEE? I'VE GOT A SOCK FOR EACH OF YOU! JUST TO SHOW YOU I'M AN ALL-RIGHT GUY, I'LL TAKE BOTH OF YOU!
2

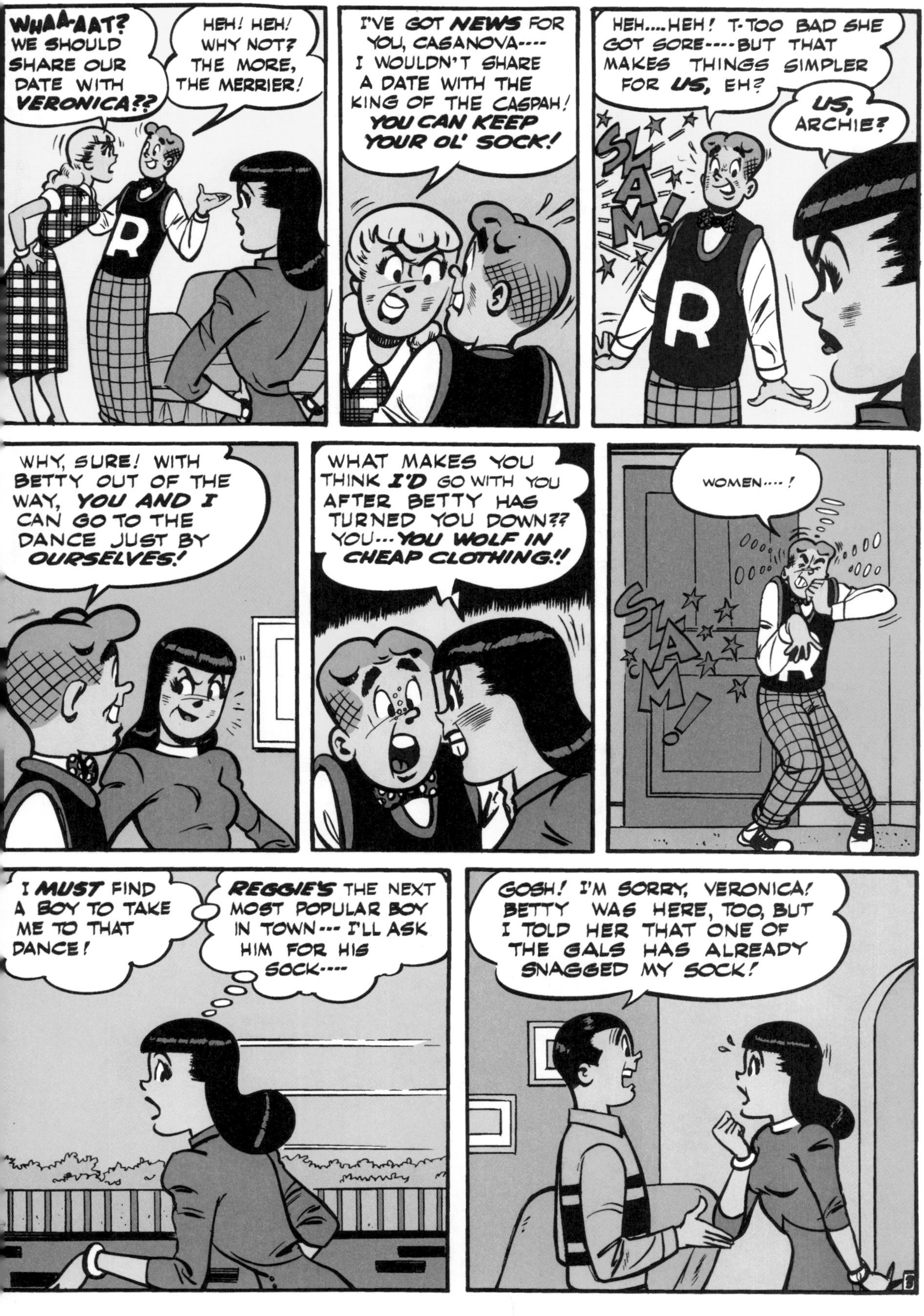
WHAA-AAT? WE SHOULD SHARE OUR DATE WITH VERONICA??
HEH! HEH! WHY NOT? THE MORE, THE MERRIER!
I'VE GOT NEWS FOR YOU, CASANOVA---- I WOULDN'T SHARE A DATE WITH THE KING OF THE CASPAH! YOU CAN KEEP YOUR OL' SOCK!
HEH....HEH! T-TOO BAD SHE GOT SORE----BUT THAT MAKES THINGS SIMPLER FOR US, EH?
SLAM!
US, ARCHIE?
WHY, SURE! WITH BETTY OUT OF THE WAY, YOU AND I CAN GO TO THE DANCE JUST BY OURSELVES!
WHAT MAKES YOU THINK I'D GO WITH YOU AFTER BETTY HAS TURNED YOU DOWN?? YOU...YOU WOLF IN CHEAP CLOTHING!!
WOMEN....!
SLAM!
I MUST FIND A BOY TO TAKE ME TO THAT DANCE!
REGGIE'S THE NEXT MOST POPULAR BOY IN TOWN--- I'LL ASK HIM FOR HIS SOCK----
GOSH! I'M SORRY, VERONICA! BETTY WAS HERE, TOO, BUT I TOLD HER THAT ONE OF THE GALS HAS ALREADY SNAGGED MY SOCK!

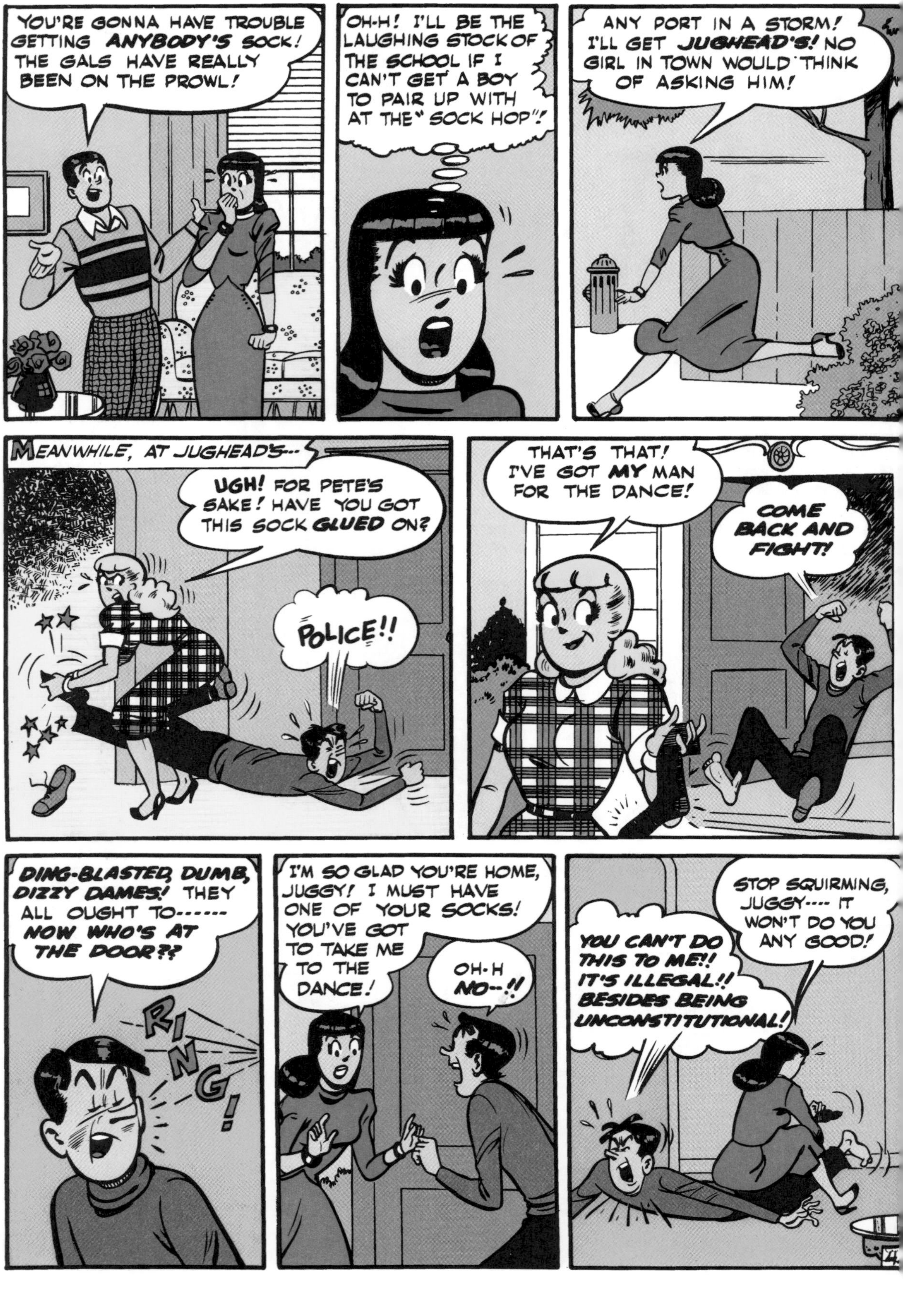
YOU'RE GONNA HAVE TROUBLE GETTING ANYBODY'S SOCK! THE GALS HAVE REALLY BEEN ON THE PROWL!
OH-H! I'LL BE THE LAUGHING STOCK OF THE SCHOOL IF I CAN'T GET A BOY TO PAIR UP WITH AT THE "SOCK HOP"!
ANY PORT IN A STORM! I'LL GET JUGHEAD'S! NO GIRL IN TOWN WOULD THINK OF ASKING HIM!
MEANWHILE, AT JUGHEAD'S---
UGH! FOR PETE'S SAKE! HAVE YOU GOT THIS SOCK GLUED ON?
POLICE!!
THAT'S THAT! I'VE GOT MY MAN FOR THE DANCE!
COME BACK AND FIGHT!
DING-BLASTED, DUMB, DIZZY DAMES! THEY ALL OUGHT TO------ NOW WHO'S AT THE DOOR??
RING!
I'M SO GLAD YOU'RE HOME, JUGGY! I MUST HAVE ONE OF YOUR SOCKS! YOU'VE GOT TO TAKE ME TO THE DANCE!
OH-H NO--!!
STOP SQUIRMING, JUGGY---- IT WON'T DO YOU ANY GOOD!
YOU CAN'T DO THIS TO ME!! IT'S ILLEGAL!! BESIDES BEING UNCONSTITUTIONAL!
4

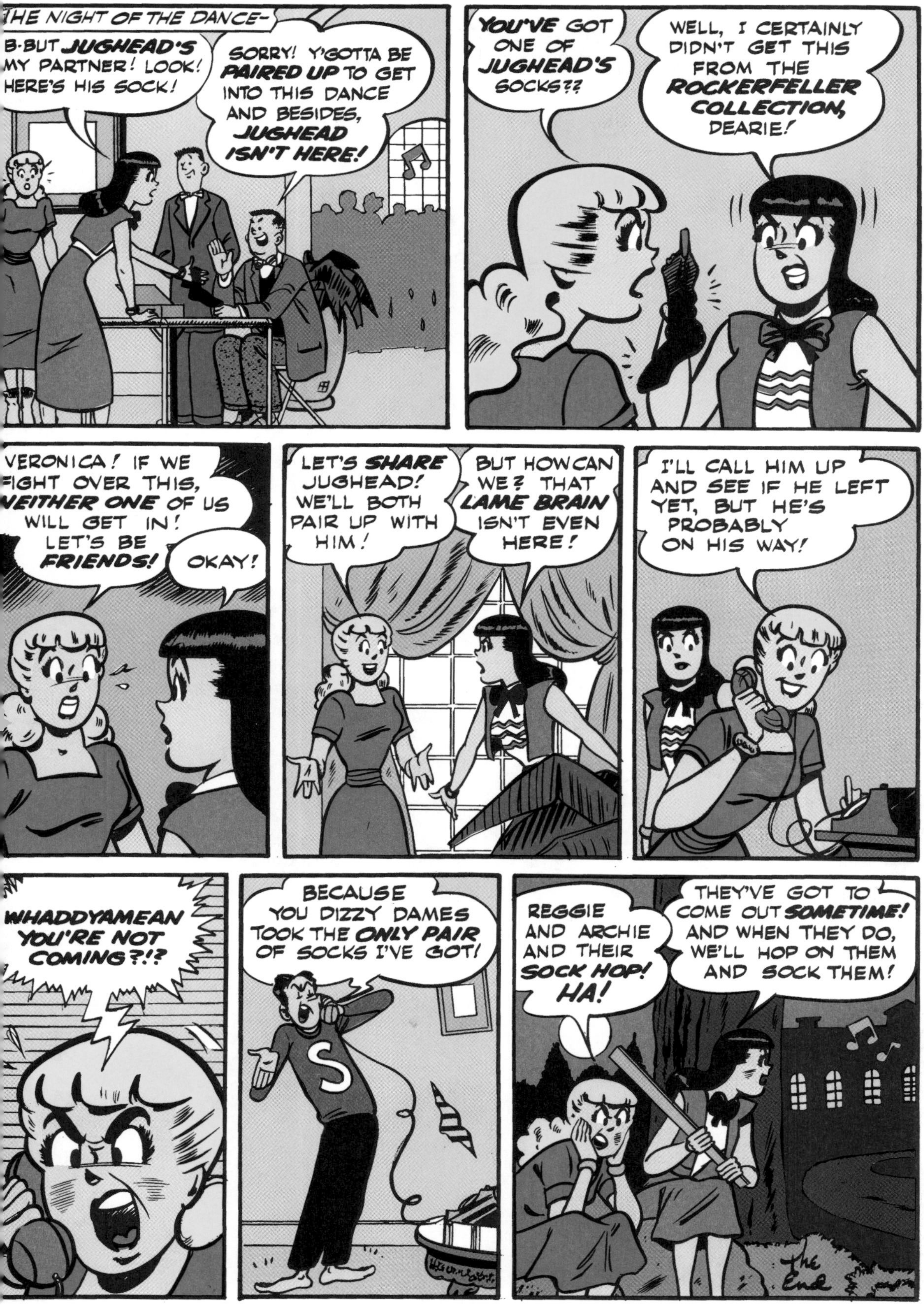
THE NIGHT OF THE DANCE—
B-BUT JUGHEAD'S MY PARTNER! LOOK! HERE'S HIS SOCK!
SORRY! Y'GOTTA BE PAIRED UP TO GET INTO THIS DANCE AND BESIDES, JUGHEAD ISN'T HERE!
YOU'VE GOT ONE OF JUGHEAD'S SOCKS??
WELL, I CERTAINLY DIDN'T GET THIS FROM THE ROCKERFELLER COLLECTION, DEARIE!
VERONICA! IF WE FIGHT OVER THIS, NEITHER ONE OF US WILL GET IN! LET'S BE FRIENDS!
OKAY!
LET'S SHARE JUGHEAD! WE'LL BOTH PAIR UP WITH HIM!
BUT HOW CAN WE? THAT LAME BRAIN ISN'T EVEN HERE!
I'LL CALL HIM UP AND SEE IF HE LEFT YET, BUT HE'S PROBABLY ON HIS WAY!
WHADDYAMEAN YOU'RE NOT COMING?!?
BECAUSE YOU DIZZY DAMES TOOK THE ONLY PAIR OF SOCKS I'VE GOT!
REGGIE AND ARCHIE AND THEIR SOCK HOP! HA!
THEY'VE GOT TO COME OUT SOMETIME! AND WHEN THEY DO, WE'LL HOP ON THEM AND SOCK THEM!
The End

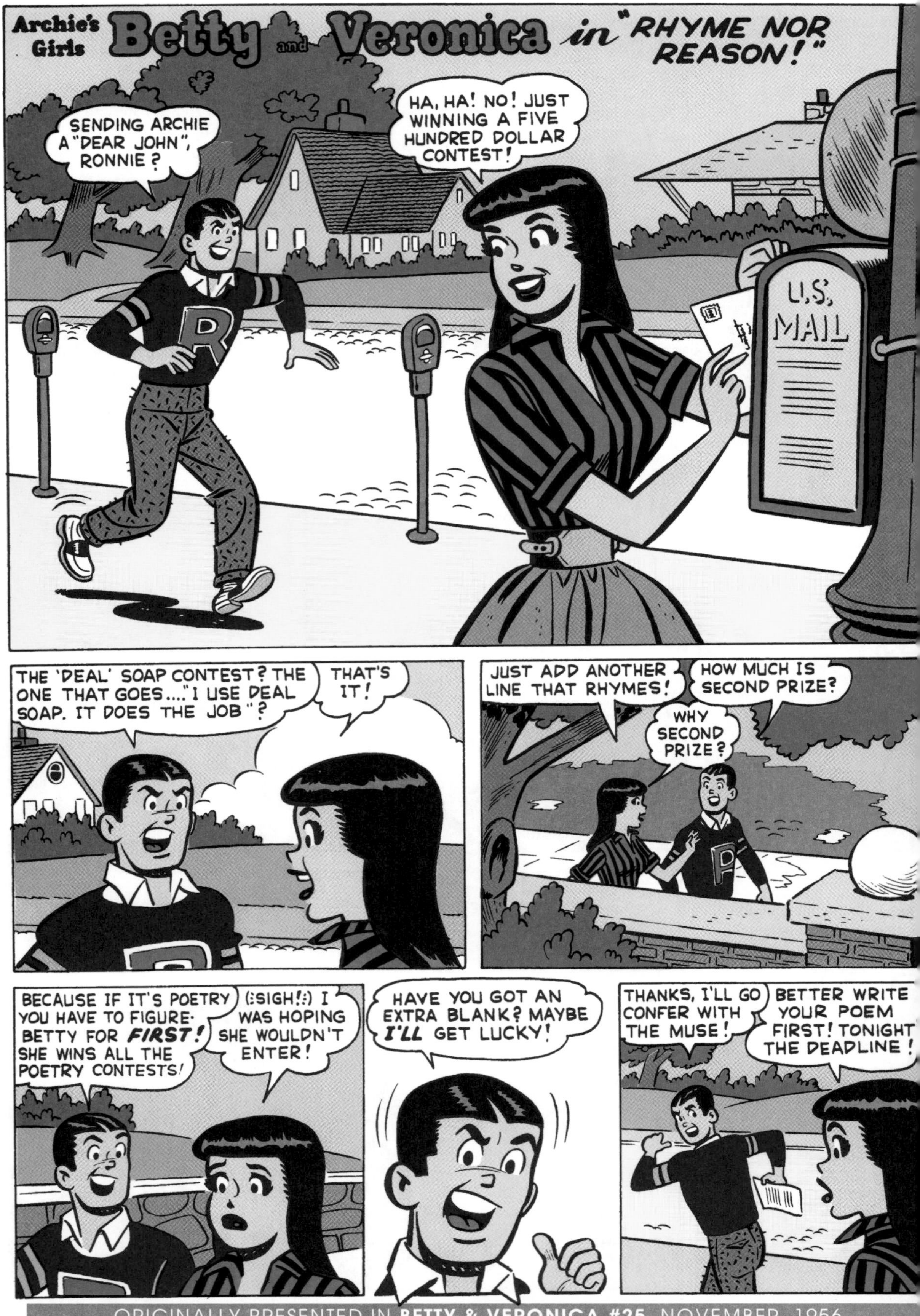
Archie's Girls Betty and Veronica in "RHYME NOR REASON!"
SENDING ARCHIE A "DEAR JOHN", RONNIE ?
HA, HA! NO! JUST WINNING A FIVE HUNDRED DOLLAR CONTEST!
U.S. MAIL
THE 'DEAL' SOAP CONTEST? THE ONE THAT GOES...."I USE DEAL SOAP. IT DOES THE JOB"?
THAT'S IT!
JUST ADD ANOTHER LINE THAT RHYMES!
HOW MUCH IS SECOND PRIZE?
WHY SECOND PRIZE?
BECAUSE IF IT'S POETRY YOU HAVE TO FIGURE BETTY FOR FIRST! SHE WINS ALL THE POETRY CONTESTS!
(:SIGH!:) I WAS HOPING SHE WOULDN'T ENTER!
HAVE YOU GOT AN EXTRA BLANK? MAYBE I'LL GET LUCKY!
THANKS, I'LL GO CONFER WITH THE MUSE!
BETTER WRITE YOUR POEM FIRST! TONIGHT THE DEADLINE!

ORIGINALLY PRESENTED IN **BETTY & VERONICA #25**, NOVEMBER, 1956.

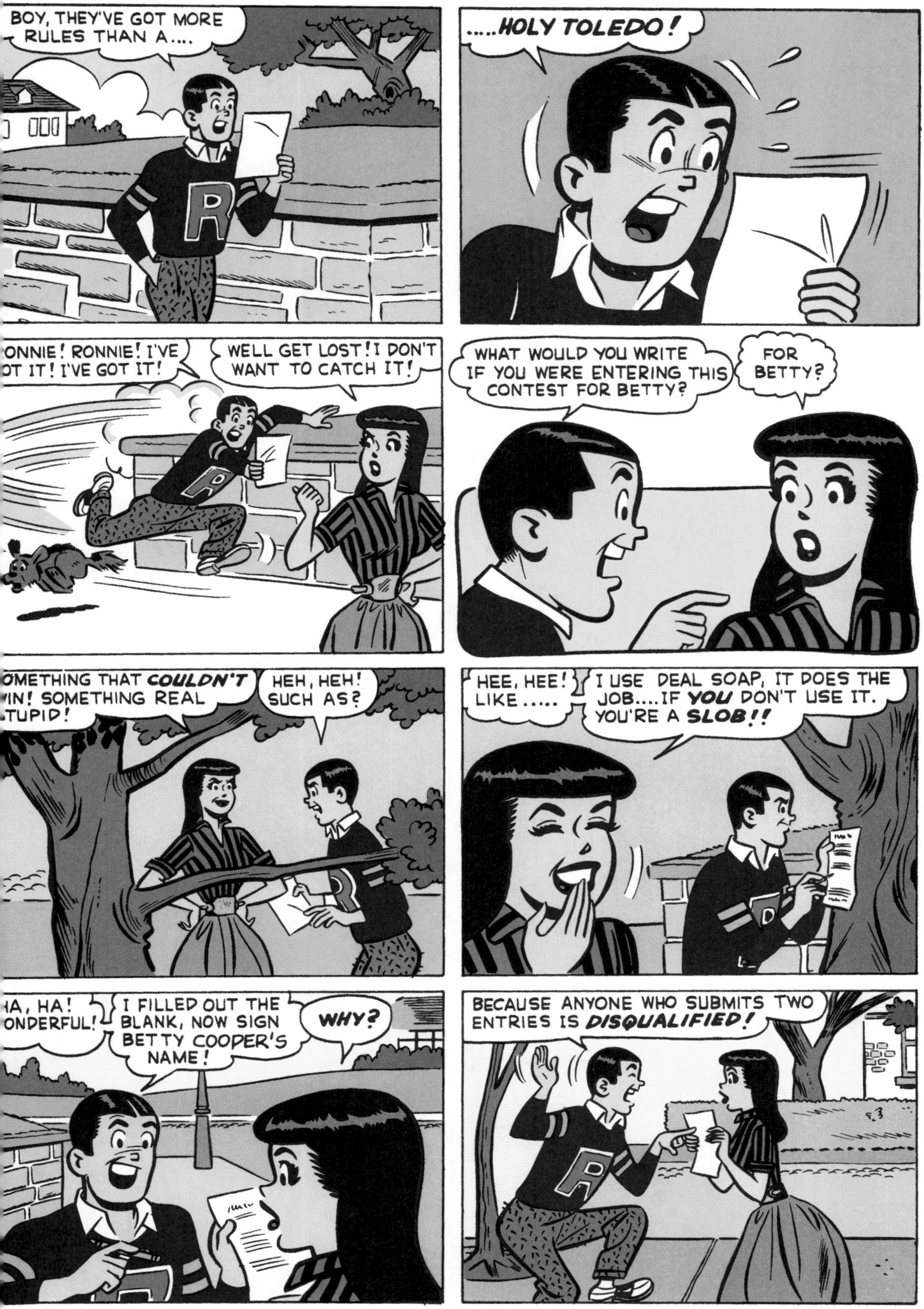
BOY, THEY'VE GOT MORE RULES THAN A....
.....HOLY TOLEDO!
ONNIE! RONNIE! I'VE OT IT! I'VE GOT IT!
WELL GET LOST! I DON'T WANT TO CATCH IT!
WHAT WOULD YOU WRITE IF YOU WERE ENTERING THIS CONTEST FOR BETTY?
FOR BETTY?
OMETHING THAT COULDN'T VIN! SOMETHING REAL TUPID!
HEH, HEH! SUCH AS?
HEE, HEE! LIKE.....
I USE DEAL SOAP, IT DOES THE JOB....IF YOU DON'T USE IT. YOU'RE A SLOB!!
HA, HA! ONDERFUL!
I FILLED OUT THE BLANK, NOW SIGN BETTY COOPER'S NAME!
WHY?
BECAUSE ANYONE WHO SUBMITS TWO ENTRIES IS DISQUALIFIED!

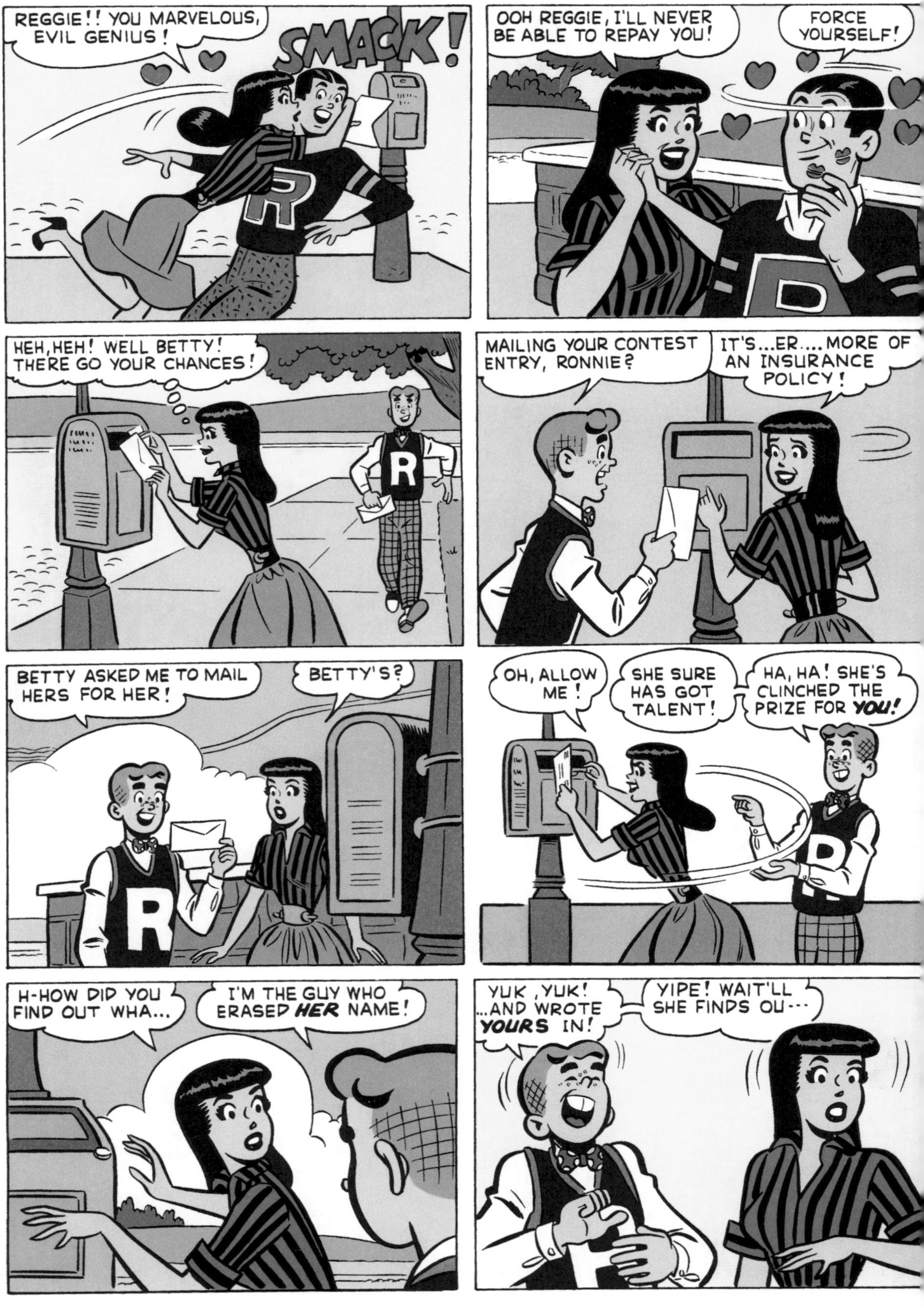
REGGIE!! YOU MARVELOUS, EVIL GENIUS!
SMACK!
OOH REGGIE, I'LL NEVER BE ABLE TO REPAY YOU!
FORCE YOURSELF!
HEH, HEH! WELL BETTY! THERE GO YOUR CHANCES!
MAILING YOUR CONTEST ENTRY, RONNIE?
IT'S...ER....MORE OF AN INSURANCE POLICY!
BETTY ASKED ME TO MAIL HERS FOR HER!
BETTY'S?
OH, ALLOW ME!
SHE SURE HAS GOT TALENT!
HA, HA! SHE'S CLINCHED THE PRIZE FOR *YOU!*
H-HOW DID YOU FIND OUT WHA...
I'M THE GUY WHO ERASED *HER* NAME!
YUK, YUK! ...AND WROTE *YOURS* IN!
YIPE! WAIT'LL SHE FINDS OU---

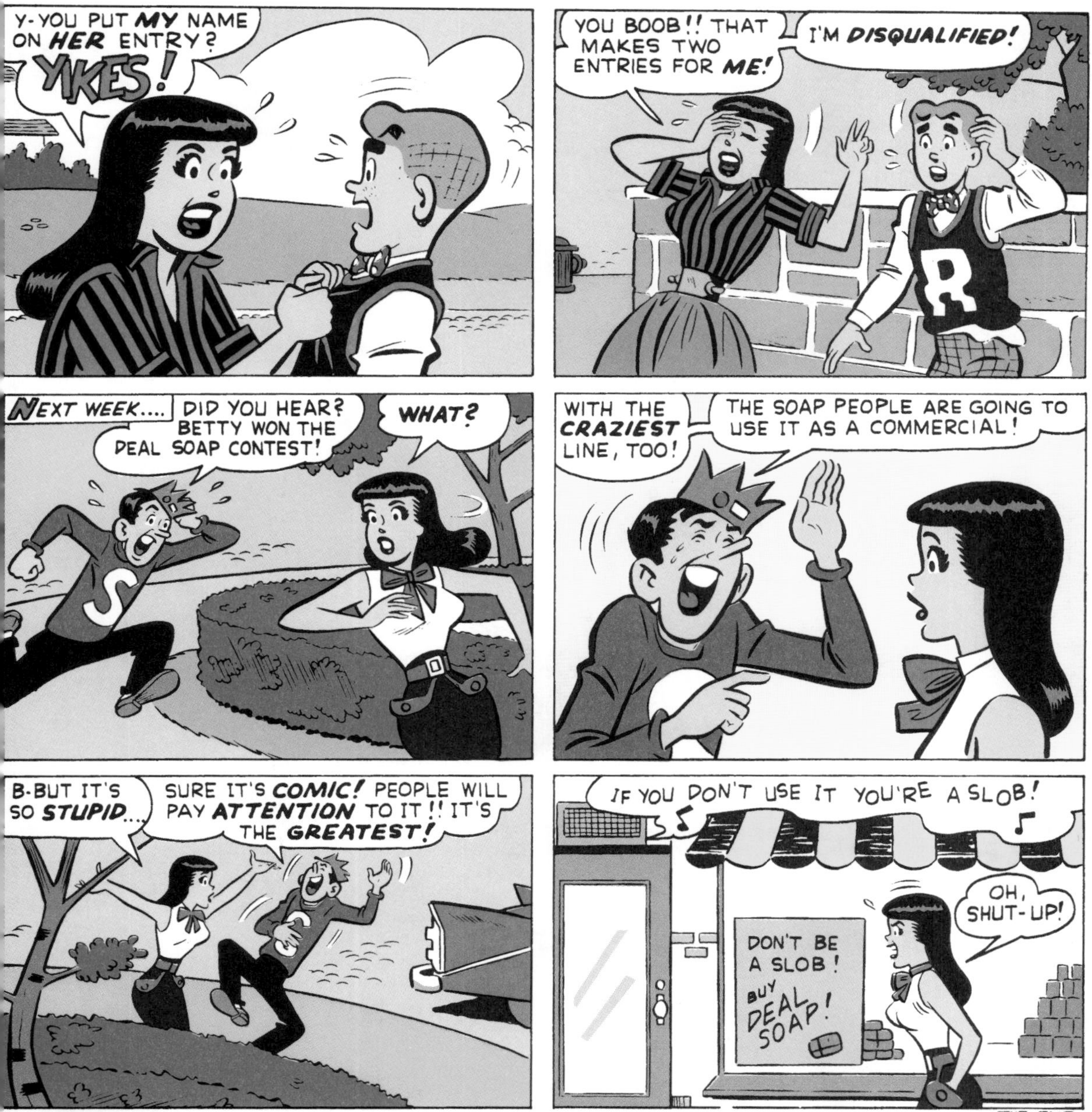
Y-YOU PUT MY NAME ON HER ENTRY? YIKES!
YOU BOOB!! THAT MAKES TWO ENTRIES FOR ME!
I'M DISQUALIFIED!
NEXT WEEK....
DID YOU HEAR? BETTY WON THE DEAL SOAP CONTEST!
WHAT?
WITH THE CRAZIEST LINE, TOO!
THE SOAP PEOPLE ARE GOING TO USE IT AS A COMMERCIAL!
B-BUT IT'S SO STUPID....
SURE IT'S COMIC! PEOPLE WILL PAY ATTENTION TO IT!! IT'S THE GREATEST!
IF YOU DON'T USE IT YOU'RE A SLOB!
DON'T BE A SLOB! BUY DEAL SOAP!
OH, SHUT-UP!
THE END

REGGIE

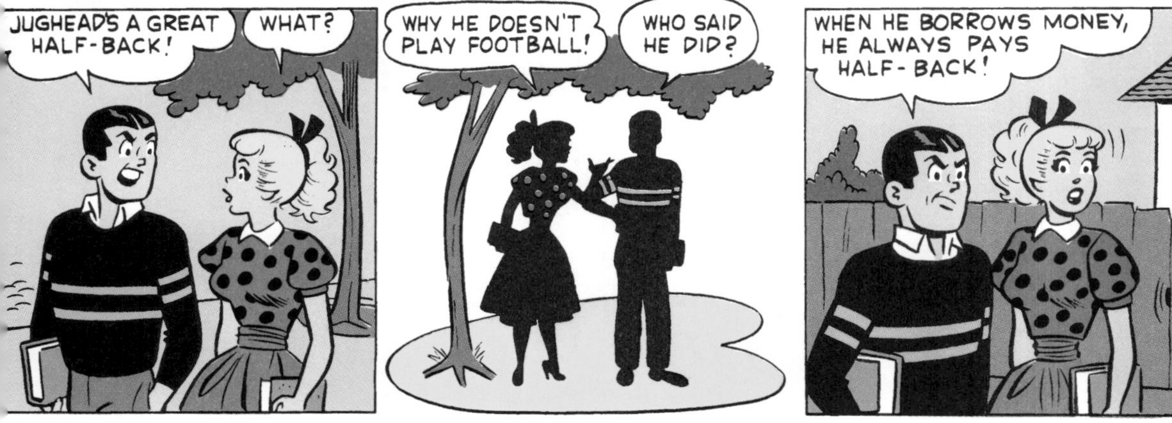
JUGHEAD'S A GREAT HALF-BACK!
WHAT?
WHY HE DOESN'T PLAY FOOTBALL!
WHO SAID HE DID?
WHEN HE BORROWS MONEY, HE ALWAYS PAYS HALF-BACK!

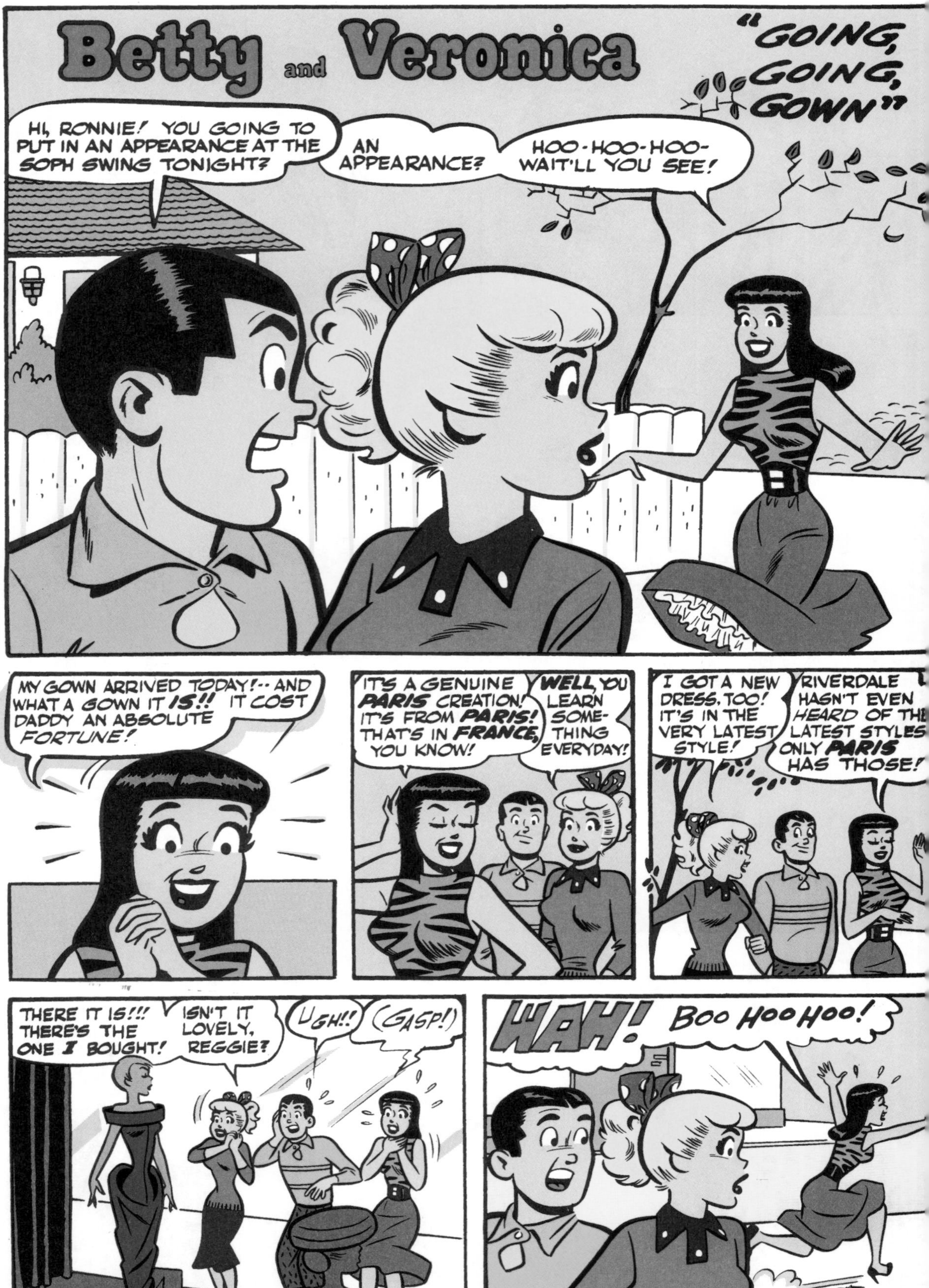
Betty and Veronica
"GOING, GOING, GOWN"
HI, RONNIE! YOU GOING TO PUT IN AN APPEARANCE AT THE SOPH SWING TONIGHT?
AN APPEARANCE?
HOO-HOO-HOO- WAIT'LL YOU SEE!
MY GOWN ARRIVED TODAY!-- AND WHAT A GOWN IT IS!! IT COST DADDY AN ABSOLUTE FORTUNE!
IT'S A GENUINE PARIS CREATION! IT'S FROM PARIS! THAT'S IN FRANCE, YOU KNOW!
WELL, YOU LEARN SOME-THING EVERYDAY!
I GOT A NEW DRESS, TOO! IT'S IN THE VERY LATEST STYLE!
RIVERDALE HASN'T EVEN HEARD OF THE LATEST STYLES ONLY PARIS HAS THOSE!
THERE IT IS!!! THERE'S THE ONE I BOUGHT!
ISN'T IT LOVELY, REGGIE?
UGH!!
(GASP!)
WAH! BOO HOO HOO!

ORIGINALLY PRESENTED IN **LAUGH COMICS #80**, APRIL, 1957.

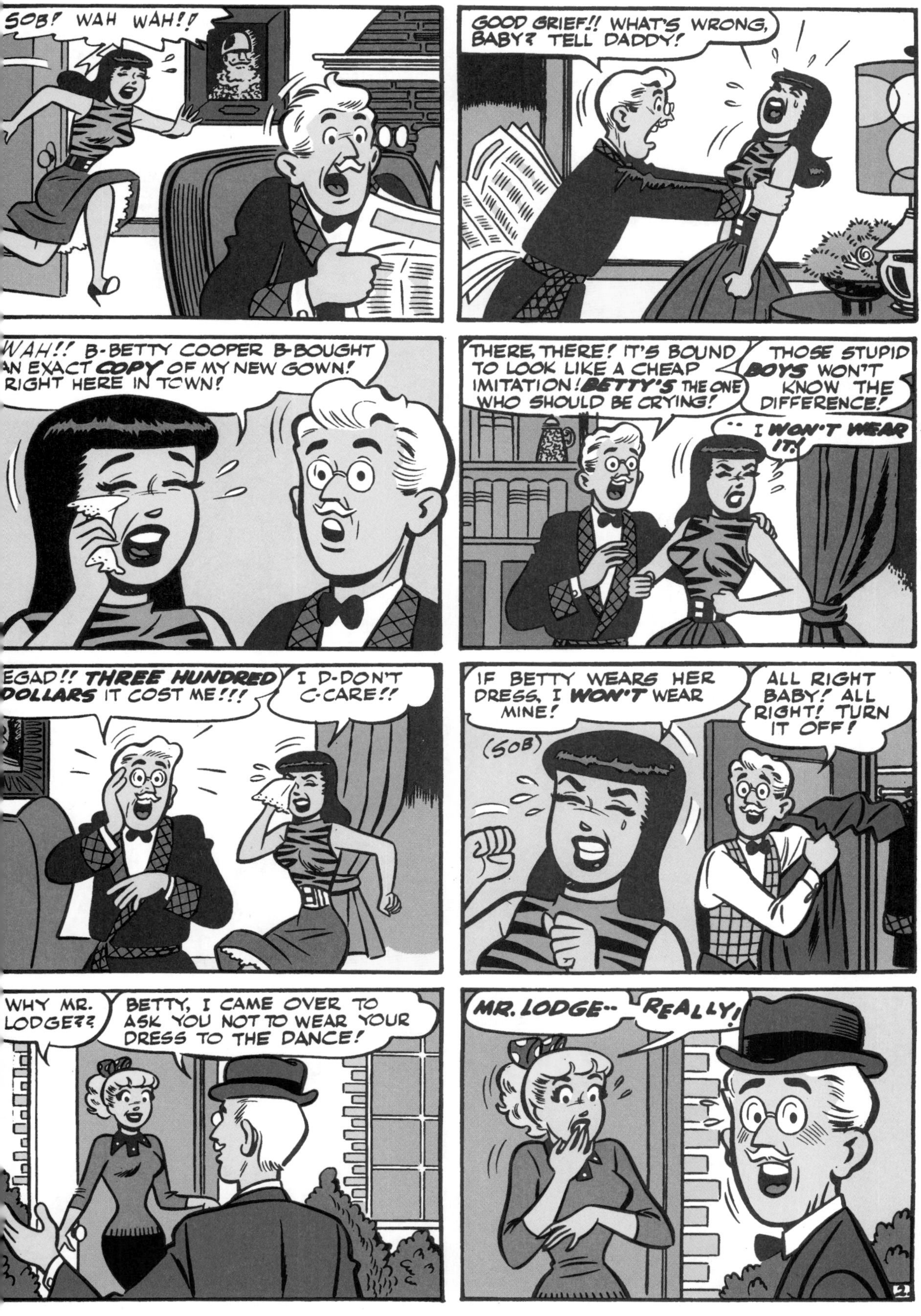
SOB! WAH WAH!!
GOOD GRIEF!! WHAT'S WRONG, BABY? TELL DADDY!
WAH!! B-BETTY COOPER B-BOUGHT AN EXACT COPY OF MY NEW GOWN! RIGHT HERE IN TOWN!
THERE, THERE! IT'S BOUND TO LOOK LIKE A CHEAP IMITATION! BETTY'S THE ONE WHO SHOULD BE CRYING!
THOSE STUPID BOYS WON'T KNOW THE DIFFERENCE!
.. I WON'T WEAR IT!
EGAD!! THREE HUNDRED DOLLARS IT COST ME!!!
I D-DON'T C-CARE!!
IF BETTY WEARS HER DRESS, I WON'T WEAR MINE!
(SOB)
ALL RIGHT BABY! ALL RIGHT! TURN IT OFF!
WHY MR. LODGE??
BETTY, I CAME OVER TO ASK YOU NOT TO WEAR YOUR DRESS TO THE DANCE!
MR. LODGE--
REALLY!
2

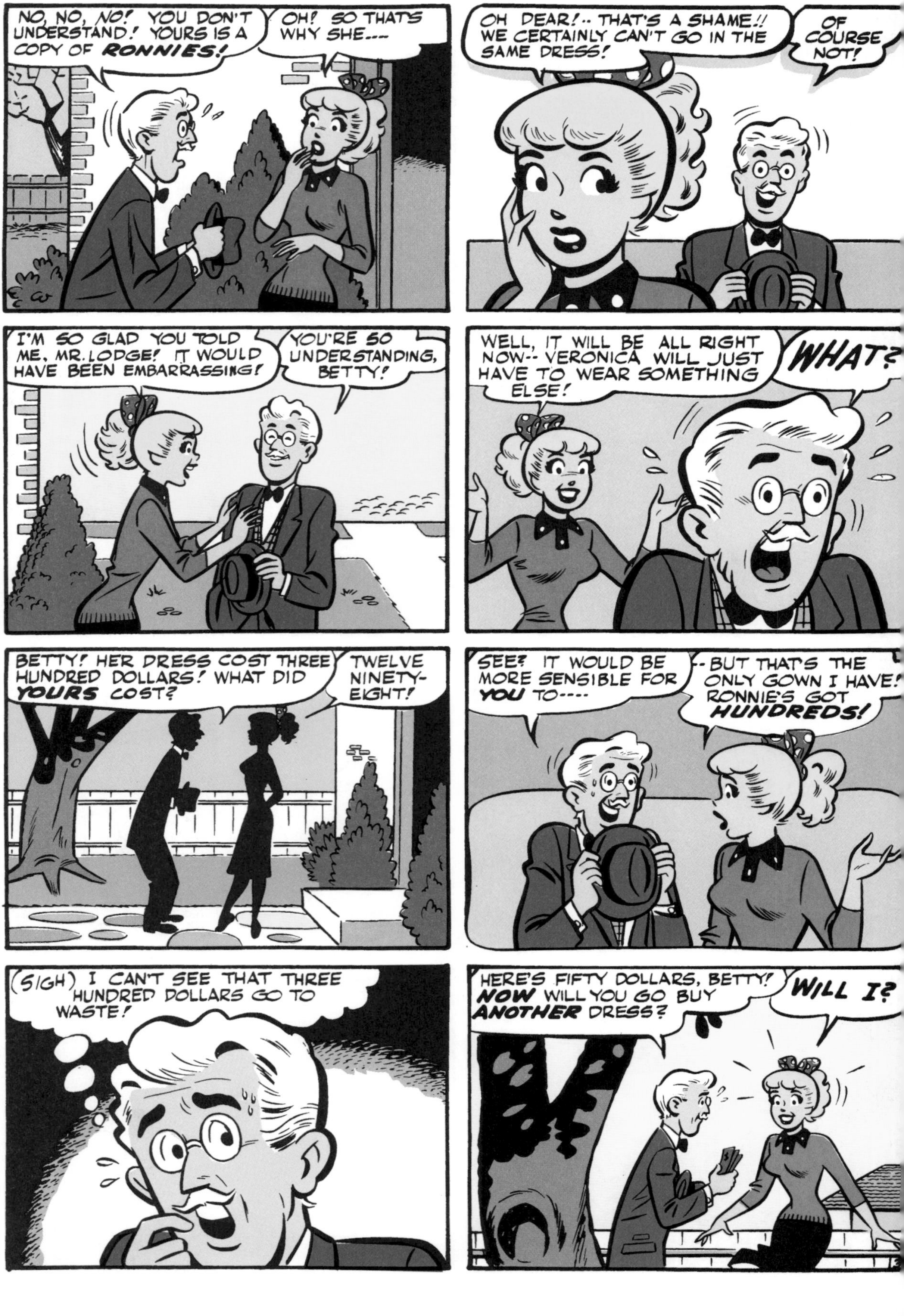
NO, NO, NO! YOU DON'T UNDERSTAND! YOURS IS A COPY OF RONNIES!
OH! SO THAT'S WHY SHE---
OH DEAR!.. THAT'S A SHAME!! WE CERTAINLY CAN'T GO IN THE SAME DRESS!
OF COURSE NOT!
I'M SO GLAD YOU TOLD ME, MR. LODGE! IT WOULD HAVE BEEN EMBARRASSING!
YOU'RE SO UNDERSTANDING, BETTY!
WELL, IT WILL BE ALL RIGHT NOW-- VERONICA WILL JUST HAVE TO WEAR SOMETHING ELSE!
WHAT?
BETTY! HER DRESS COST THREE HUNDRED DOLLARS! WHAT DID YOURS COST?
TWELVE NINETY-EIGHT!
SEE? IT WOULD BE MORE SENSIBLE FOR YOU TO----
-- BUT THAT'S THE ONLY GOWN I HAVE! RONNIE'S GOT HUNDREDS!
(SIGH) I CAN'T SEE THAT THREE HUNDRED DOLLARS GO TO WASTE!
HERE'S FIFTY DOLLARS, BETTY! NOW WILL YOU GO BUY ANOTHER DRESS?
WILL I?

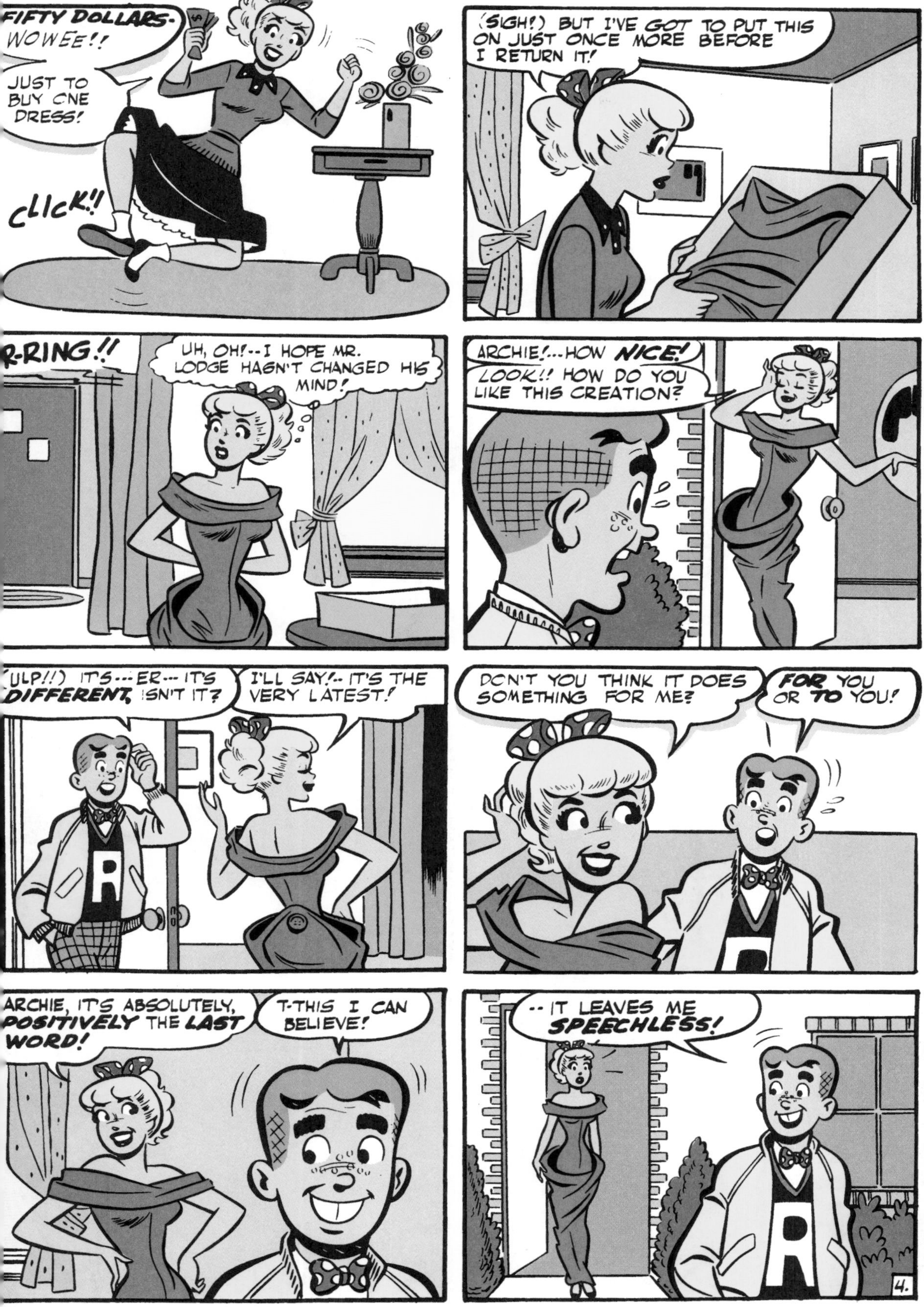
FIFTY DOLLARS- WOWEE!!
JUST TO BUY CNE DRESS!
CLICK!!
(SIGH!) BUT I'VE GOT TO PUT THIS ON JUST ONCE MORE BEFORE I RETURN IT!
R-RING!!
UH, OH!--I HOPE MR. LODGE HASN'T CHANGED HIS MIND!
ARCHIE!...HOW NICE!
LOOK!! HOW DO YOU LIKE THIS CREATION?
(ULP!!) IT'S...ER...IT'S DIFFERENT, ISN'T IT?
I'LL SAY!-- IT'S THE VERY LATEST!
DON'T YOU THINK IT DOES SOMETHING FOR ME?
FOR YOU OR TO YOU!
ARCHIE, IT'S ABSOLUTELY, POSITIVELY THE LAST WORD!
T-THIS I CAN BELIEVE!
-- IT LEAVES ME SPEECHLESS!
4.

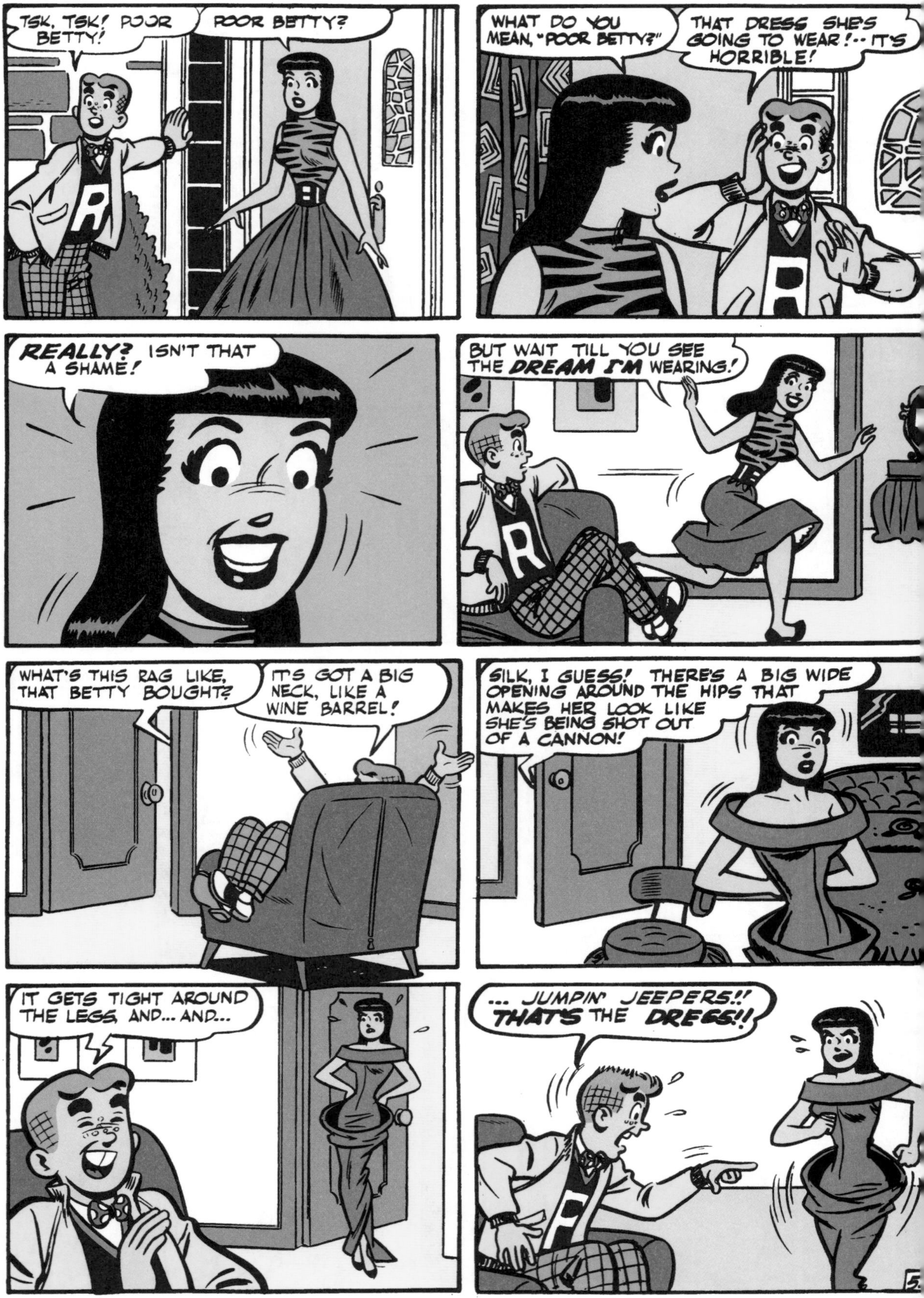
TSK, TSK! POOR BETTY!
POOR BETTY?
WHAT DO YOU MEAN, "POOR BETTY?"
THAT DRESS SHE'S GOING TO WEAR!-- IT'S HORRIBLE!
REALLY? ISN'T THAT A SHAME!
BUT WAIT TILL YOU SEE THE DREAM I'M WEARING!
WHAT'S THIS RAG LIKE, THAT BETTY BOUGHT?
IT'S GOT A BIG NECK, LIKE A WINE BARREL!
SILK, I GUESS! THERE'S A BIG WIDE OPENING AROUND THE HIPS THAT MAKES HER LOOK LIKE SHE'S BEING SHOT OUT OF A CANNON!
IT GETS TIGHT AROUND THE LEGS AND... AND...
... JUMPIN' JEEPERS!! THAT'S THE DRESS!!
5

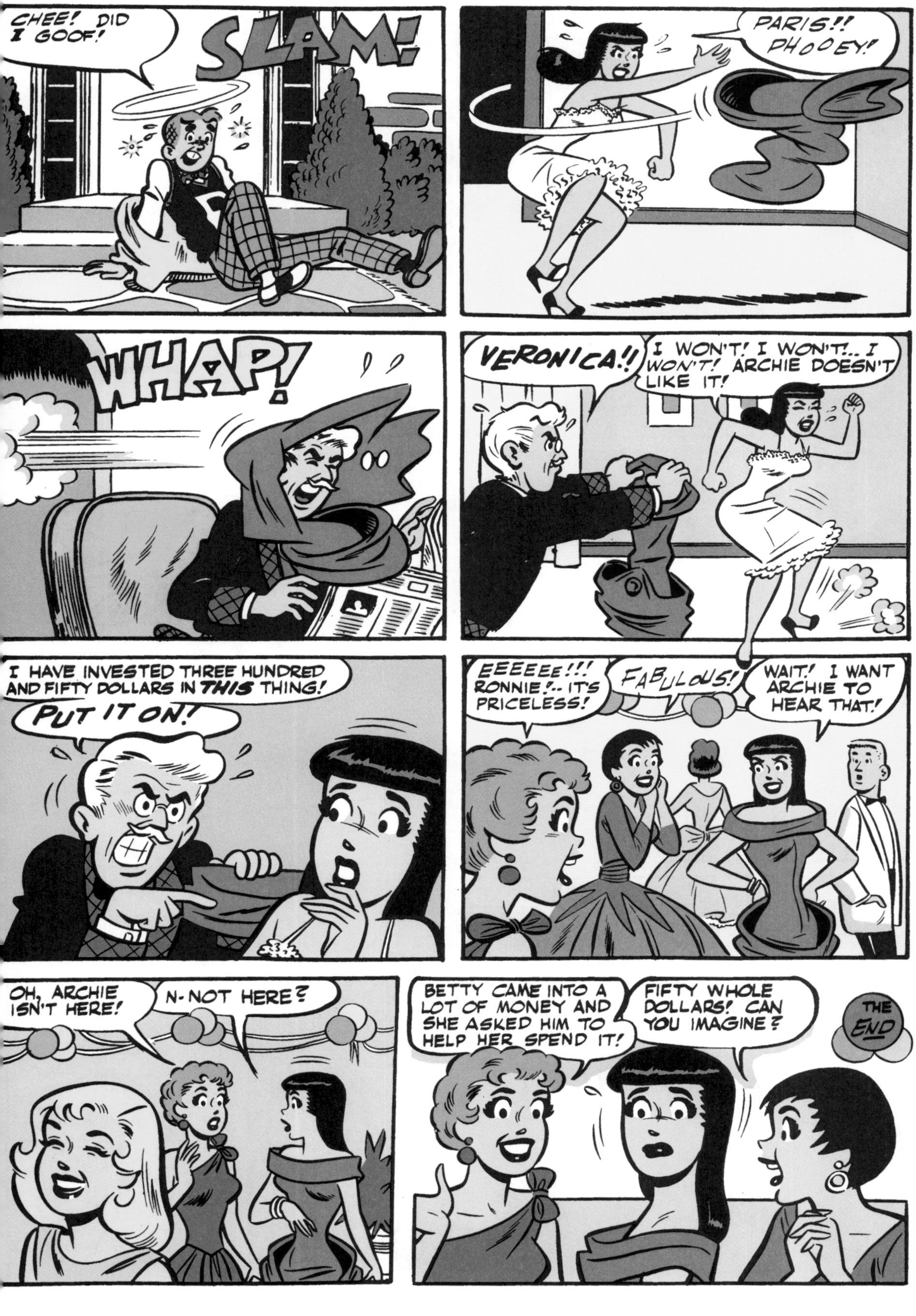
CHEE! DID I GOOF!
SLAM!
PARIS!! PHOOEY!
WHAP!
VERONICA!!
I WON'T! I WON'T!.. I WON'T! ARCHIE DOESN'T LIKE IT!
I HAVE INVESTED THREE HUNDRED AND FIFTY DOLLARS IN THIS THING!
PUT IT ON!
EEEEEE!!! RONNIE!.. IT'S PRICELESS!
FABULOUS!
WAIT! I WANT ARCHIE TO HEAR THAT!
OH, ARCHIE ISN'T HERE!
N-NOT HERE?
BETTY CAME INTO A LOT OF MONEY AND SHE ASKED HIM TO HELP HER SPEND IT!
FIFTY WHOLE DOLLARS! CAN YOU IMAGINE?
THE END

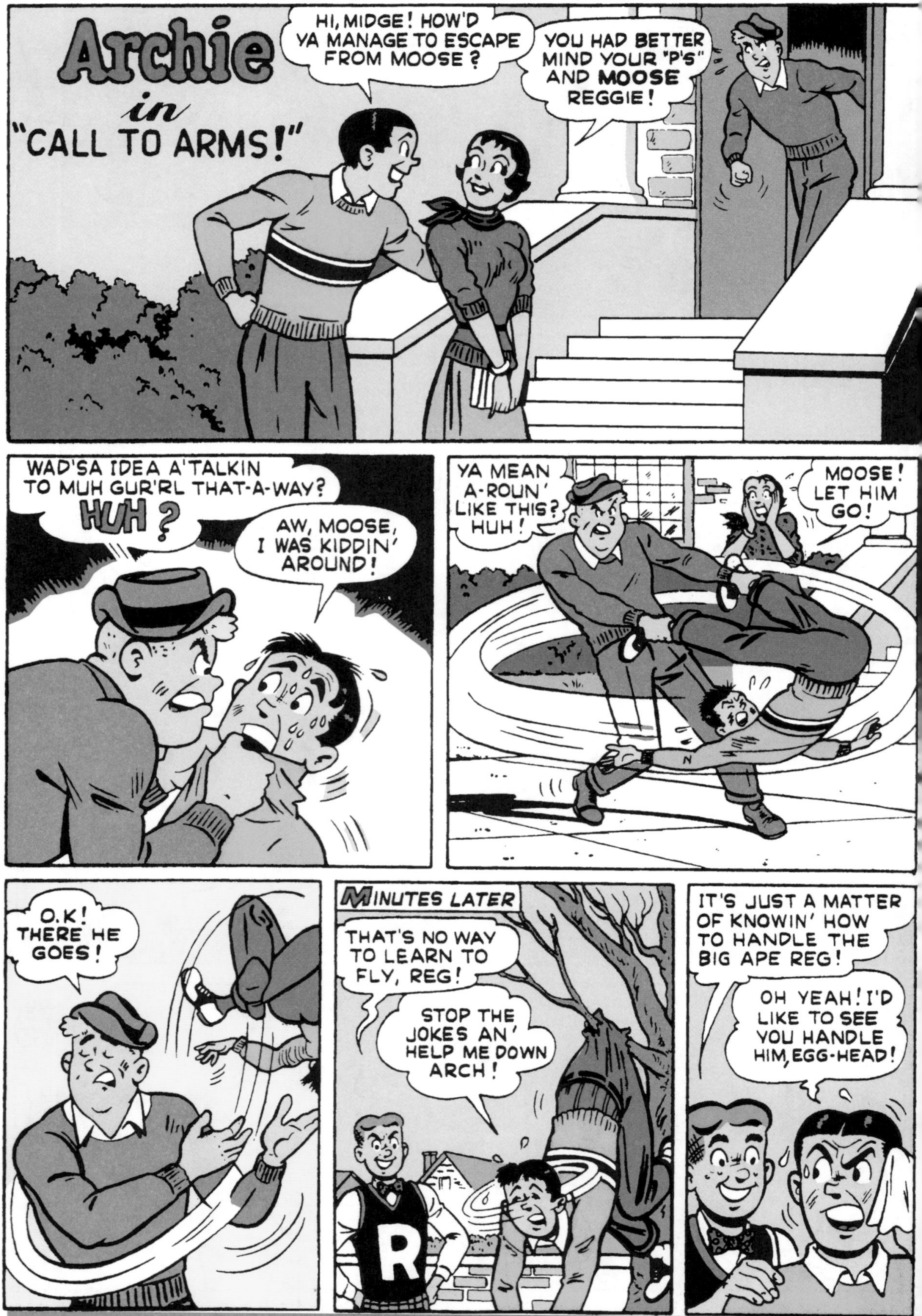
Archie
in
"CALL TO ARMS!"
HI, MIDGE! HOW'D YA MANAGE TO ESCAPE FROM MOOSE?
YOU HAD BETTER MIND YOUR "P'S" AND MOOSE REGGIE!
WAD'SA IDEA A'TALKIN TO MUH GUR'RL THAT-A-WAY? HUH?
AW, MOOSE, I WAS KIDDIN' AROUND!
YA MEAN A-ROUN' LIKE THIS? HUH!
MOOSE! LET HIM GO!
O.K! THERE HE GOES!
MINUTES LATER
THAT'S NO WAY TO LEARN TO FLY, REG!
STOP THE JOKES AN' HELP ME DOWN ARCH!
IT'S JUST A MATTER OF KNOWIN' HOW TO HANDLE THE BIG APE REG!
OH YEAH! I'D LIKE TO SEE YOU HANDLE HIM, EGG-HEAD!
R

ORIGINALLY PRESENTED IN **ARCHIE COMICS #86**, MAY-JUNE, 1957.

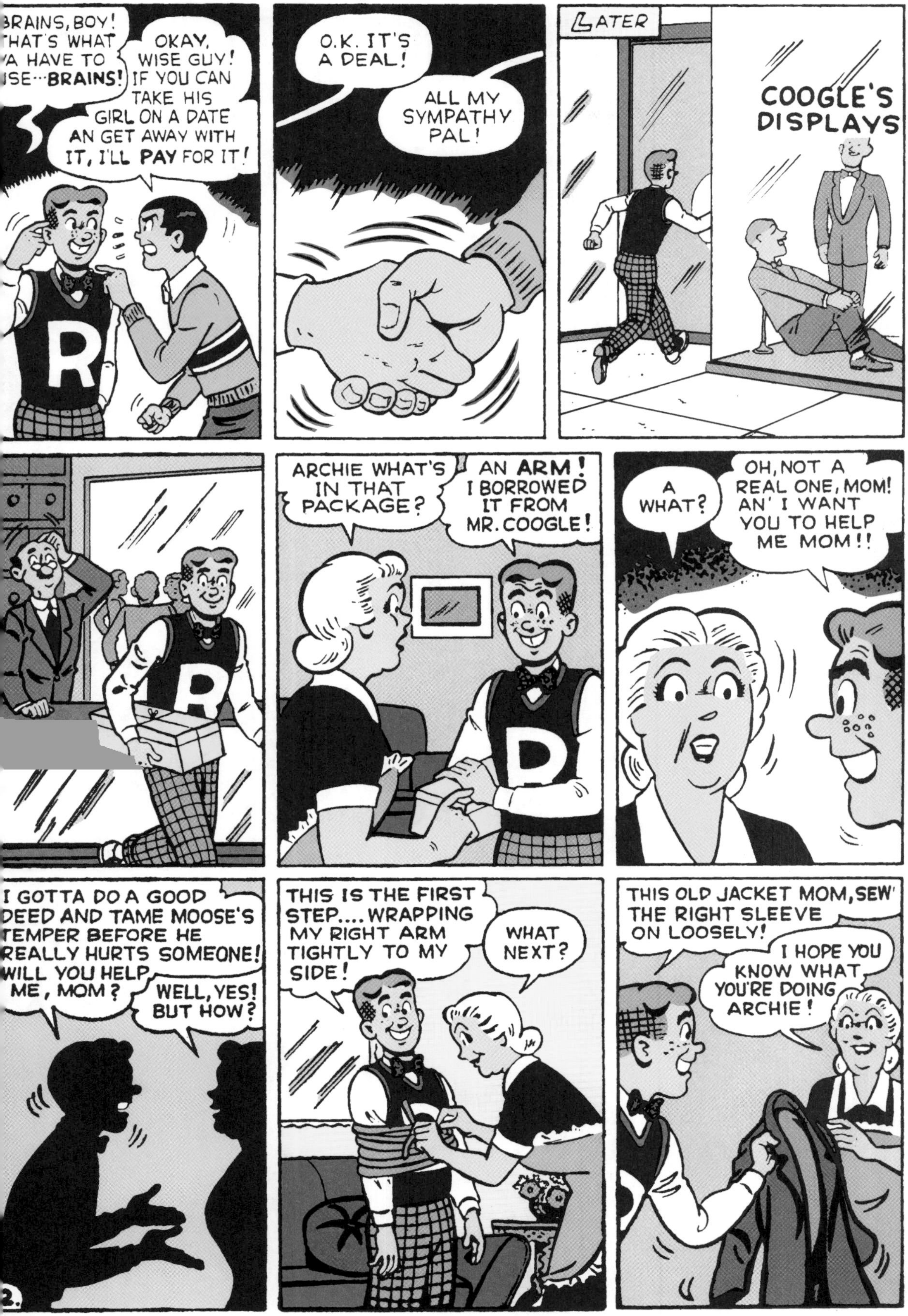
BRAINS, BOY! THAT'S WHAT YA HAVE TO USE···BRAINS!
OKAY, WISE GUY! IF YOU CAN TAKE HIS GIRL ON A DATE AN GET AWAY WITH IT, I'LL PAY FOR IT!
O.K. IT'S A DEAL!
ALL MY SYMPATHY PAL!
LATER
COOGLE'S DISPLAYS
ARCHIE WHAT'S IN THAT PACKAGE?
AN ARM! I BORROWED IT FROM MR. COOGLE!
A WHAT?
OH, NOT A REAL ONE, MOM! AN' I WANT YOU TO HELP ME MOM!!
I GOTTA DO A GOOD DEED AND TAME MOOSE'S TEMPER BEFORE HE REALLY HURTS SOMEONE! WILL YOU HELP ME, MOM?
WELL, YES! BUT HOW?
THIS IS THE FIRST STEP....WRAPPING MY RIGHT ARM TIGHTLY TO MY SIDE!
WHAT NEXT?
THIS OLD JACKET MOM, SEW THE RIGHT SLEEVE ON LOOSELY!
I HOPE YOU KNOW WHAT YOU'RE DOING ARCHIE!

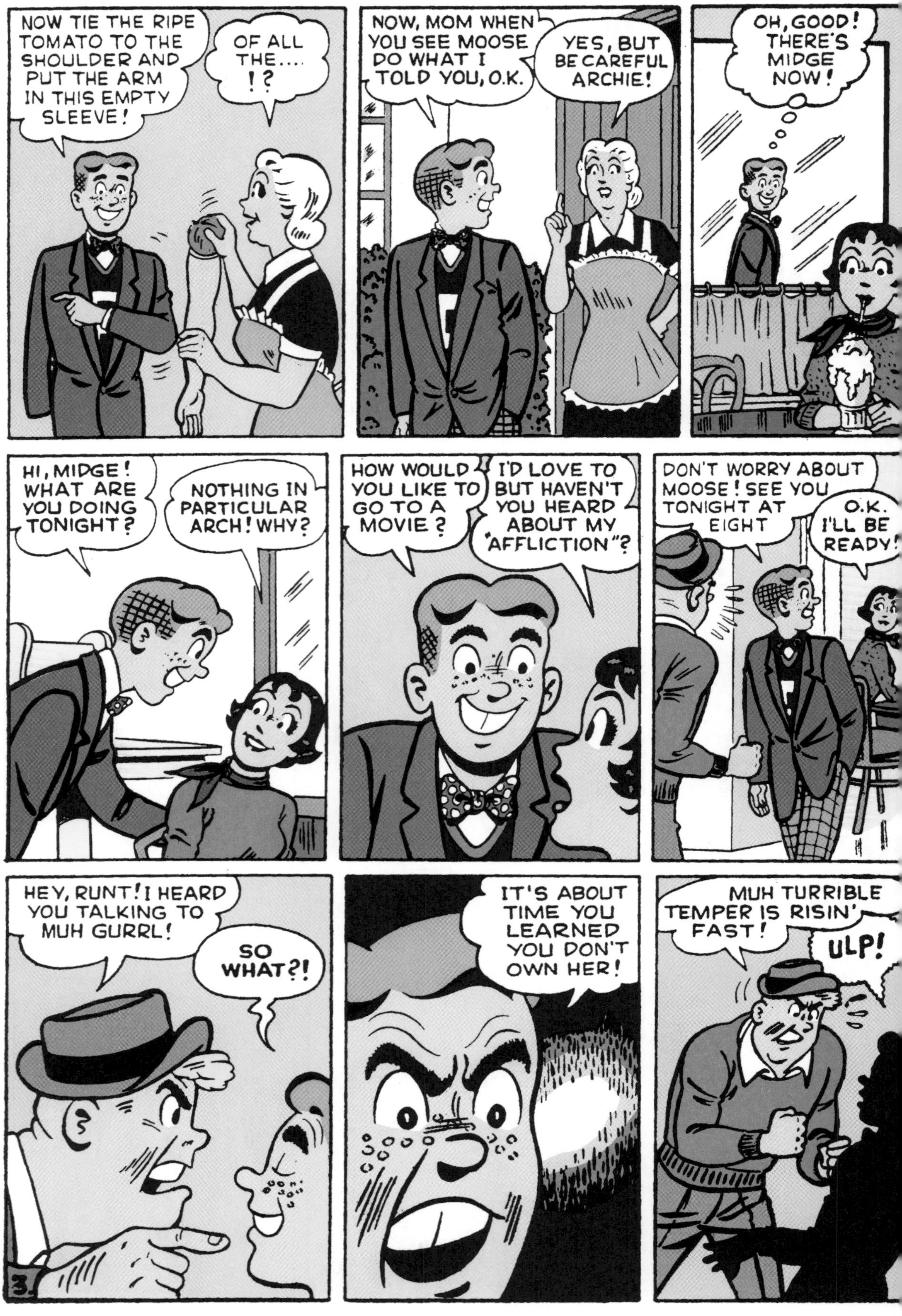
NOW TIE THE RIPE TOMATO TO THE SHOULDER AND PUT THE ARM IN THIS EMPTY SLEEVE!
OF ALL THE.... !?
NOW, MOM WHEN YOU SEE MOOSE DO WHAT I TOLD YOU, O.K.
YES, BUT BE CAREFUL ARCHIE!
OH, GOOD! THERE'S MIDGE NOW!
HI, MIDGE! WHAT ARE YOU DOING TONIGHT?
NOTHING IN PARTICULAR ARCH! WHY?
HOW WOULD YOU LIKE TO GO TO A MOVIE?
I'D LOVE TO BUT HAVEN'T YOU HEARD ABOUT MY "AFFLICTION"?
DON'T WORRY ABOUT MOOSE! SEE YOU TONIGHT AT EIGHT
O.K. I'LL BE READY!
HEY, RUNT! I HEARD YOU TALKING TO MUH GURRL!
SO WHAT?!
IT'S ABOUT TIME YOU LEARNED YOU DON'T OWN HER!
MUH TURRIBLE TEMPER IS RISIN' FAST!
ULP!

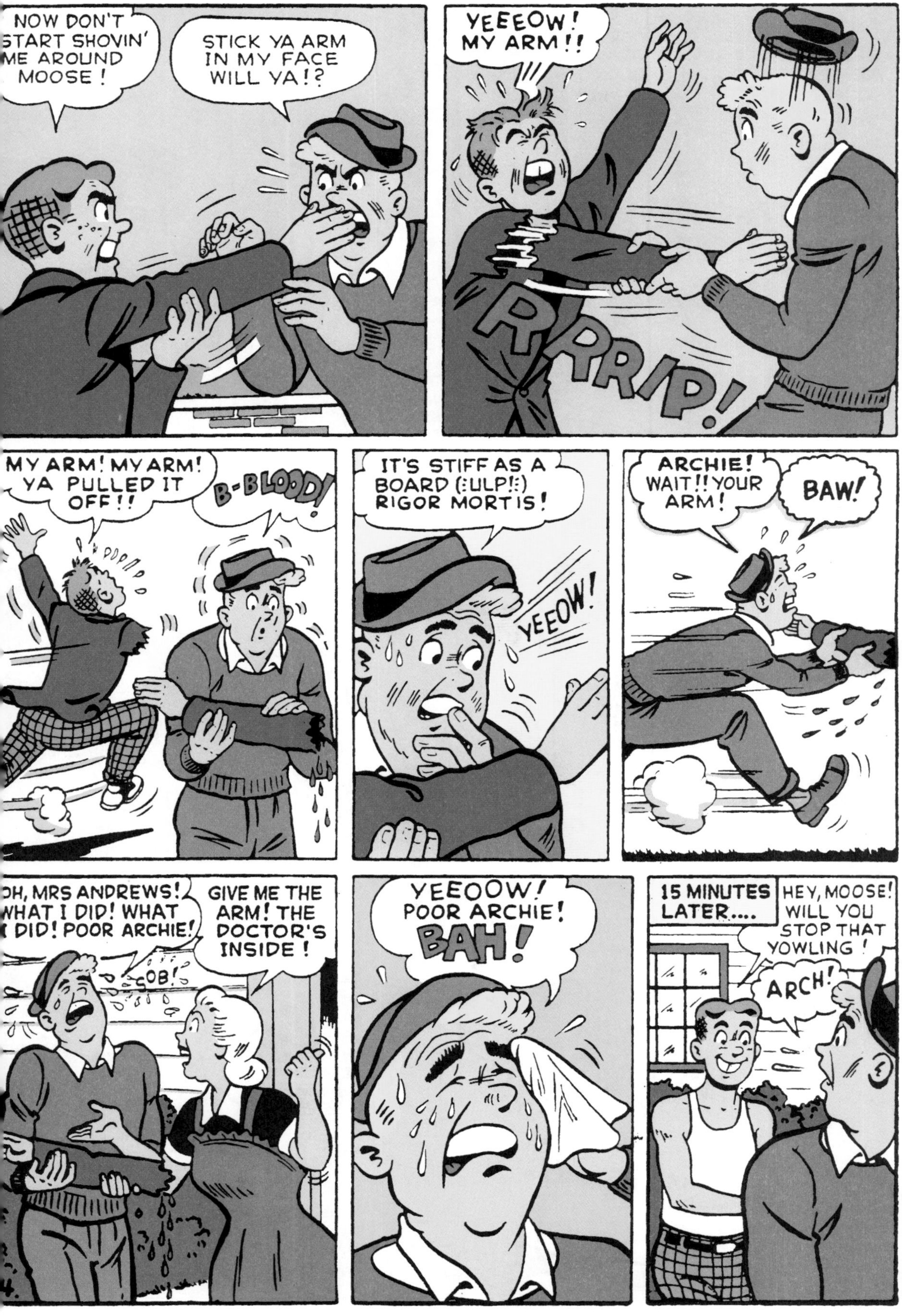
NOW DON'T START SHOVIN' ME AROUND MOOSE!
STICK YA ARM IN MY FACE WILL YA!?
YEEEOW! MY ARM!!
RRRIP!
MY ARM! MY ARM! YA PULLED IT OFF!!
B-BLOOD!
IT'S STIFF AS A BOARD (:ULP!:) RIGOR MORTIS!
YEEOW!
ARCHIE! WAIT!! YOUR ARM!
BAW!
OH, MRS ANDREWS! WHAT I DID! WHAT I DID! POOR ARCHIE!
SOB!
GIVE ME THE ARM! THE DOCTOR'S INSIDE!
YEEOOW! POOR ARCHIE! BAH!
15 MINUTES LATER....
HEY, MOOSE! WILL YOU STOP THAT YOWLING!
ARCH!

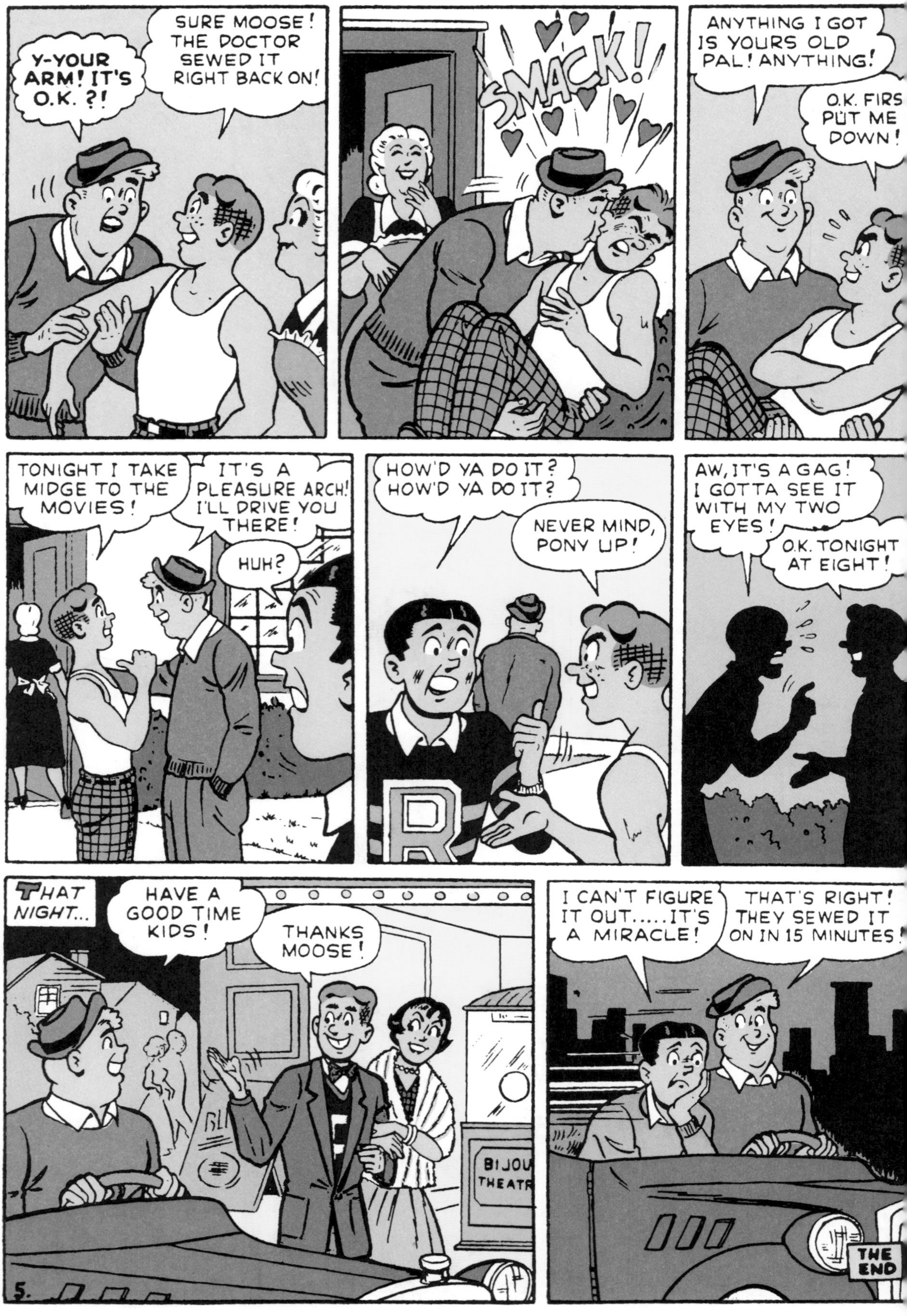
Y-YOUR ARM! IT'S O.K. ?!
SURE MOOSE! THE DOCTOR SEWED IT RIGHT BACK ON!
SMACK!
ANYTHING I GOT IS YOURS OLD PAL! ANYTHING!
O.K. FIRS PUT ME DOWN!
TONIGHT I TAKE MIDGE TO THE MOVIES!
IT'S A PLEASURE ARCH! I'LL DRIVE YOU THERE!
HUH?
HOW'D YA DO IT? HOW'D YA DO IT?
NEVER MIND, PONY UP!
AW, IT'S A GAG! I GOTTA SEE IT WITH MY TWO EYES!
O.K. TONIGHT AT EIGHT!
THAT NIGHT...
HAVE A GOOD TIME KIDS!
THANKS MOOSE!
BIJOU THEATR
5.
I CAN'T FIGURE IT OUT.....IT'S A MIRACLE!
THAT'S RIGHT! THEY SEWED IT ON IN 15 MINUTES!
THE END

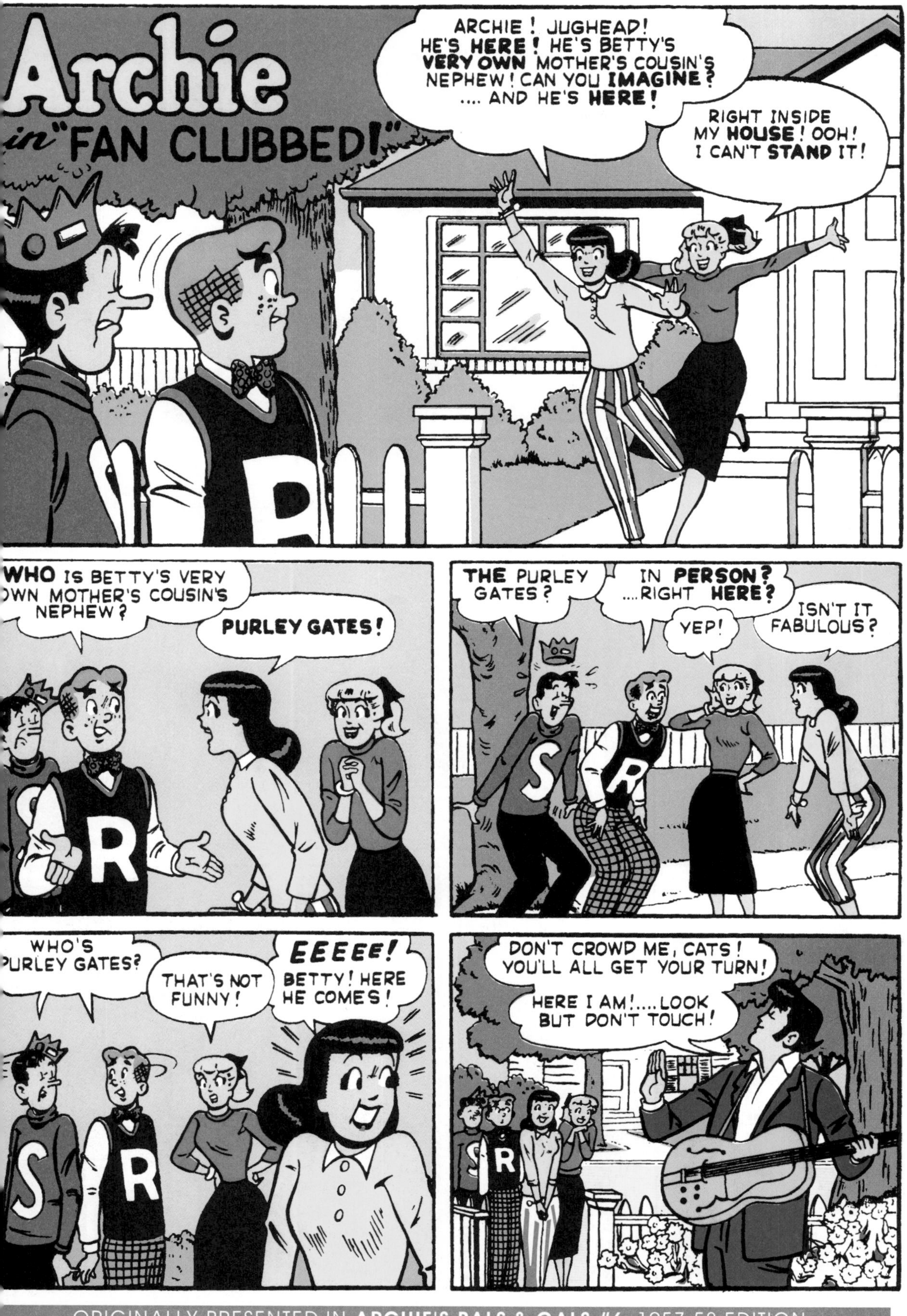
Archie in "FAN CLUBBED!"
ARCHIE! JUGHEAD! HE'S HERE! HE'S BETTY'S VERY OWN MOTHER'S COUSIN'S NEPHEW! CAN YOU IMAGINE? .... AND HE'S HERE!
RIGHT INSIDE MY HOUSE! OOH! I CAN'T STAND IT!
WHO IS BETTY'S VERY OWN MOTHER'S COUSIN'S NEPHEW?
PURLEY GATES!
THE PURLEY GATES?
IN PERSON? ....RIGHT HERE?
YEP!
ISN'T IT FABULOUS?
WHO'S PURLEY GATES?
THAT'S NOT FUNNY!
EEEEE! BETTY! HERE HE COMES!
DON'T CROWD ME, CATS! YOU'LL ALL GET YOUR TURN!
HERE I AM!....LOOK BUT DON'T TOUCH!

ORIGINALLY PRESENTED IN **ARCHIE'S PALS & GALS #6**, 1957-58 EDITION.

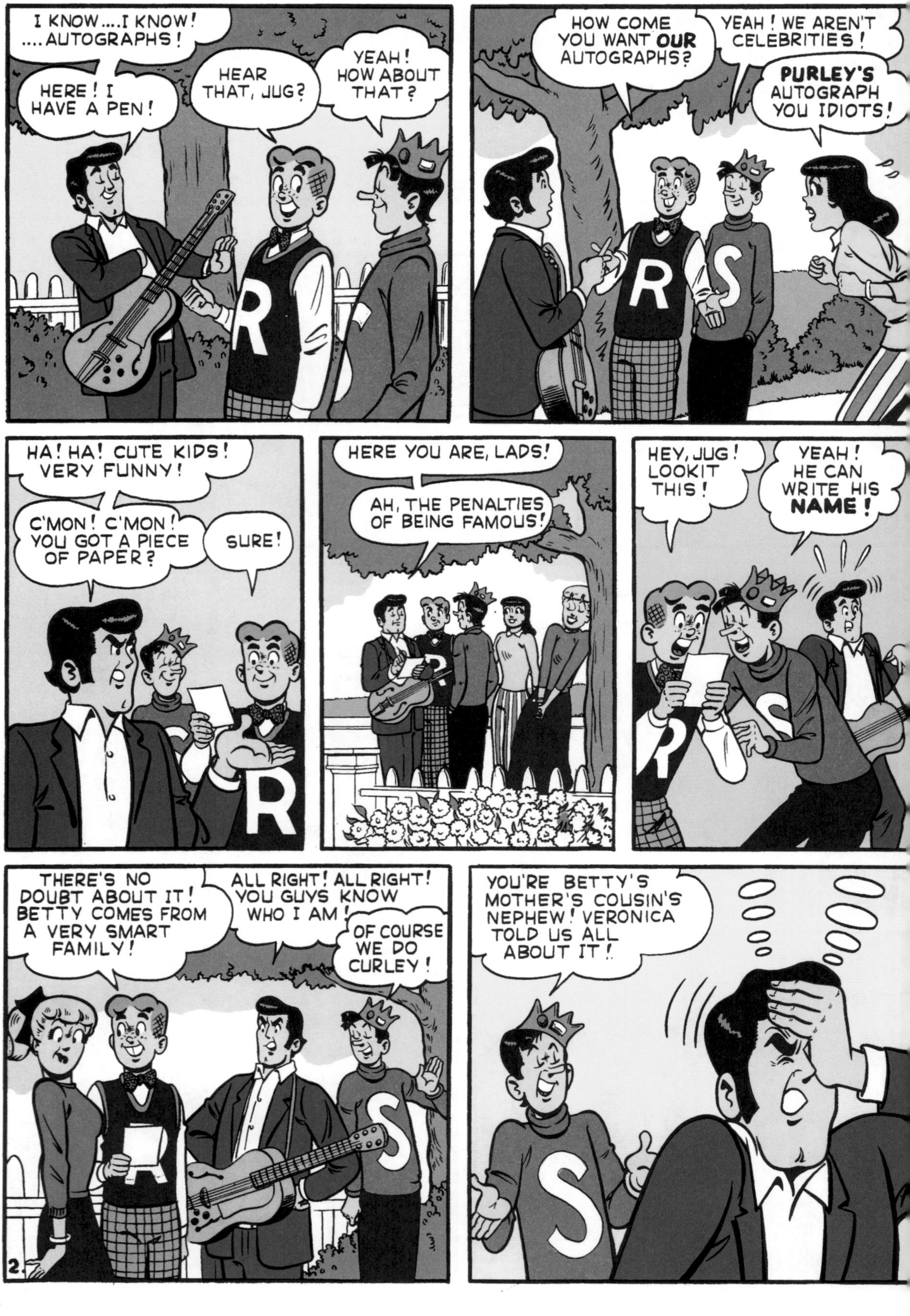
I KNOW....I KNOW! ....AUTOGRAPHS!
HERE! I HAVE A PEN!
HEAR THAT, JUG?
YEAH! HOW ABOUT THAT?
HOW COME YOU WANT **OUR** AUTOGRAPHS?
YEAH! WE AREN'T CELEBRITIES!
PURLEY'S AUTOGRAPH YOU IDIOTS!
HA! HA! CUTE KIDS! VERY FUNNY!
C'MON! C'MON! YOU GOT A PIECE OF PAPER?
SURE!
HERE YOU ARE, LADS!
AH, THE PENALTIES OF BEING FAMOUS!
HEY, JUG! LOOKIT THIS!
YEAH! HE CAN WRITE HIS **NAME**!
THERE'S NO DOUBT ABOUT IT! BETTY COMES FROM A VERY SMART FAMILY!
ALL RIGHT! ALL RIGHT! YOU GUYS KNOW WHO I AM!
OF COURSE WE DO CURLEY!
2
YOU'RE BETTY'S MOTHER'S COUSIN'S NEPHEW! VERONICA TOLD US ALL ABOUT IT!

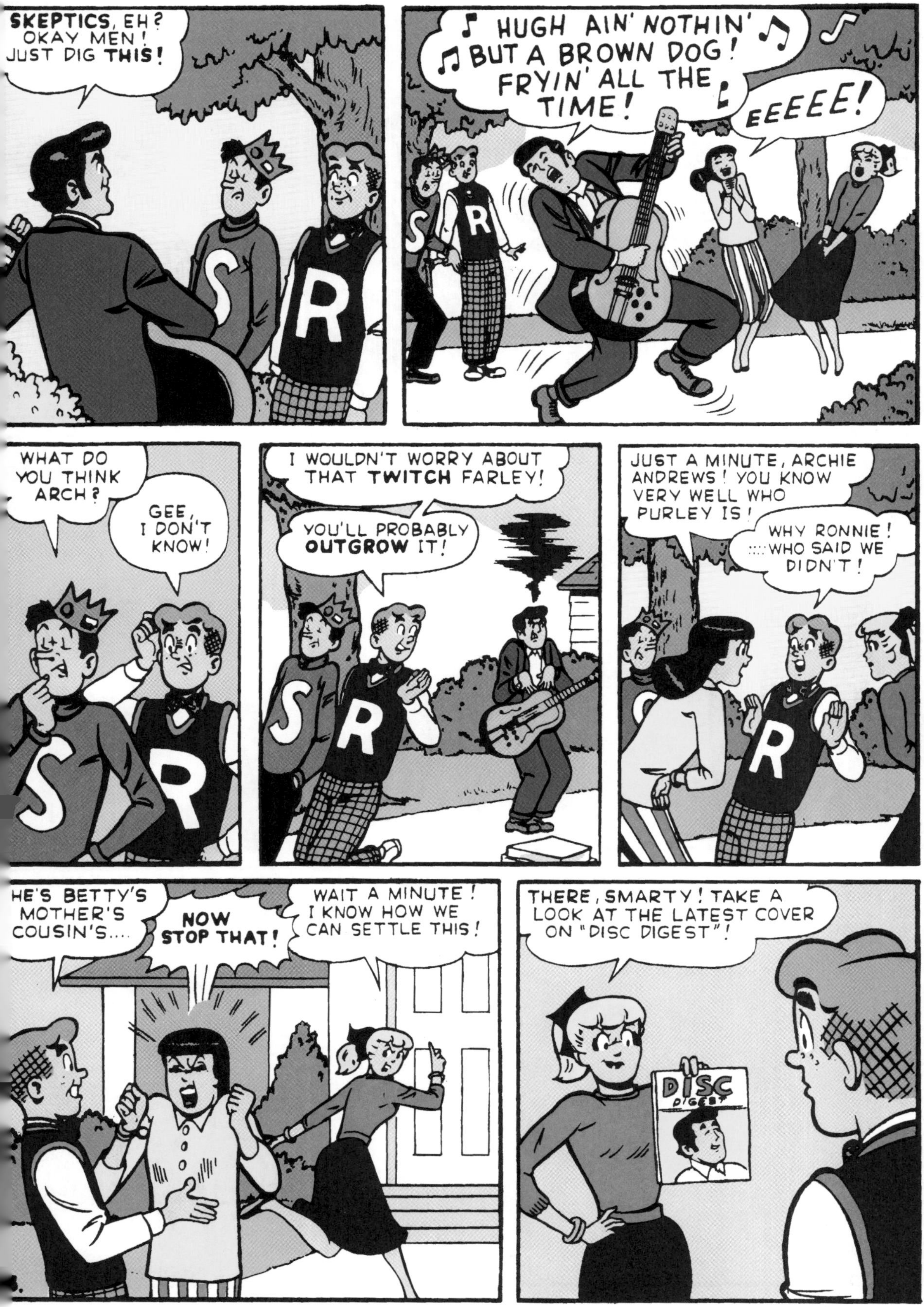
SKEPTICS, EH? OKAY MEN! JUST DIG THIS!
HUGH AIN' NOTHIN' BUT A BROWN DOG! FRYIN' ALL THE TIME!
EEEEE!
WHAT DO YOU THINK ARCH?
GEE, I DON'T KNOW!
I WOULDN'T WORRY ABOUT THAT TWITCH FARLEY!
YOU'LL PROBABLY OUTGROW IT!
JUST A MINUTE, ARCHIE ANDREWS! YOU KNOW VERY WELL WHO PURLEY IS!
WHY RONNIE! WHO SAID WE DIDN'T!
HE'S BETTY'S MOTHER'S COUSIN'S....
NOW STOP THAT!
WAIT A MINUTE! I KNOW HOW WE CAN SETTLE THIS!
THERE, SMARTY! TAKE A LOOK AT THE LATEST COVER ON "DISC DIGEST"!
DISC DIGEST

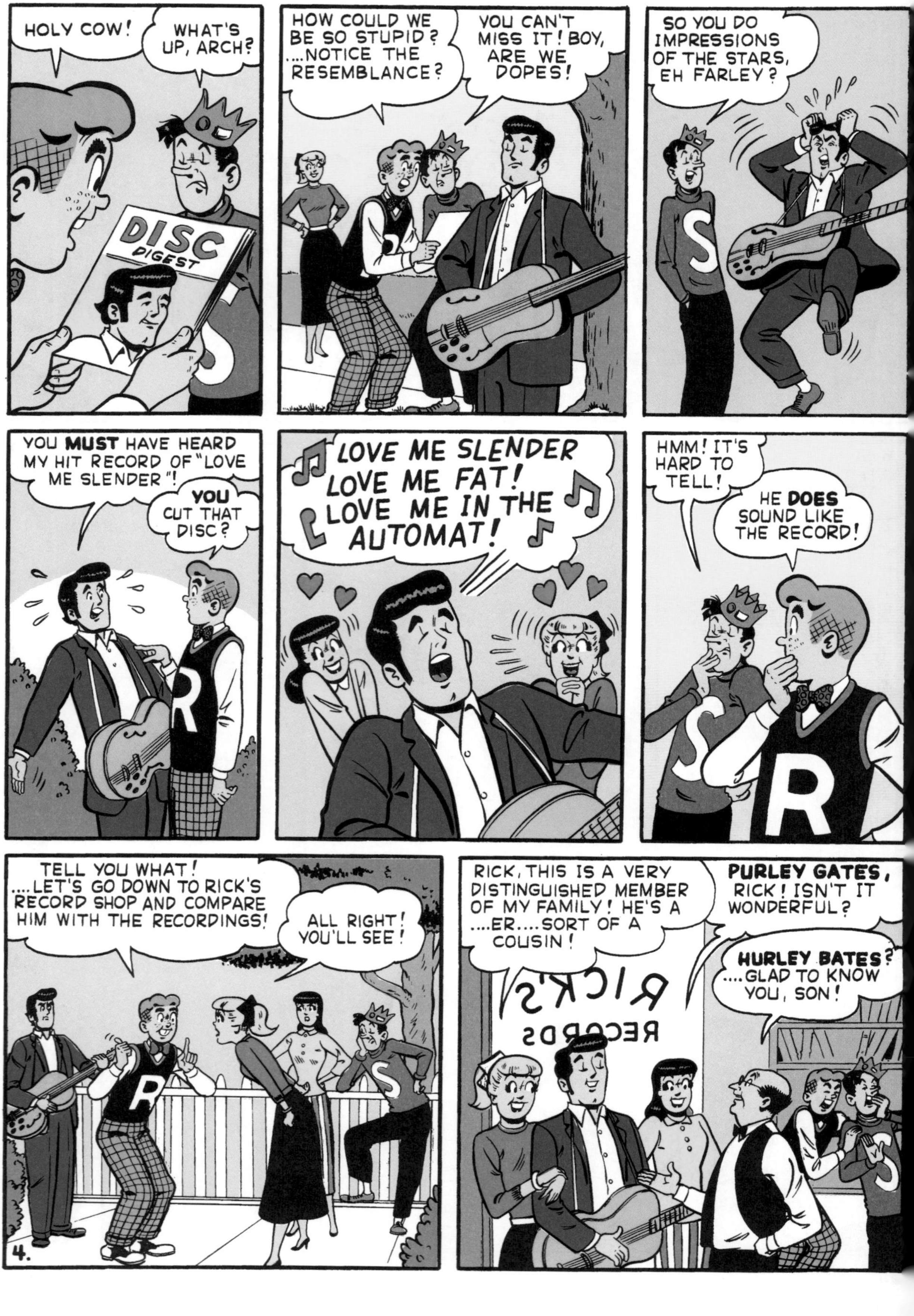
HOLY COW!
WHAT'S UP, ARCH?
DISC DIGEST
HOW COULD WE BE SO STUPID? ....NOTICE THE RESEMBLANCE?
YOU CAN'T MISS IT! BOY, ARE WE DOPES!
SO YOU DO IMPRESSIONS OF THE STARS, EH FARLEY?
YOU MUST HAVE HEARD MY HIT RECORD OF "LOVE ME SLENDER"!
YOU CUT THAT DISC?
LOVE ME SLENDER LOVE ME FAT! LOVE ME IN THE AUTOMAT!
HMM! IT'S HARD TO TELL!
HE DOES SOUND LIKE THE RECORD!
TELL YOU WHAT! ....LET'S GO DOWN TO RICK'S RECORD SHOP AND COMPARE HIM WITH THE RECORDINGS!
ALL RIGHT! YOU'LL SEE!
4.
RICK, THIS IS A VERY DISTINGUISHED MEMBER OF MY FAMILY! HE'S A ....ER....SORT OF A COUSIN!
PURLEY GATES, RICK! ISN'T IT WONDERFUL?
HURLEY BATES? ....GLAD TO KNOW YOU, SON!
RICK'S RECORDS

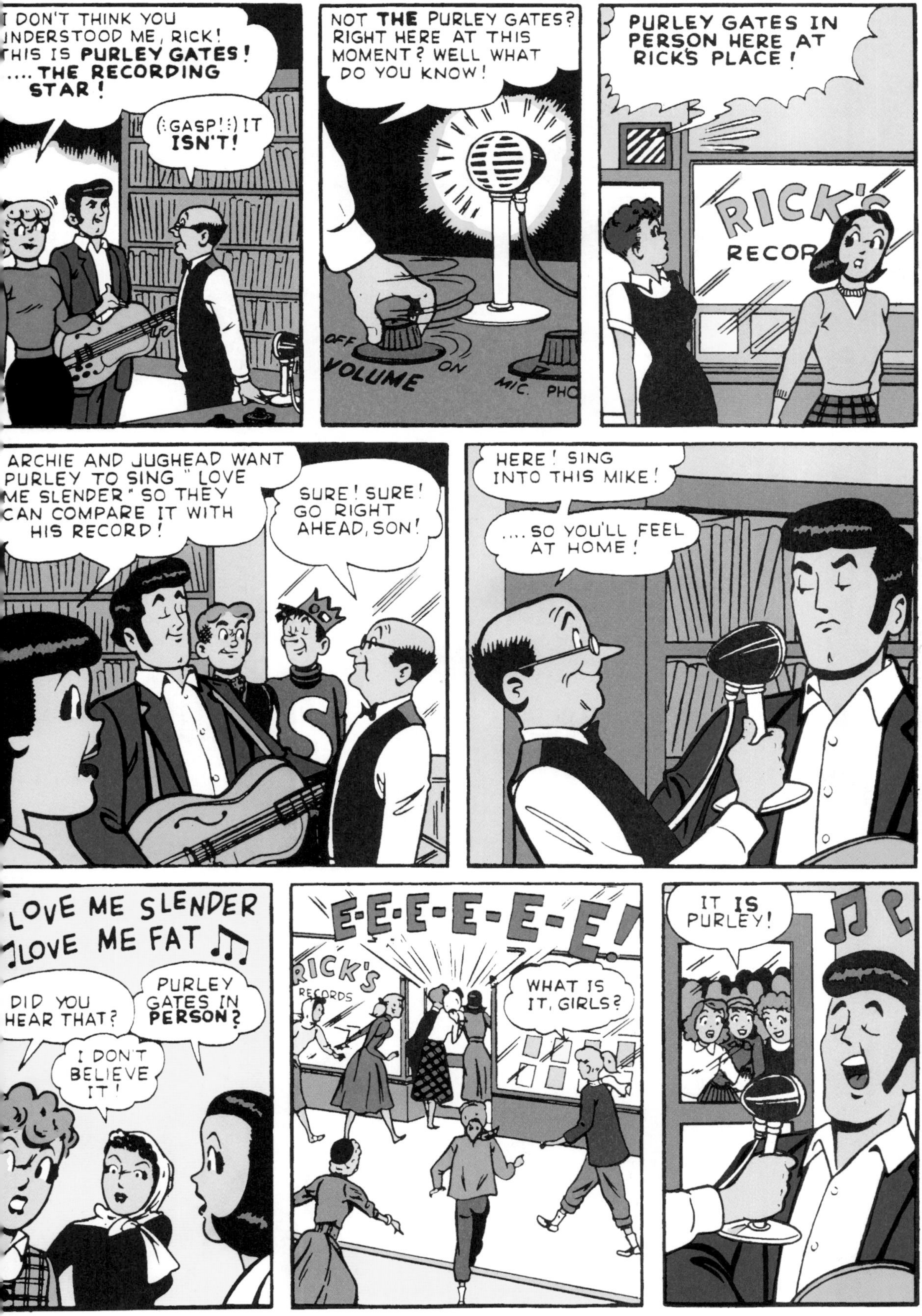
I DON'T THINK YOU UNDERSTOOD ME, RICK! THIS IS PURLEY GATES! .... THE RECORDING STAR!
(GASP!) IT ISN'T!
NOT THE PURLEY GATES? RIGHT HERE AT THIS MOMENT? WELL WHAT DO YOU KNOW!
OFF
VOLUME
ON
MIC.
PHO
PURLEY GATES IN PERSON HERE AT RICK'S PLACE!
RICK'S
RECOR
ARCHIE AND JUGHEAD WANT PURLEY TO SING "LOVE ME SLENDER" SO THEY CAN COMPARE IT WITH HIS RECORD!
SURE! SURE! GO RIGHT AHEAD, SON!
HERE! SING INTO THIS MIKE!
.... SO YOU'LL FEEL AT HOME!
LOVE ME SLENDER LOVE ME FAT
DID YOU HEAR THAT?
PURLEY GATES IN PERSON?
I DON'T BELIEVE IT!
E-E-E-E-E-E!
RICK'S RECORDS
WHAT IS IT, GIRLS?
IT IS PURLEY!

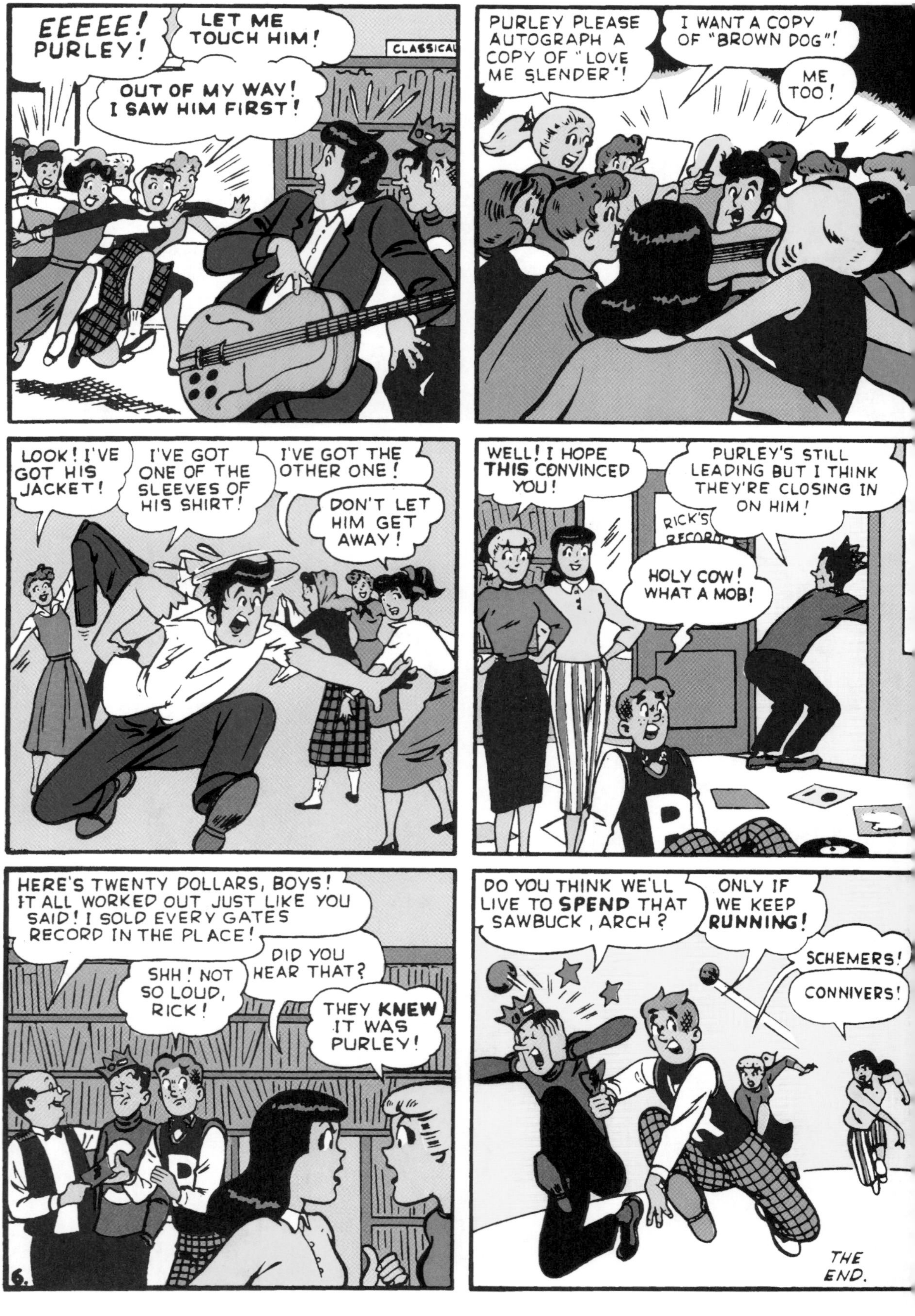
EEEEE! PURLEY!
LET ME TOUCH HIM!
CLASSICAL
OUT OF MY WAY! I SAW HIM FIRST!
PURLEY PLEASE AUTOGRAPH A COPY OF "LOVE ME SLENDER"!
I WANT A COPY OF "BROWN DOG"!
ME TOO!
LOOK! I'VE GOT HIS JACKET!
I'VE GOT ONE OF THE SLEEVES OF HIS SHIRT!
I'VE GOT THE OTHER ONE!
DON'T LET HIM GET AWAY!
WELL! I HOPE **THIS** CONVINCED YOU!
PURLEY'S STILL LEADING BUT I THINK THEY'RE CLOSING IN ON HIM!
HOLY COW! WHAT A MOB!
HERE'S TWENTY DOLLARS, BOYS! IT ALL WORKED OUT JUST LIKE YOU SAID! I SOLD EVERY GATES RECORD IN THE PLACE!
SHH! NOT SO LOUD, RICK!
DID YOU HEAR THAT?
THEY **KNEW** IT WAS PURLEY!
6.
DO YOU THINK WE'LL LIVE TO **SPEND** THAT SAWBUCK, ARCH?
ONLY IF WE KEEP **RUNNING**!
SCHEMERS!
CONNIVERS!
THE END.

A CLASSIC 1950'S ARCHIE AD!

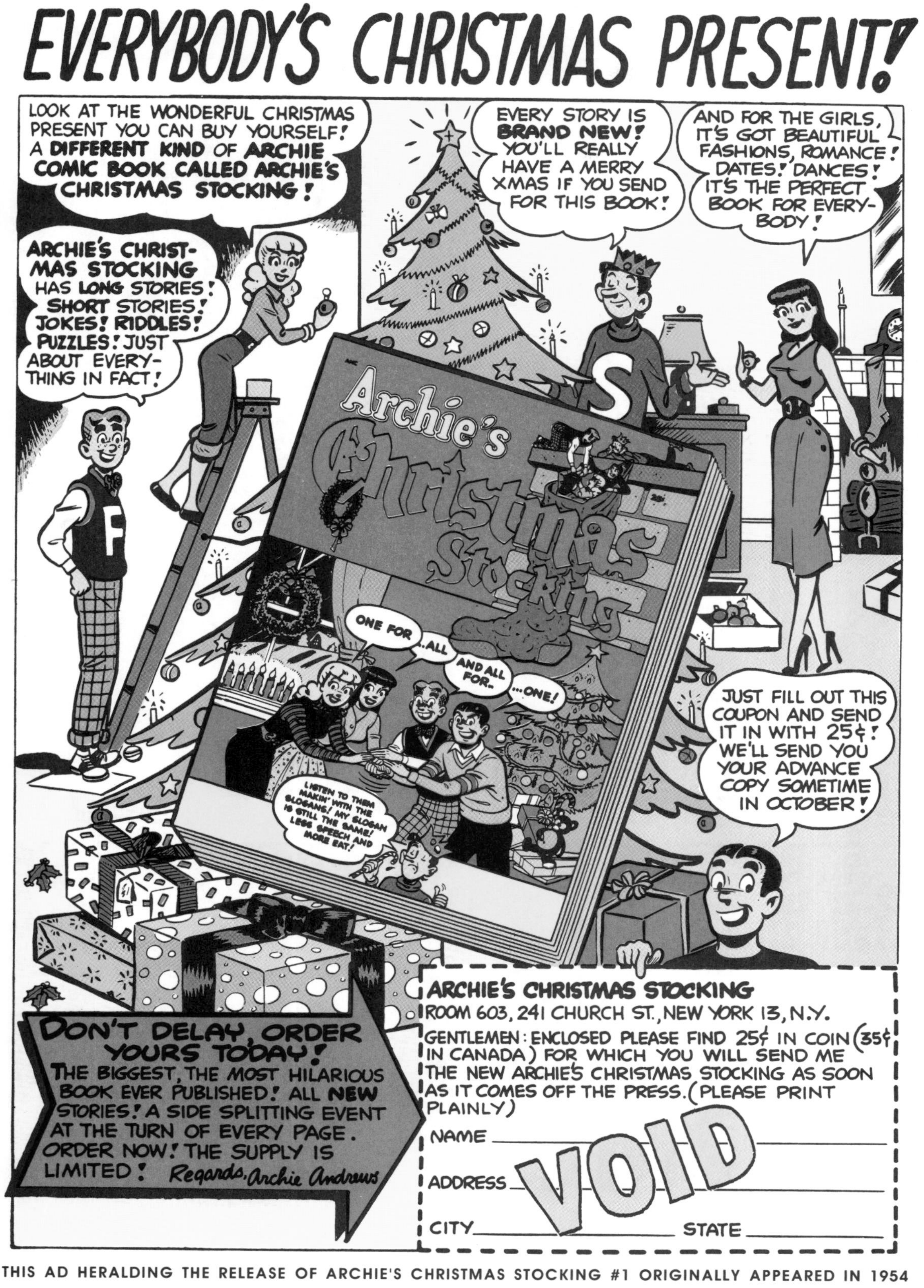
EVERYBODY'S CHRISTMAS PRESENT!
LOOK AT THE WONDERFUL CHRISTMAS PRESENT YOU CAN BUY YOURSELF! A DIFFERENT KIND OF ARCHIE COMIC BOOK CALLED ARCHIE'S CHRISTMAS STOCKING!
EVERY STORY IS BRAND NEW! YOU'LL REALLY HAVE A MERRY XMAS IF YOU SEND FOR THIS BOOK!
AND FOR THE GIRLS, IT'S GOT BEAUTIFUL FASHIONS, ROMANCE! DATES! DANCES! IT'S THE PERFECT BOOK FOR EVERY-BODY!
ARCHIE'S CHRIST-MAS STOCKING HAS LONG STORIES! SHORT STORIES! JOKES! RIDDLES! PUZZLES! JUST ABOUT EVERY-THING IN FACT!
Archie's Christmas Stocking
ONE FOR
..ALL
AND ALL FOR..
...ONE!
LISTEN TO THEM MAKIN' WITH THE SLOGANS! MY SLOGAN IS STILL THE SAME! LESS SPEECH AND MORE EAT!
JUST FILL OUT THIS COUPON AND SEND IT IN WITH 25¢! WE'LL SEND YOU YOUR ADVANCE COPY SOMETIME IN OCTOBER!
DON'T DELAY, ORDER YOURS TODAY!
THE BIGGEST, THE MOST HILARIOUS BOOK EVER PUBLISHED! ALL NEW STORIES! A SIDE SPLITTING EVENT AT THE TURN OF EVERY PAGE. ORDER NOW! THE SUPPLY IS LIMITED! Regards, Archie Andrews
ARCHIE'S CHRISTMAS STOCKING
ROOM 603, 241 CHURCH ST., NEW YORK 13, N.Y.
GENTLEMEN: ENCLOSED PLEASE FIND 25¢ IN COIN (35¢ IN CANADA) FOR WHICH YOU WILL SEND ME THE NEW ARCHIE'S CHRISTMAS STOCKING AS SOON AS IT COMES OFF THE PRESS. (PLEASE PRINT PLAINLY)
NAME
ADDRESS
CITY
STATE
VOID

THIS AD HERALDING THE RELEASE OF ARCHIE'S CHRISTMAS STOCKING #1 ORIGINALLY APPEARED IN 1954

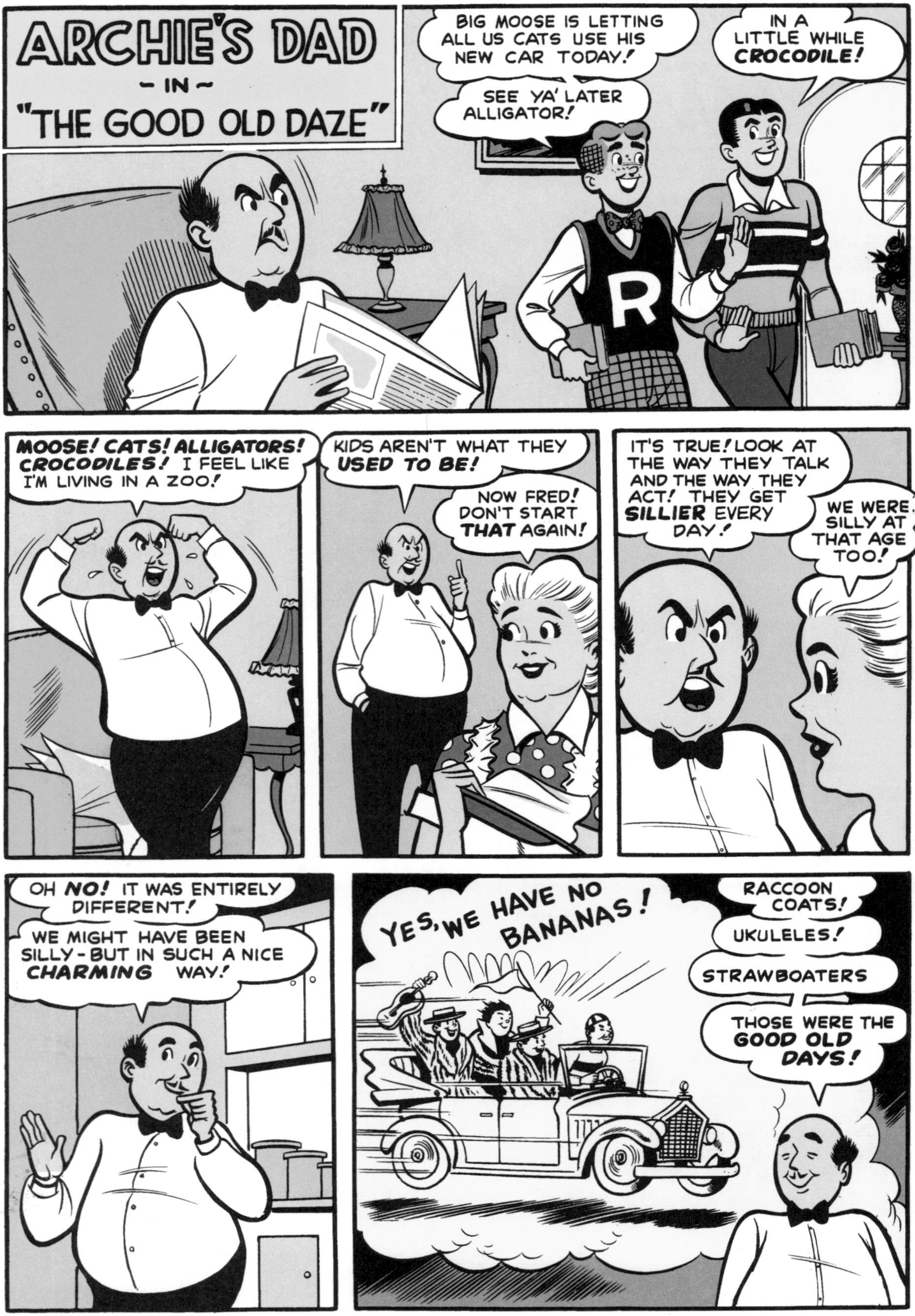
ARCHIE'S DAD
- IN -
"THE GOOD OLD DAZE"
BIG MOOSE IS LETTING ALL US CATS USE HIS NEW CAR TODAY!
SEE YA' LATER ALLIGATOR!
IN A LITTLE WHILE CROCODILE!
R
MOOSE! CATS! ALLIGATORS! CROCODILES! I FEEL LIKE I'M LIVING IN A ZOO!
KIDS AREN'T WHAT THEY USED TO BE!
NOW FRED! DON'T START THAT AGAIN!
IT'S TRUE! LOOK AT THE WAY THEY TALK AND THE WAY THEY ACT! THEY GET SILLIER EVERY DAY!
WE WERE SILLY AT THAT AGE TOO!
OH NO! IT WAS ENTIRELY DIFFERENT!
WE MIGHT HAVE BEEN SILLY - BUT IN SUCH A NICE CHARMING WAY!
YES, WE HAVE NO BANANAS!
RACCOON COATS!
UKULELES!
STRAWBOATERS
THOSE WERE THE GOOD OLD DAYS!

ORIGINALLY PRESENTED IN **BETTY & VERONICA #38**, SEPTEMBER, 1958.

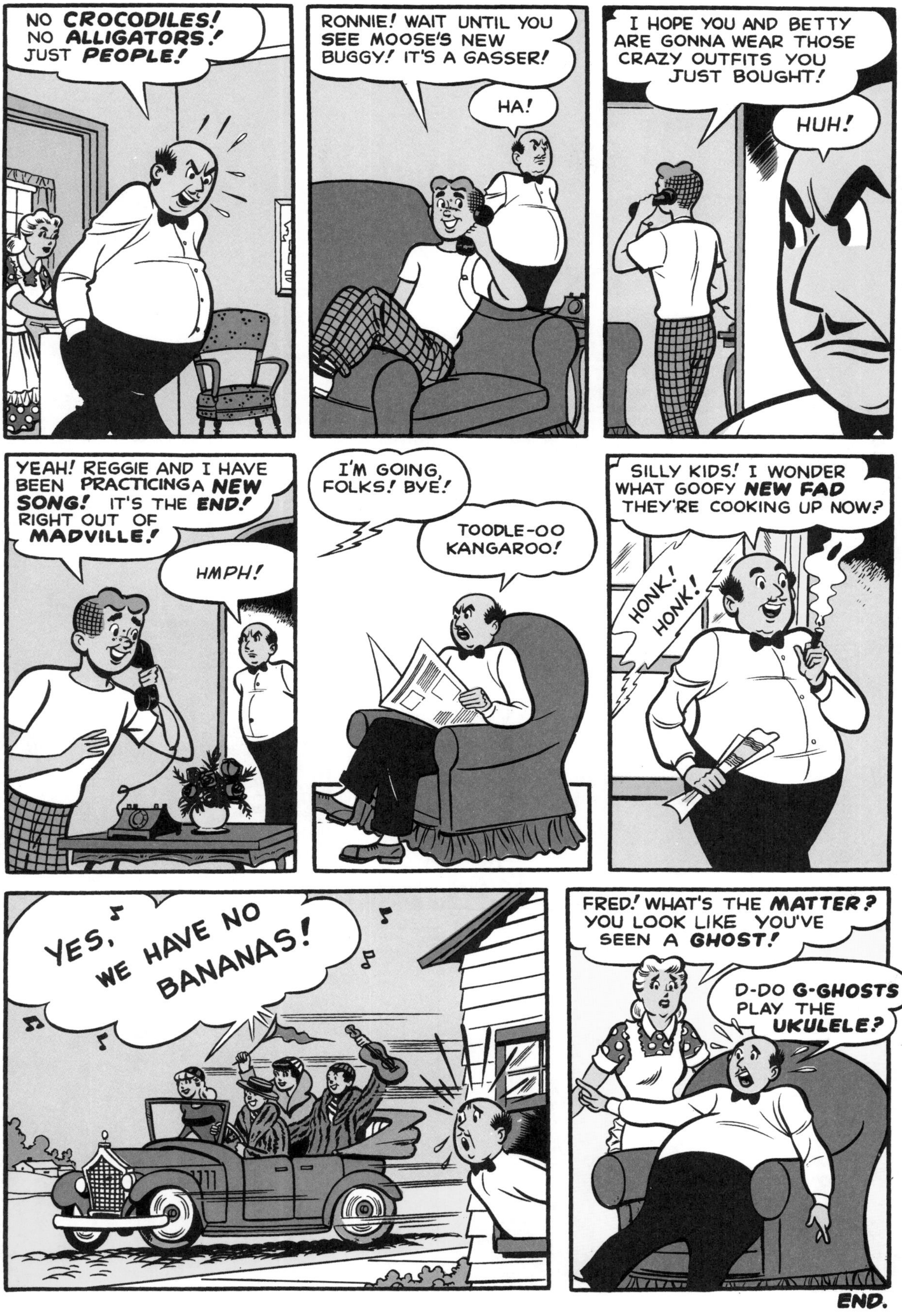
NO CROCODILES! NO ALLIGATORS! JUST PEOPLE!
RONNIE! WAIT UNTIL YOU SEE MOOSE'S NEW BUGGY! IT'S A GASSER!
HA!
I HOPE YOU AND BETTY ARE GONNA WEAR THOSE CRAZY OUTFITS YOU JUST BOUGHT!
HUH!
YEAH! REGGIE AND I HAVE BEEN PRACTICING A NEW SONG! IT'S THE END! RIGHT OUT OF MADVILLE!
HMPH!
I'M GOING, FOLKS! BYE!
TOODLE-OO KANGAROO!
SILLY KIDS! I WONDER WHAT GOOFY NEW FAD THEY'RE COOKING UP NOW?
HONK! HONK!
YES, WE HAVE NO BANANAS!
FRED! WHAT'S THE MATTER? YOU LOOK LIKE YOU'VE SEEN A GHOST!
D-DO G-GHOSTS PLAY THE UKULELE?
END.

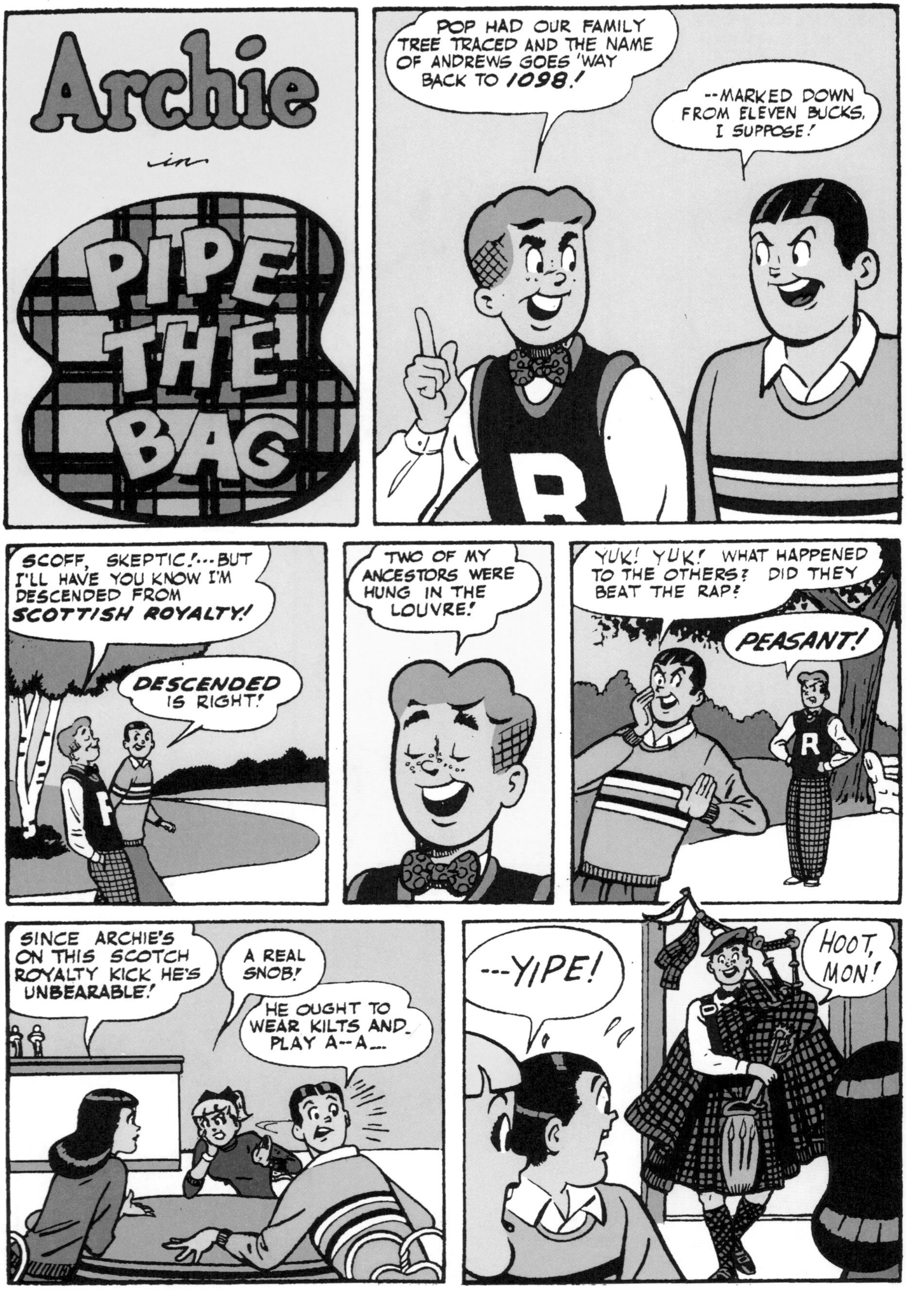
Archie
in
PIPE THE BAG
POP HAD OUR FAMILY TREE TRACED AND THE NAME OF ANDREWS GOES 'WAY BACK TO 1098!
--MARKED DOWN FROM ELEVEN BUCKS, I SUPPOSE!
SCOFF, SKEPTIC!---BUT I'LL HAVE YOU KNOW I'M DESCENDED FROM SCOTTISH ROYALTY!
DESCENDED IS RIGHT!
TWO OF MY ANCESTORS WERE HUNG IN THE LOUVRE!
YUK! YUK! WHAT HAPPENED TO THE OTHERS? DID THEY BEAT THE RAP?
PEASANT!
SINCE ARCHIE'S ON THIS SCOTCH ROYALTY KICK HE'S UNBEARABLE!
A REAL SNOB!
HE OUGHT TO WEAR KILTS AND PLAY A--A...
---YIPE!
HOOT, MON!

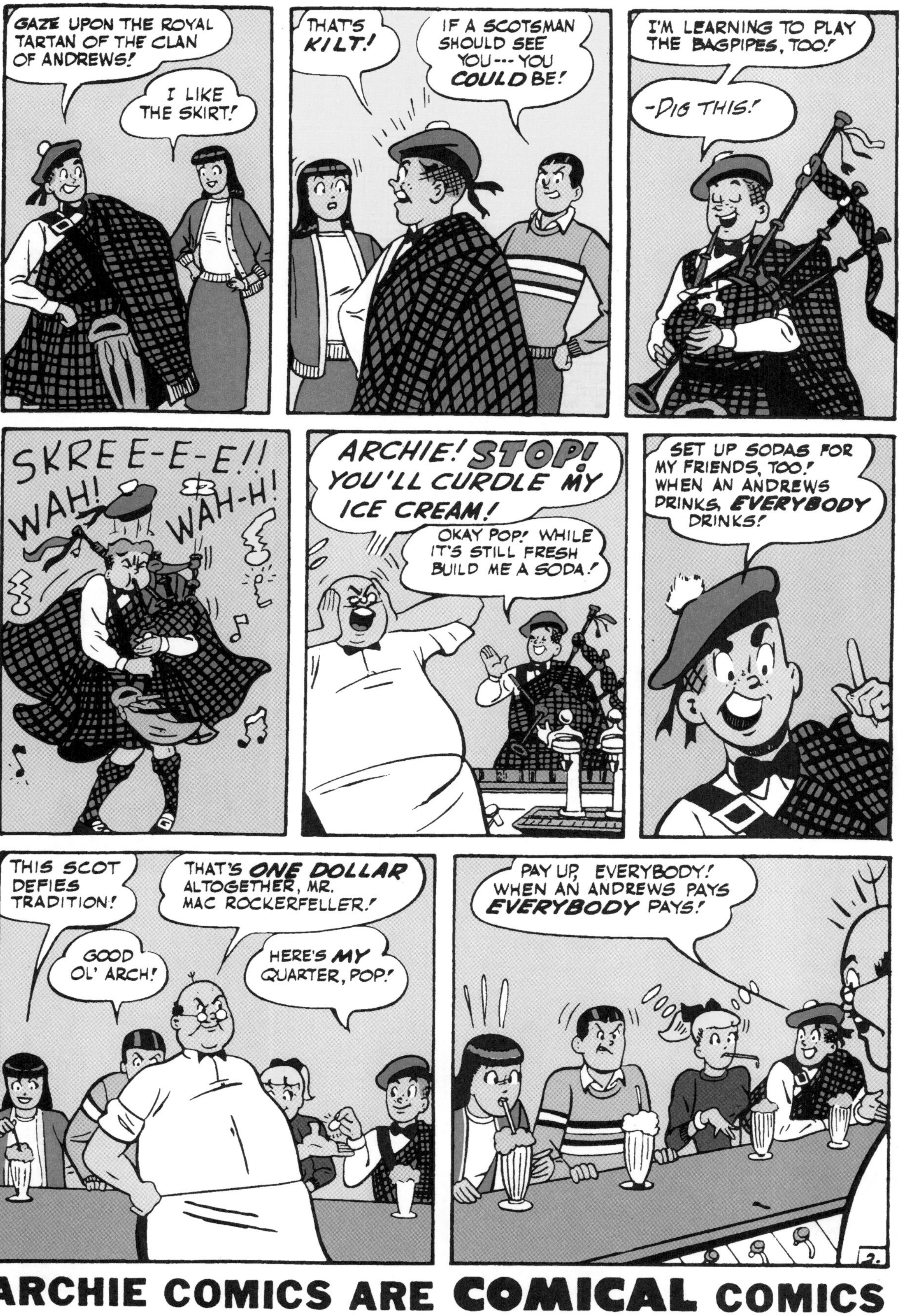
GAZE UPON THE ROYAL TARTAN OF THE CLAN OF ANDREWS!
I LIKE THE SKIRT!
THAT'S KILT!
IF A SCOTSMAN SHOULD SEE YOU --- YOU COULD BE!
I'M LEARNING TO PLAY THE BAGPIPES, TOO!
-DIG THIS!
SKREE-E-E!!
WAH!
WAH-H!
ARCHIE! STOP! YOU'LL CURDLE MY ICE CREAM!
OKAY POP! WHILE IT'S STILL FRESH BUILD ME A SODA!
SET UP SODAS FOR MY FRIENDS, TOO! WHEN AN ANDREWS DRINKS, EVERYBODY DRINKS!
THIS SCOT DEFIES TRADITION!
GOOD OL' ARCH!
THAT'S ONE DOLLAR ALTOGETHER, MR. MAC ROCKERFELLER!
HERE'S MY QUARTER, POP!
PAY UP, EVERYBODY! WHEN AN ANDREWS PAYS EVERYBODY PAYS!
2.

ARCHIE COMICS ARE COMICAL COMICS

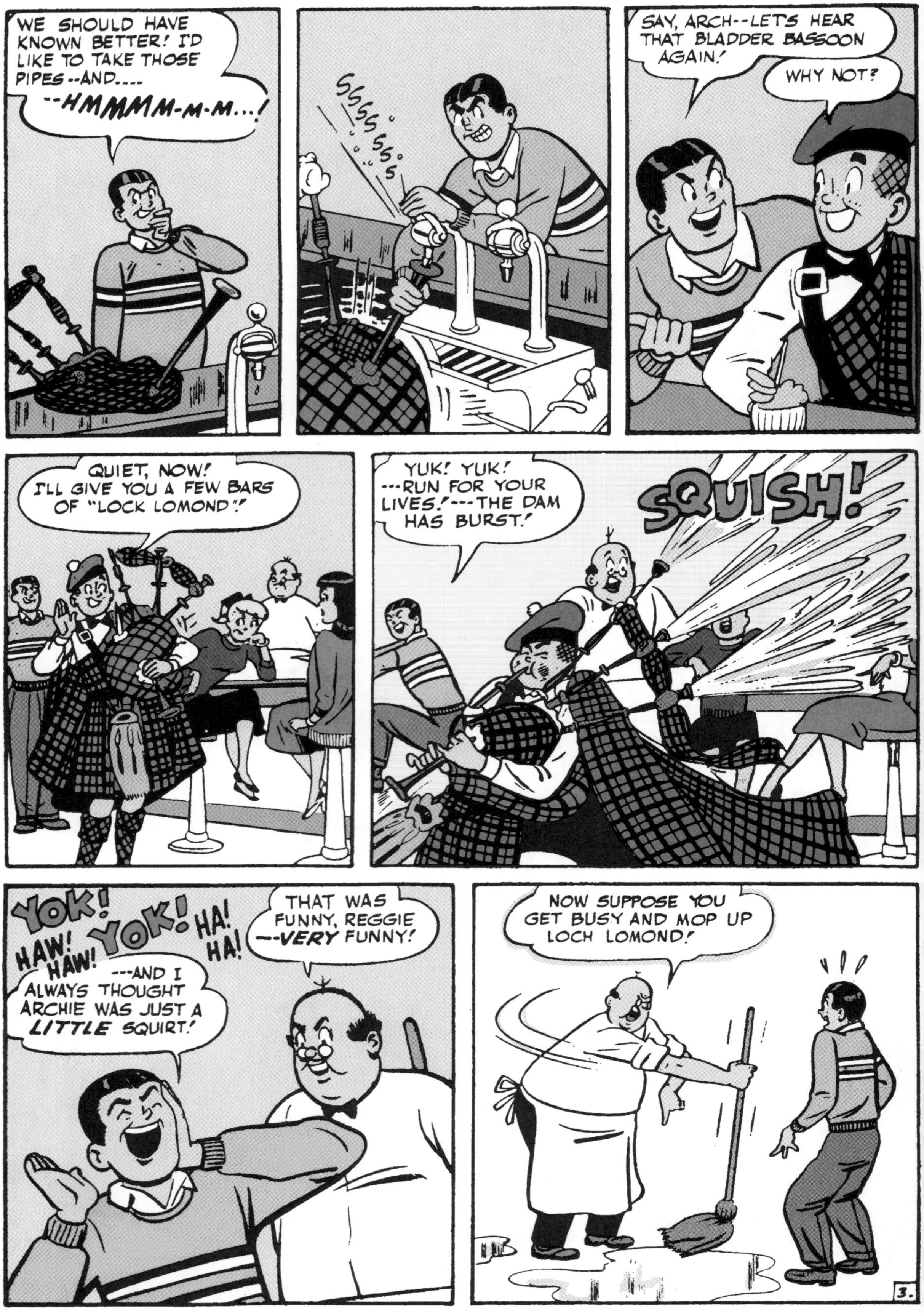
WE SHOULD HAVE KNOWN BETTER! I'D LIKE TO TAKE THOSE PIPES--AND....
--HMMMM-M-M...!
SSSSSSSS
SAY, ARCH--LET'S HEAR THAT BLADDER BASSOON AGAIN!
WHY NOT?
QUIET, NOW! I'LL GIVE YOU A FEW BARS OF "LOCK LOMOND"!
YUK! YUK! ---RUN FOR YOUR LIVES!---THE DAM HAS BURST!
SQUISH!
YOK! HAW! HAW! YOK! HA! HA!
---AND I ALWAYS THOUGHT ARCHIE WAS JUST A LITTLE SQUIRT!
THAT WAS FUNNY, REGGIE --VERY FUNNY!
NOW SUPPOSE YOU GET BUSY AND MOP UP LOCH LOMOND!
3.

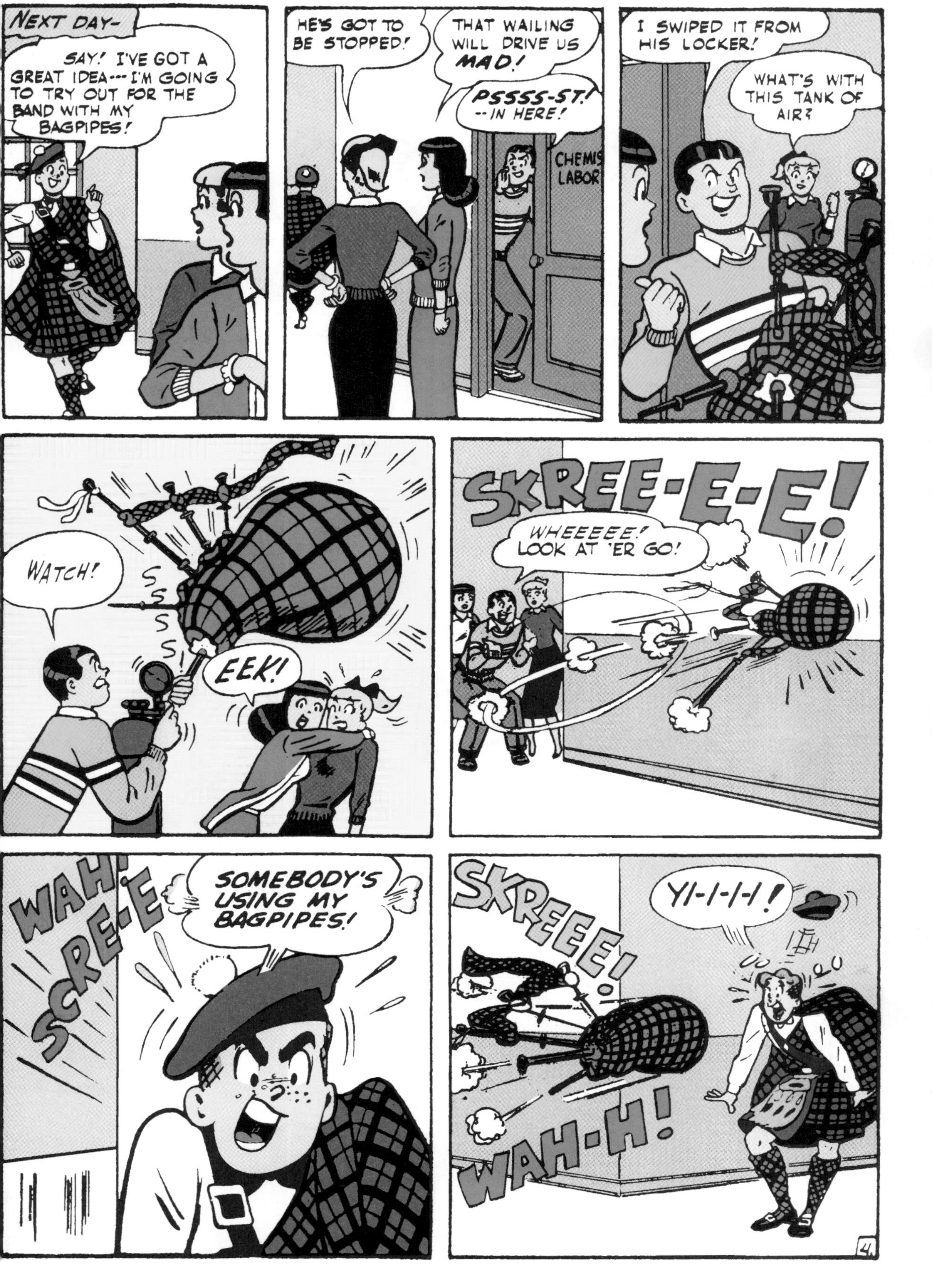
NEXT DAY-
SAY! I'VE GOT A GREAT IDEA--- I'M GOING TO TRY OUT FOR THE BAND WITH MY BAGPIPES!
HE'S GOT TO BE STOPPED!
THAT WAILING WILL DRIVE US MAD!
PSSSS-ST! --IN HERE!
CHEMIS LABOR
I SWIPED IT FROM HIS LOCKER!
WHAT'S WITH THIS TANK OF AIR?
WATCH!
S S S S
EEK!
SKREE-E-E!
WHEEEEE! LOOK AT 'ER GO!
WAH! SCRE-E
SOMEBODY'S USING MY BAGPIPES!
SKREEEE!
YI-I-I-I!
WAH-H!
4

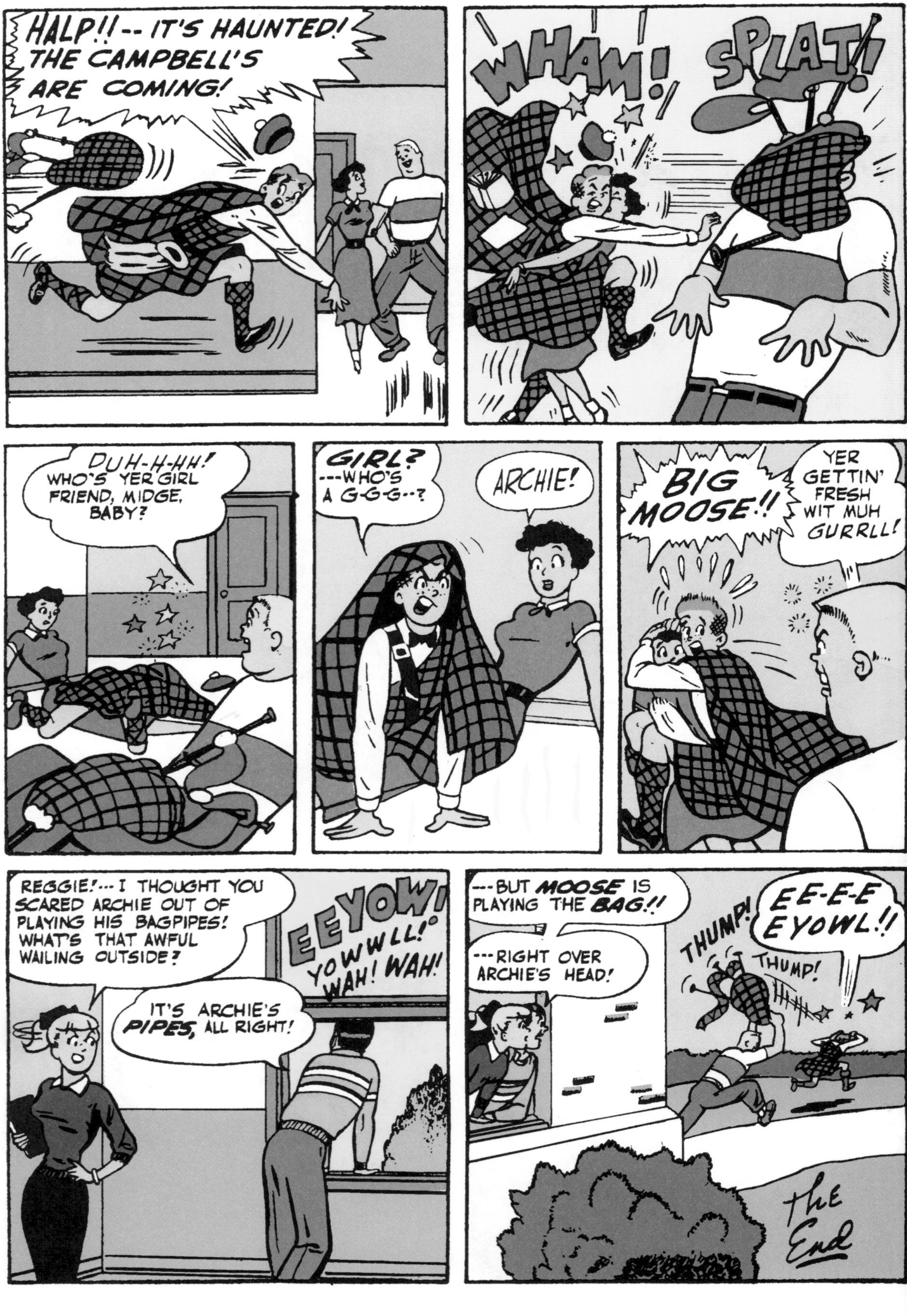
HALP!! -- IT'S HAUNTED! THE CAMPBELL'S ARE COMING!
WHAM!
SPLAT!
DUH-H-HH! WHO'S YER GIRL FRIEND, MIDGE, BABY?
GIRL? ---WHO'S A G-G-G--?
ARCHIE!
BIG MOOSE!!
YER GETTIN' FRESH WIT MUH GURRLL!
REGGIE!--- I THOUGHT YOU SCARED ARCHIE OUT OF PLAYING HIS BAGPIPES! WHAT'S THAT AWFUL WAILING OUTSIDE?
EEYOW!
YOWWLL!
WAH! WAH!
IT'S ARCHIE'S PIPES, ALL RIGHT!
---BUT MOOSE IS PLAYING THE BAG!!
---RIGHT OVER ARCHIE'S HEAD!
THUMP!
EE-E-E EYOWL!!
THUMP!
The End

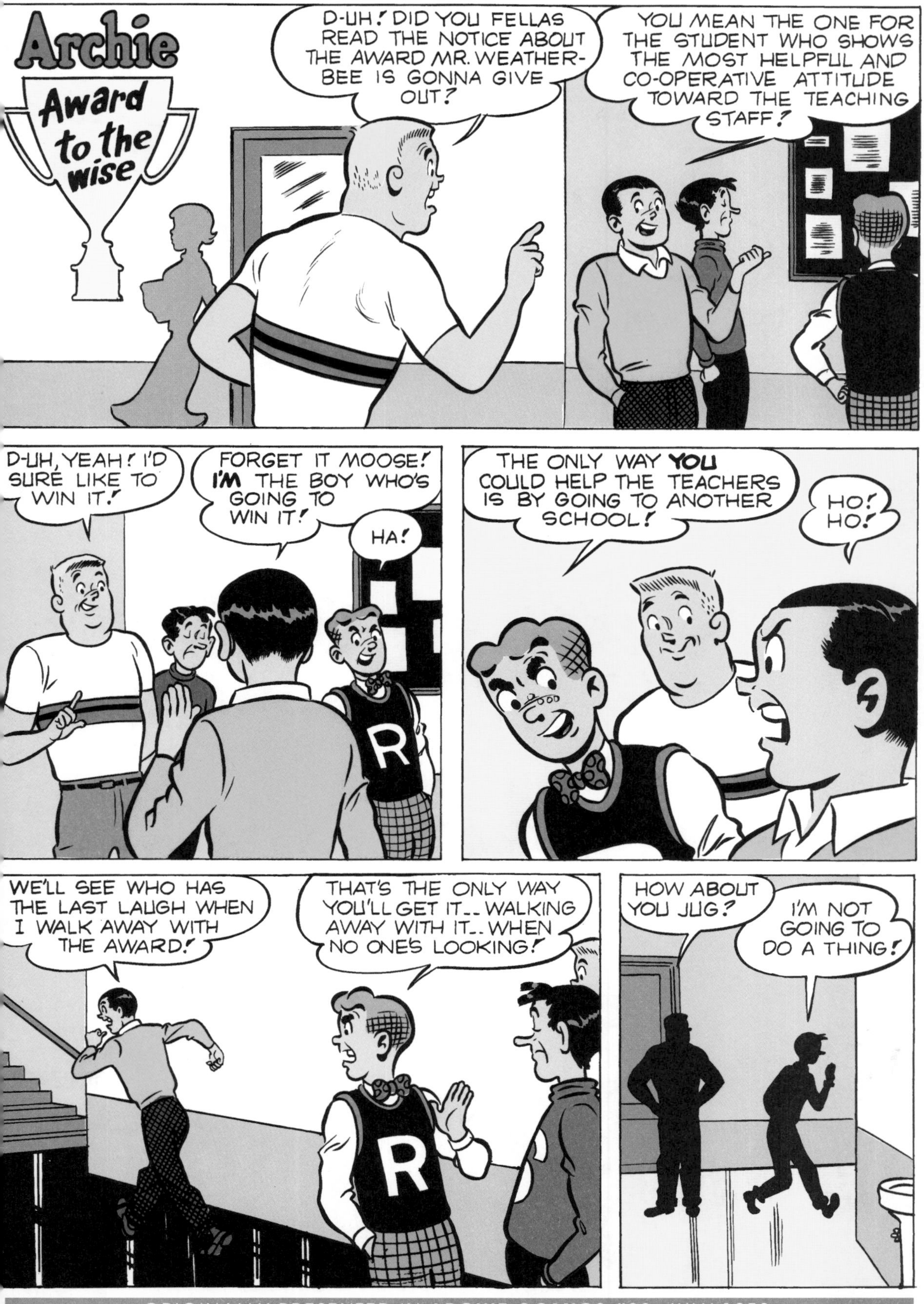
Archie
Award to the wise
D-UH! DID YOU FELLAS READ THE NOTICE ABOUT THE AWARD MR. WEATHER-BEE IS GONNA GIVE OUT?
YOU MEAN THE ONE FOR THE STUDENT WHO SHOWS THE MOST HELPFUL AND CO-OPERATIVE ATTITUDE TOWARD THE TEACHING STAFF?
D-UH, YEAH! I'D SURE LIKE TO WIN IT!
FORGET IT MOOSE! I'M THE BOY WHO'S GOING TO WIN IT!
HA!
THE ONLY WAY YOU COULD HELP THE TEACHERS IS BY GOING TO ANOTHER SCHOOL!
HO! HO!
WE'LL SEE WHO HAS THE LAST LAUGH WHEN I WALK AWAY WITH THE AWARD!
THAT'S THE ONLY WAY YOU'LL GET IT-- WALKING AWAY WITH IT-- WHEN NO ONE'S LOOKING!
HOW ABOUT YOU JUG?
I'M NOT GOING TO DO A THING!

ORIGINALLY PRESENTED IN **ARCHIE COMICS #93**, JULY 1958.

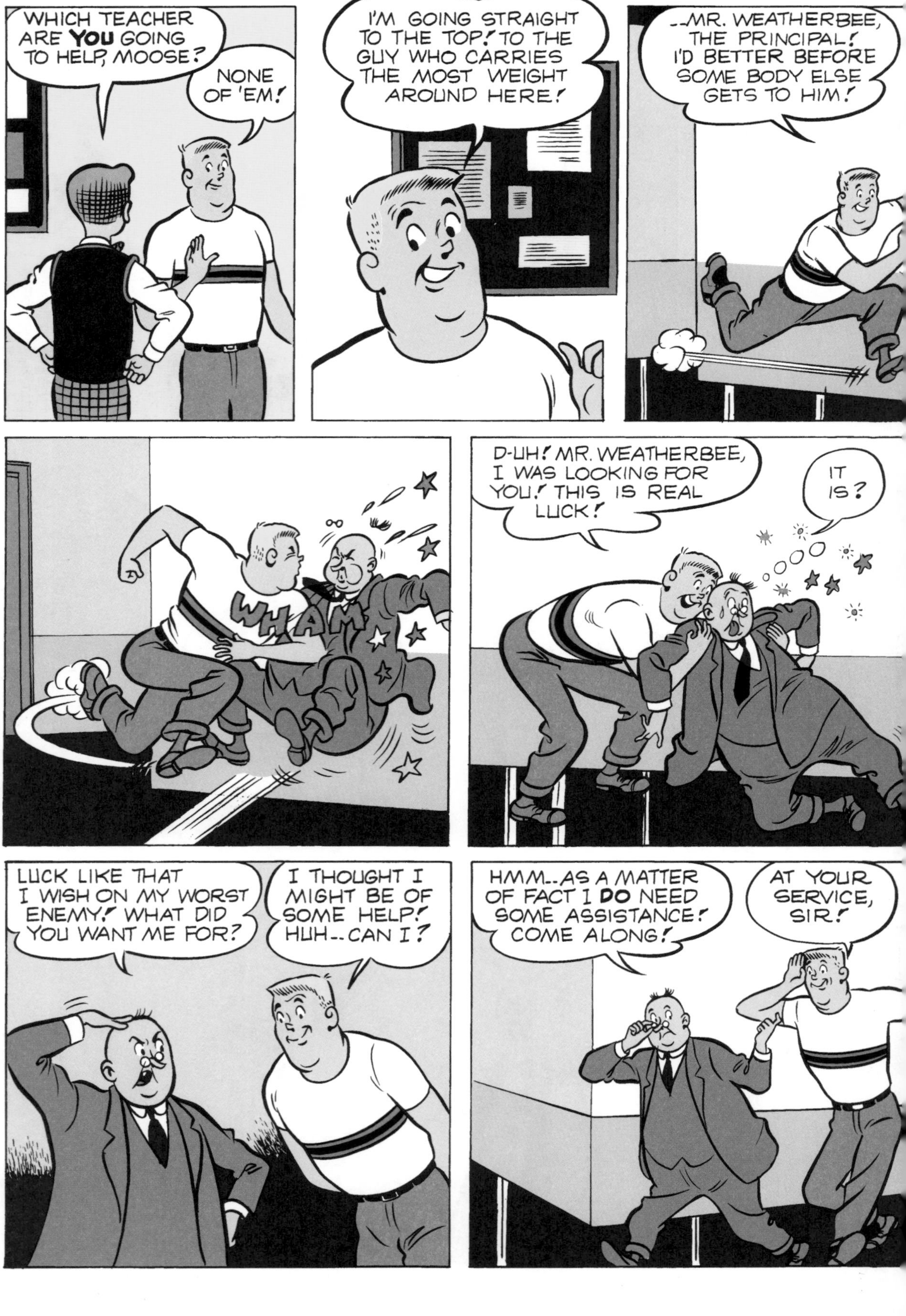
WHICH TEACHER ARE YOU GOING TO HELP, MOOSE?
NONE OF 'EM!
I'M GOING STRAIGHT TO THE TOP! TO THE GUY WHO CARRIES THE MOST WEIGHT AROUND HERE!
--MR. WEATHERBEE, THE PRINCIPAL! I'D BETTER BEFORE SOME BODY ELSE GETS TO HIM!
WHAM
D-UH! MR. WEATHERBEE, I WAS LOOKING FOR YOU! THIS IS REAL LUCK!
IT IS?
LUCK LIKE THAT I WISH ON MY WORST ENEMY! WHAT DID YOU WANT ME FOR?
I THOUGHT I MIGHT BE OF SOME HELP! HUH--CAN I?
HMM--AS A MATTER OF FACT I DO NEED SOME ASSISTANCE! COME ALONG!
AT YOUR SERVICE, SIR!

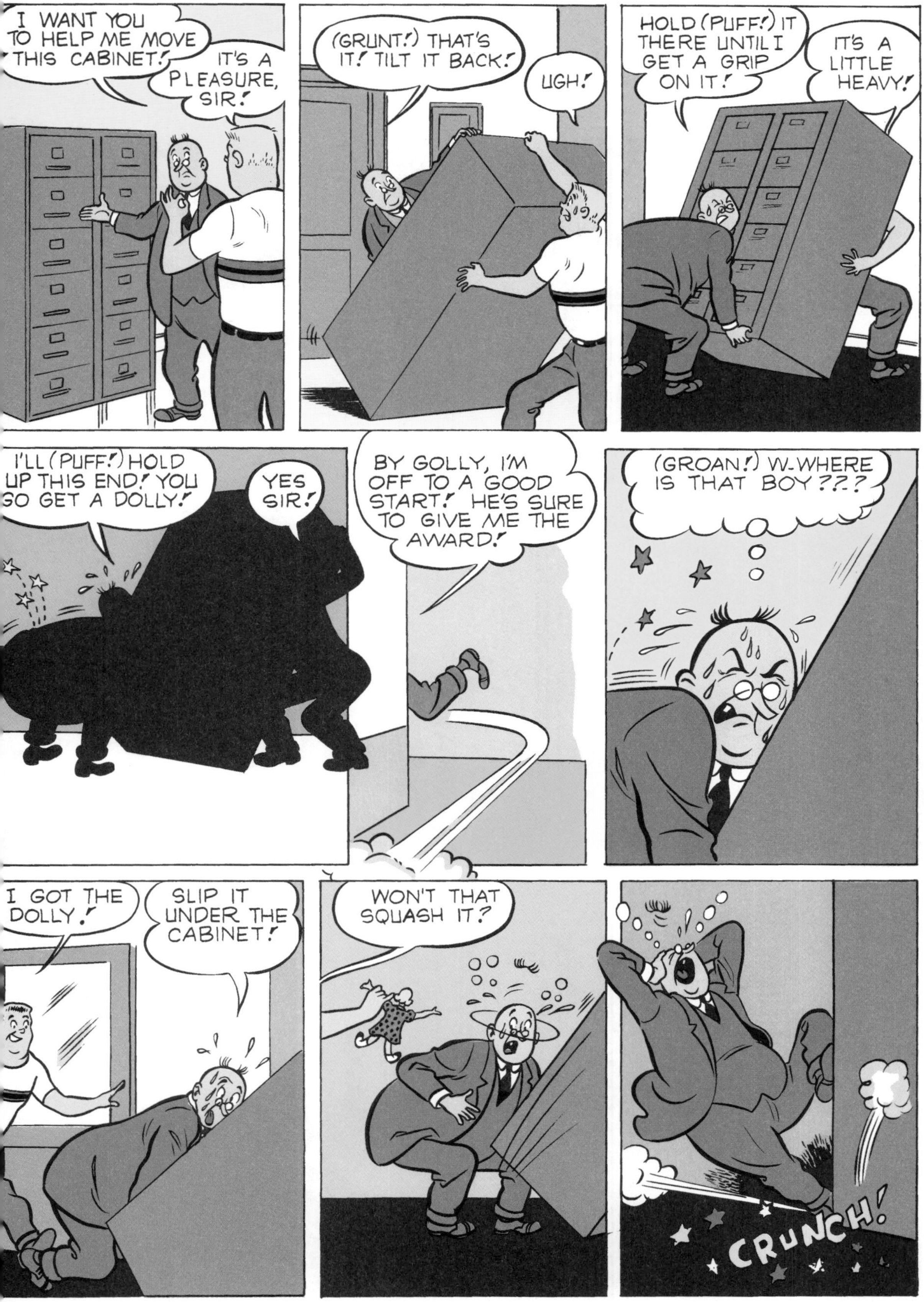
I WANT YOU TO HELP ME MOVE THIS CABINET!
IT'S A PLEASURE, SIR!
(GRUNT!) THAT'S IT! TILT IT BACK!
UGH!
HOLD (PUFF!) IT THERE UNTIL I GET A GRIP ON IT!
IT'S A LITTLE HEAVY!
I'LL (PUFF!) HOLD UP THIS END! YOU GO GET A DOLLY!
YES SIR!
BY GOLLY, I'M OFF TO A GOOD START! HE'S SURE TO GIVE ME THE AWARD!
(GROAN!) W-WHERE IS THAT BOY???
I GOT THE DOLLY!
SLIP IT UNDER THE CABINET!
WON'T THAT SQUASH IT?
CRUNCH!

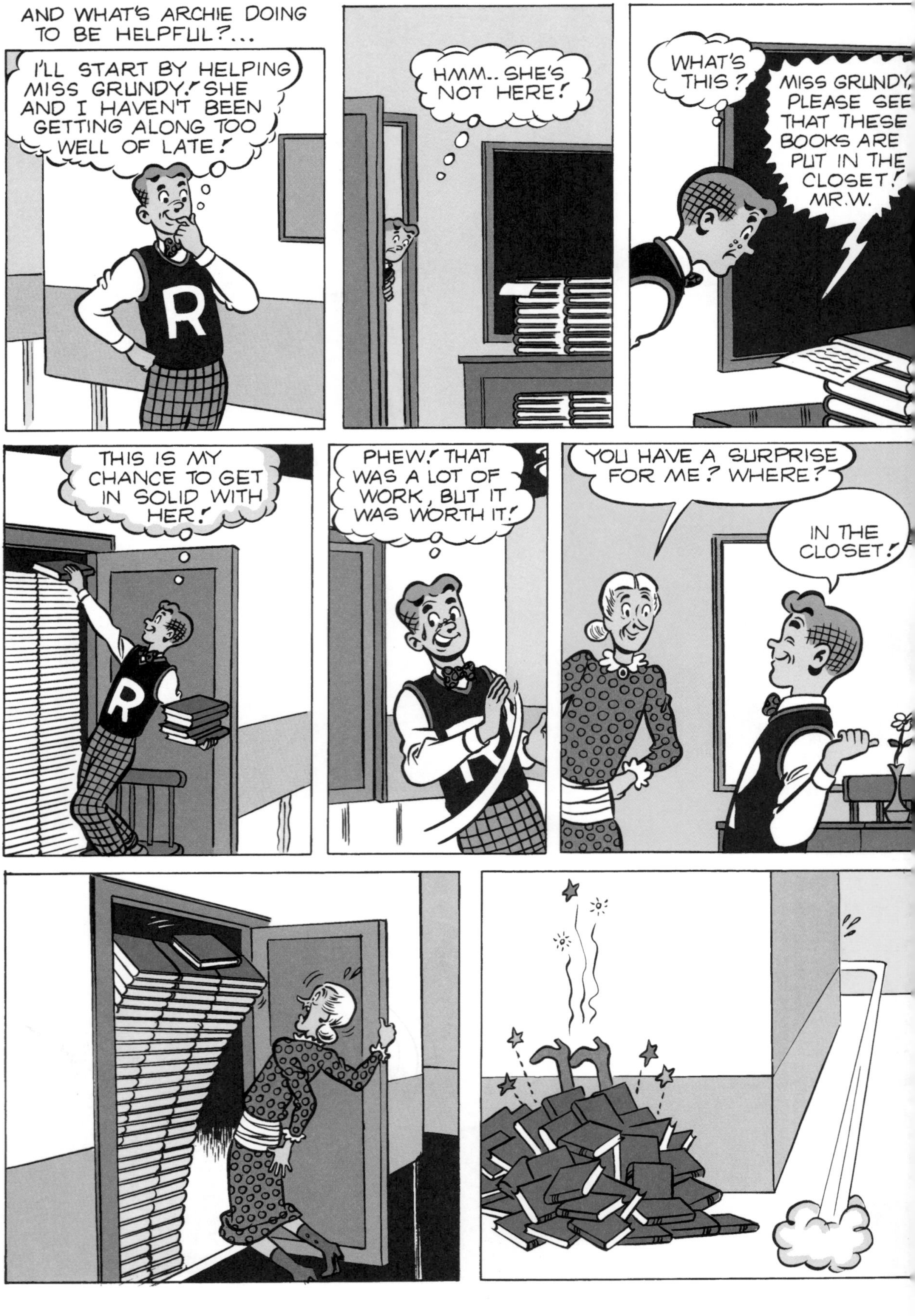
AND WHAT'S ARCHIE DOING TO BE HELPFUL?...
I'LL START BY HELPING MISS GRUNDY! SHE AND I HAVEN'T BEEN GETTING ALONG TOO WELL OF LATE!
HMM.. SHE'S NOT HERE!
WHAT'S THIS?
MISS GRUNDY, PLEASE SEE THAT THESE BOOKS ARE PUT IN THE CLOSET! MR.W.
THIS IS MY CHANCE TO GET IN SOLID WITH HER!
PHEW! THAT WAS A LOT OF WORK, BUT IT WAS WORTH IT!
YOU HAVE A SURPRISE FOR ME? WHERE?
IN THE CLOSET!

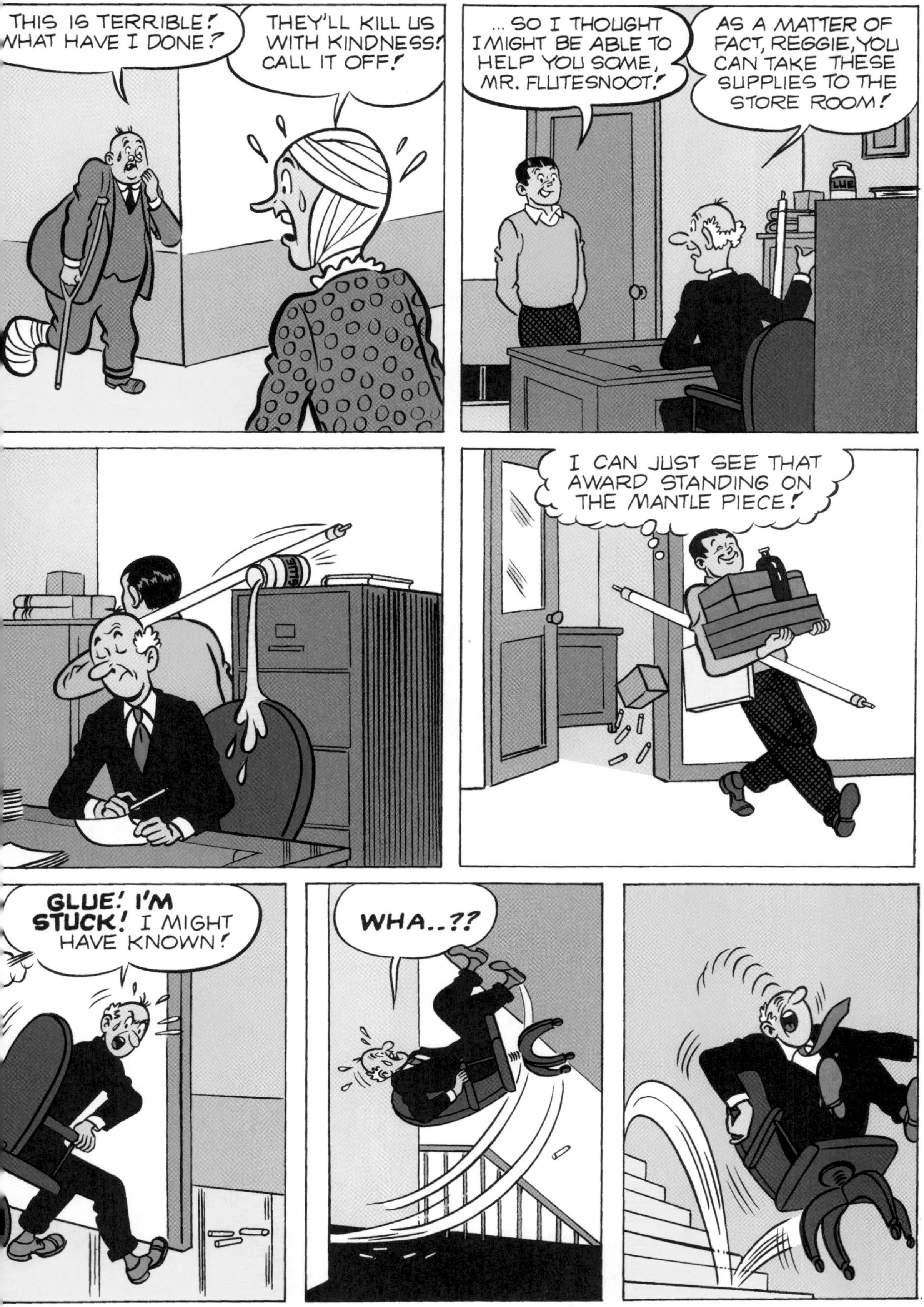
THIS IS TERRIBLE! WHAT HAVE I DONE?
THEY'LL KILL US WITH KINDNESS! CALL IT OFF!
...SO I THOUGHT I MIGHT BE ABLE TO HELP YOU SOME, MR. FLUTESNOOT!
AS A MATTER OF FACT, REGGIE, YOU CAN TAKE THESE SUPPLIES TO THE STORE ROOM!
GLUE
I CAN JUST SEE THAT AWARD STANDING ON THE MANTLE PIECE!
GLUE! I'M STUCK! I MIGHT HAVE KNOWN!
WHA..??

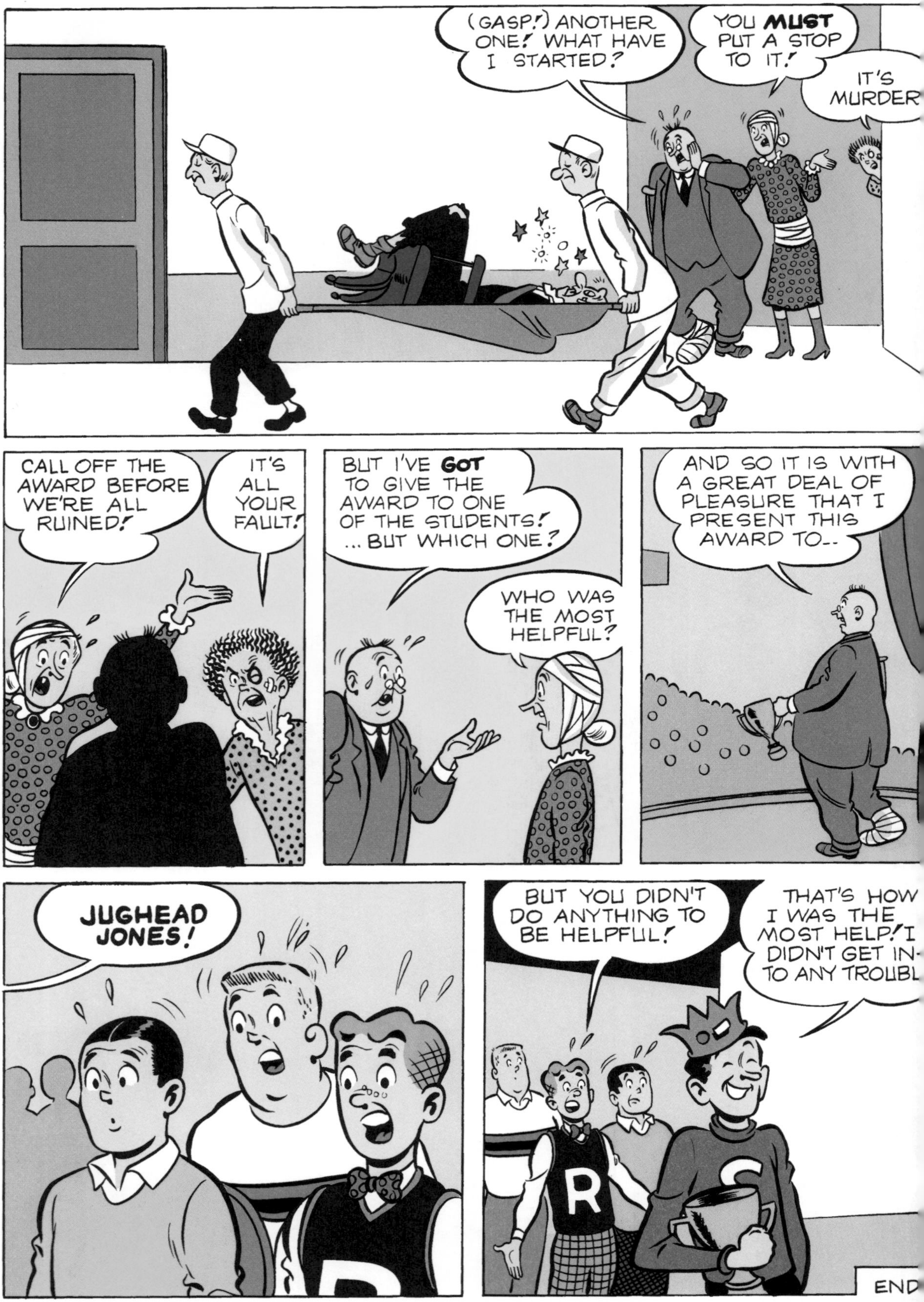
(GASP!) ANOTHER ONE! WHAT HAVE I STARTED?
YOU MUST PUT A STOP TO IT!
IT'S MURDER
CALL OFF THE AWARD BEFORE WE'RE ALL RUINED!
IT'S ALL YOUR FAULT!
BUT I'VE GOT TO GIVE THE AWARD TO ONE OF THE STUDENTS! ... BUT WHICH ONE?
WHO WAS THE MOST HELPFUL?
AND SO IT IS WITH A GREAT DEAL OF PLEASURE THAT I PRESENT THIS AWARD TO--
JUGHEAD JONES!
BUT YOU DIDN'T DO ANYTHING TO BE HELPFUL!
THAT'S HOW I WAS THE MOST HELP! I DIDN'T GET IN-TO ANY TROUBL
END

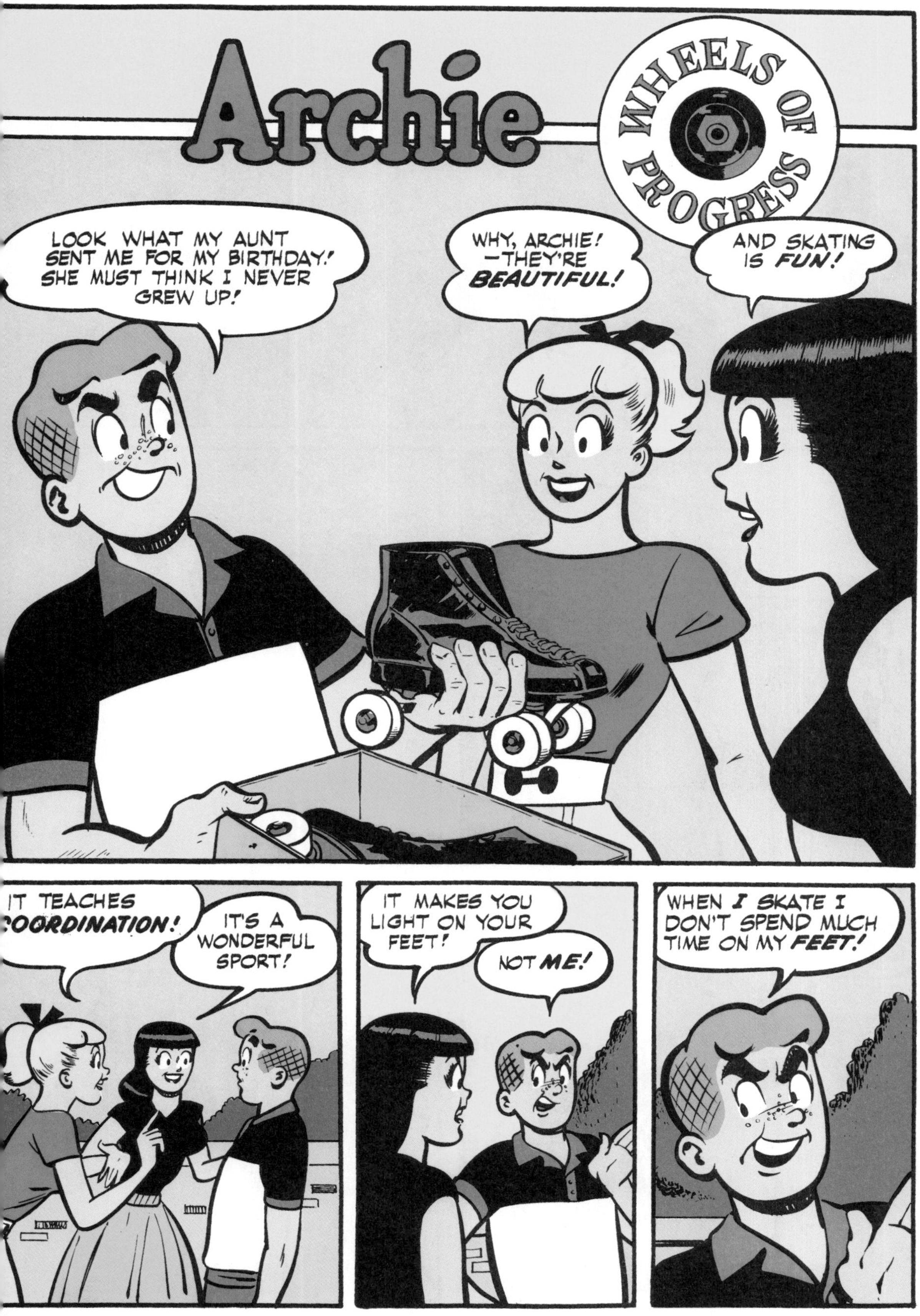

Archie
WHEELS OF PROGRESS
LOOK WHAT MY AUNT SENT ME FOR MY BIRTHDAY! SHE MUST THINK I NEVER GREW UP!
WHY, ARCHIE! —THEY'RE BEAUTIFUL!
AND SKATING IS FUN!
IT TEACHES COORDINATION!
IT'S A WONDERFUL SPORT!
IT MAKES YOU LIGHT ON YOUR FEET!
NOT ME!
WHEN I SKATE I DON'T SPEND MUCH TIME ON MY FEET!

ORIGINALLY PRESENTED IN **LAUGH COMICS #98**, MAY 1958.

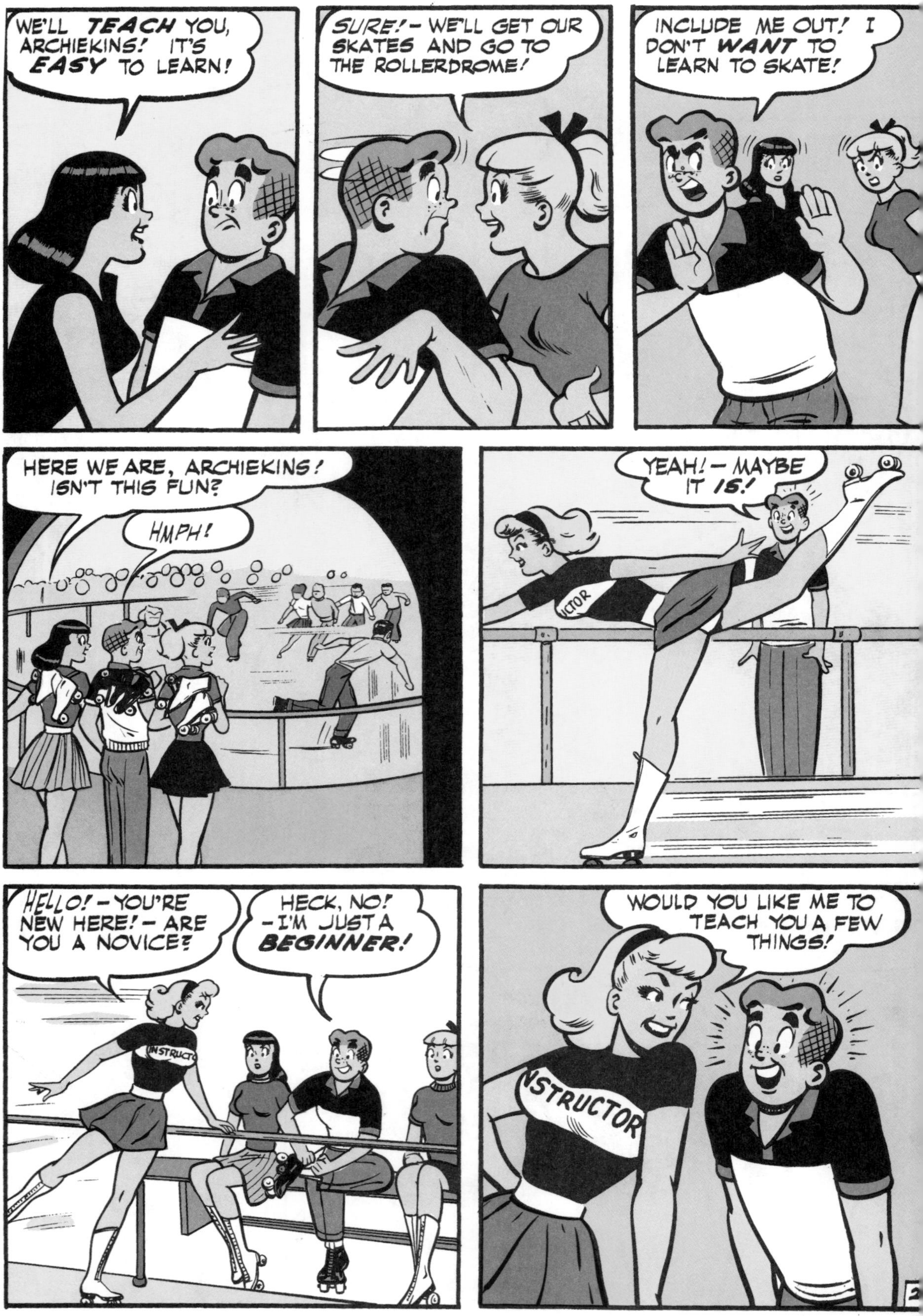
WE'LL TEACH YOU, ARCHIEKINS! IT'S EASY TO LEARN!
SURE! – WE'LL GET OUR SKATES AND GO TO THE ROLLERDROME!
INCLUDE ME OUT! I DON'T WANT TO LEARN TO SKATE!
HERE WE ARE, ARCHIEKINS! ISN'T THIS FUN?
HMPH!
YEAH! – MAYBE IT IS!
HELLO! – YOU'RE NEW HERE! – ARE YOU A NOVICE?
HECK, NO! – I'M JUST A BEGINNER!
INSTRUCTOR
WOULD YOU LIKE ME TO TEACH YOU A FEW THINGS!
INSTRUCTOR

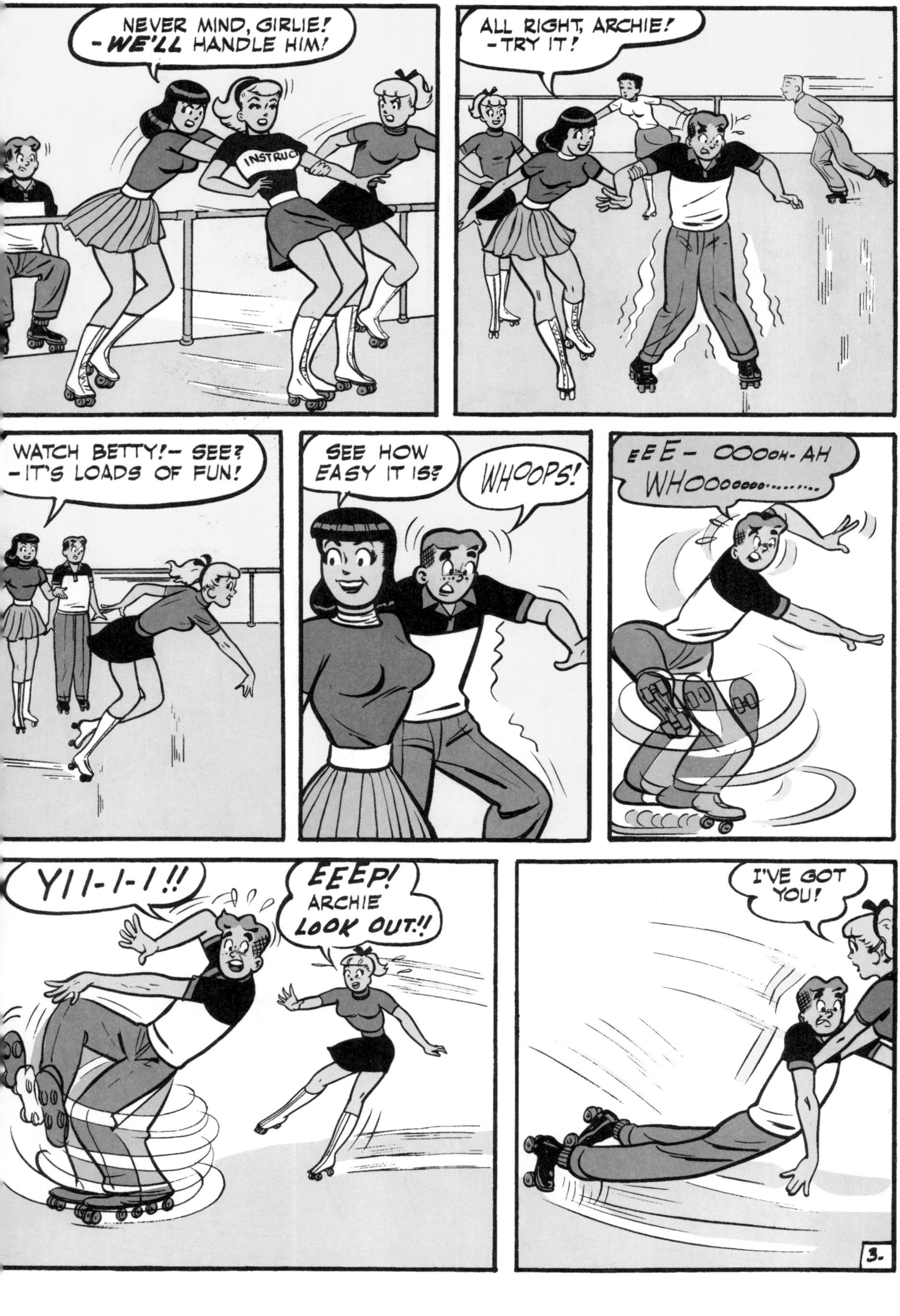
NEVER MIND, GIRLIE! -WE'LL HANDLE HIM!
INSTRUC
ALL RIGHT, ARCHIE! -TRY IT!
WATCH BETTY!- SEE? -IT'S LOADS OF FUN!
SEE HOW EASY IT IS?
WHOOPS!
EEE- OOOOH- AH WHOooooo........
YII-I-I!!
EEEP! ARCHIE LOOK OUT!!
I'VE GOT YOU!
3.

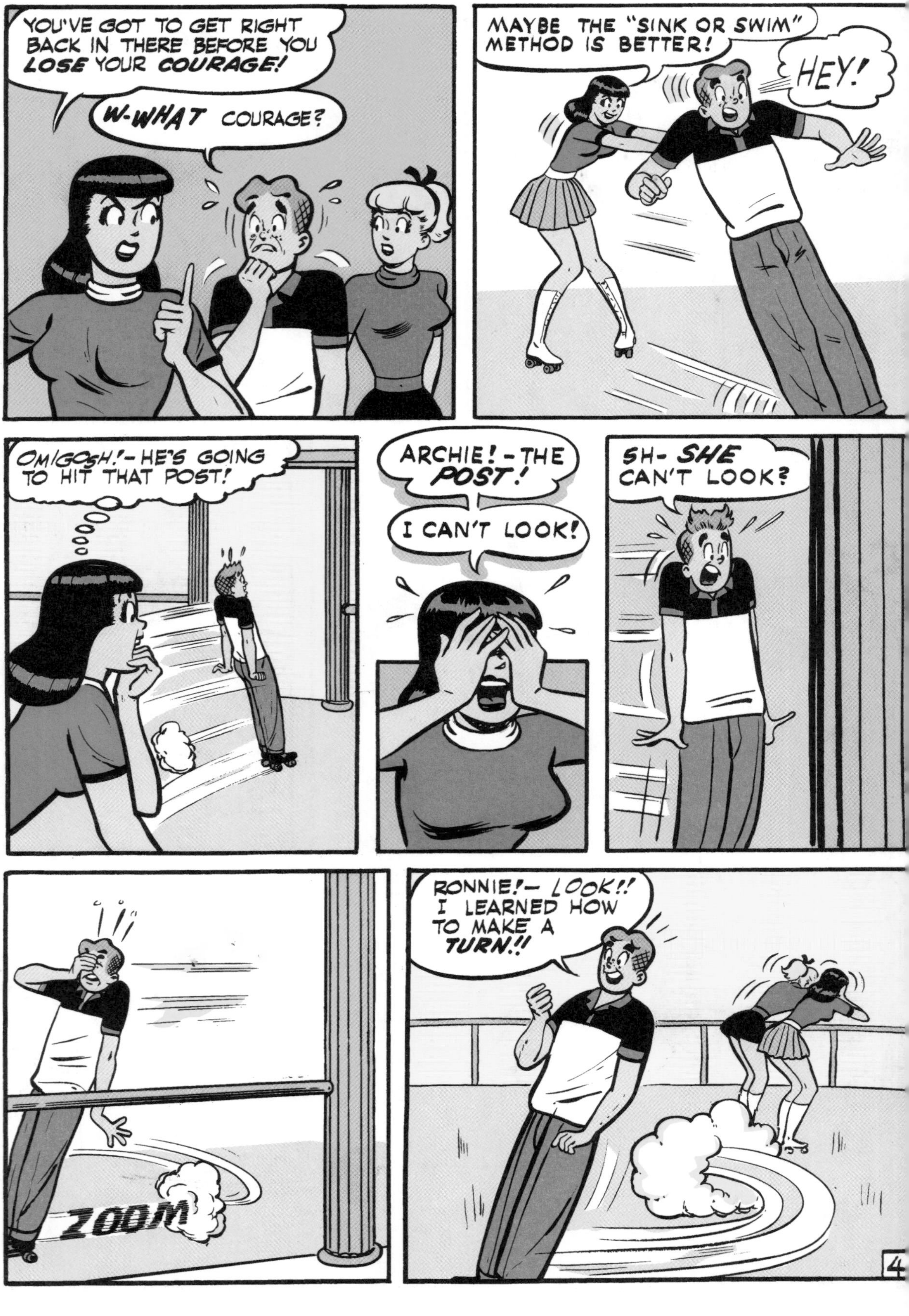
YOU'VE GOT TO GET RIGHT BACK IN THERE BEFORE YOU LOSE YOUR COURAGE!
W-WHAT COURAGE?
MAYBE THE "SINK OR SWIM" METHOD IS BETTER!
HEY!
OMIGOSH!- HE'S GOING TO HIT THAT POST!
ARCHIE! - THE POST!
I CAN'T LOOK!
SH- SHE CAN'T LOOK?
ZOOM
RONNIE!- LOOK!! I LEARNED HOW TO MAKE A TURN!!
4

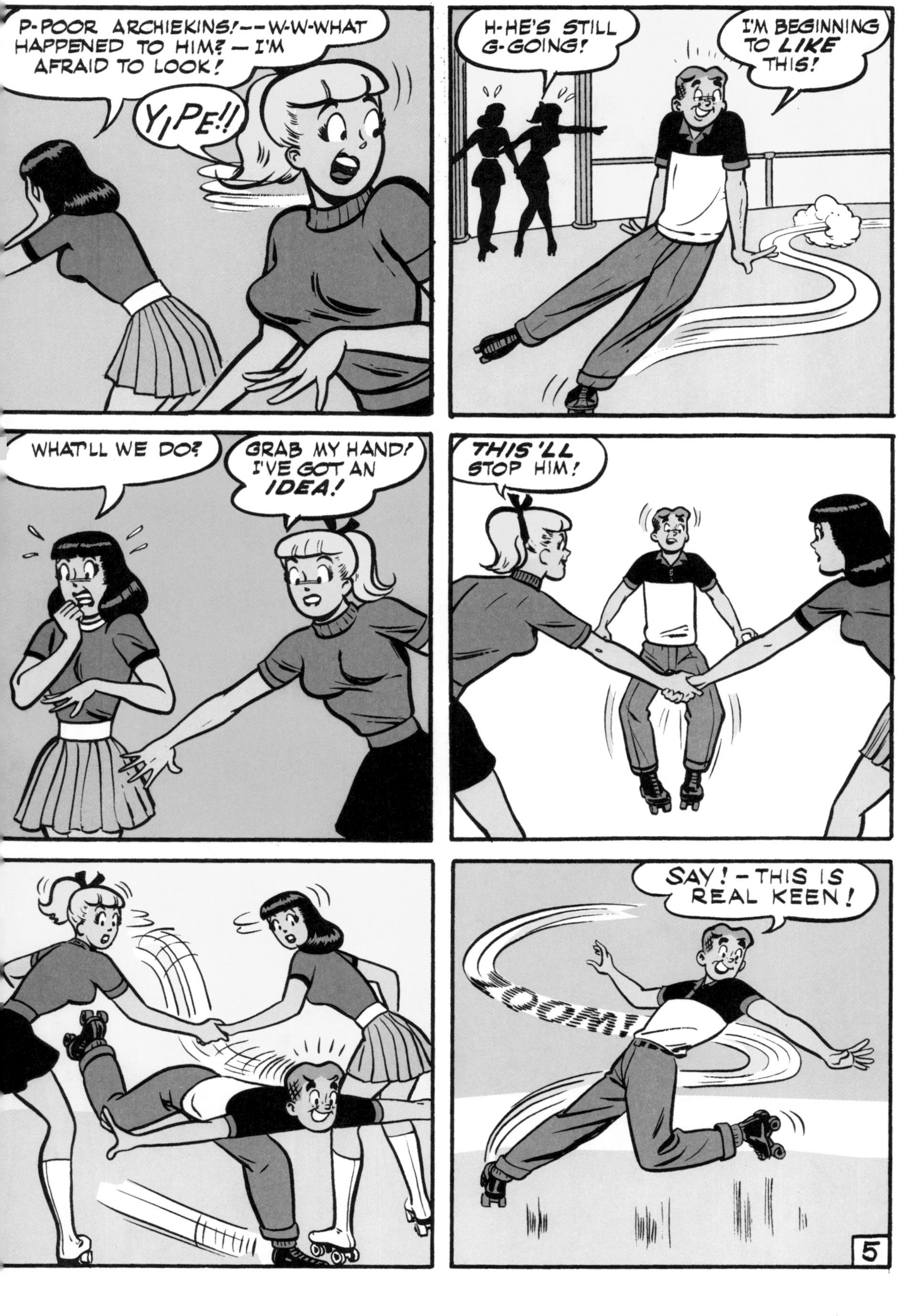
P-POOR ARCHIEKINS! -- W-W-WHAT HAPPENED TO HIM? — I'M AFRAID TO LOOK!
YIPE!!
H-HE'S STILL G-GOING!
I'M BEGINNING TO LIKE THIS!
WHAT'LL WE DO?
GRAB MY HAND! I'VE GOT AN IDEA!
THIS'LL STOP HIM!
SAY! - THIS IS REAL KEEN!
ZOOM!
5

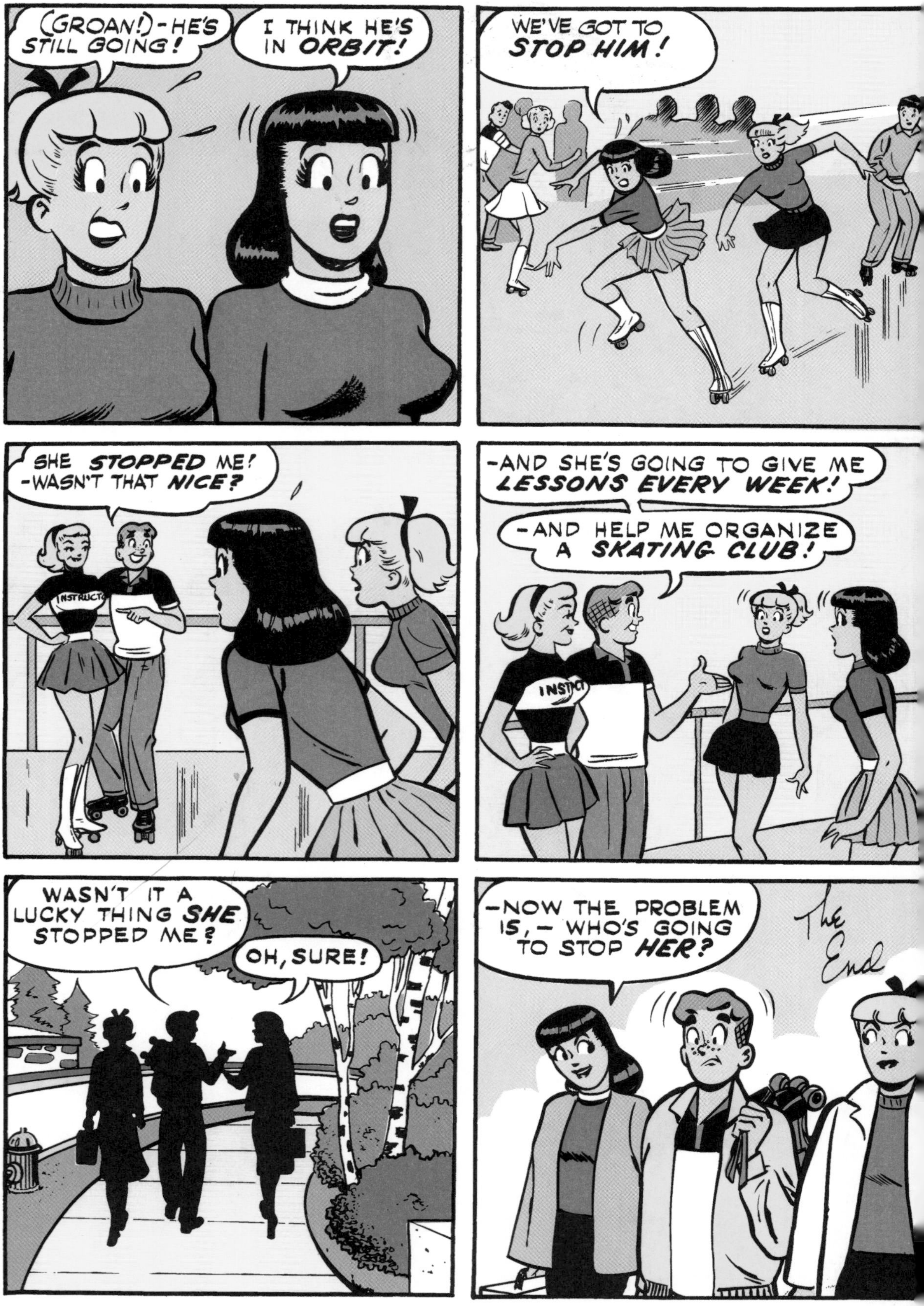
(GROAN!) - HE'S STILL GOING!
I THINK HE'S IN ORBIT!
WE'VE GOT TO STOP HIM!
SHE STOPPED ME! -WASN'T THAT NICE?
INSTRUCTO
-AND SHE'S GOING TO GIVE ME LESSONS EVERY WEEK!
-AND HELP ME ORGANIZE A SKATING CLUB!
INSTR
WASN'T IT A LUCKY THING SHE STOPPED ME?
OH, SURE!
-NOW THE PROBLEM IS, - WHO'S GOING TO STOP HER?
The End

A GALLERY OF CLASSIC 50s COVER GAGS BY BOB MONTANA

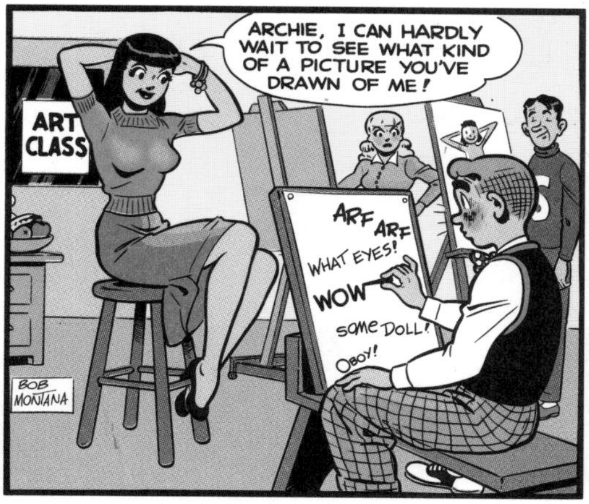
ARCHIE, I CAN HARDLY WAIT TO SEE WHAT KIND OF A PICTURE YOU'VE DRAWN OF ME!
ART CLASS
ARF ARF
WHAT EYES!
WOW
SOME DOLL!
OBOY!
BOB MONTANA

ARCHIE COMICS #44,
May-June, 1950.

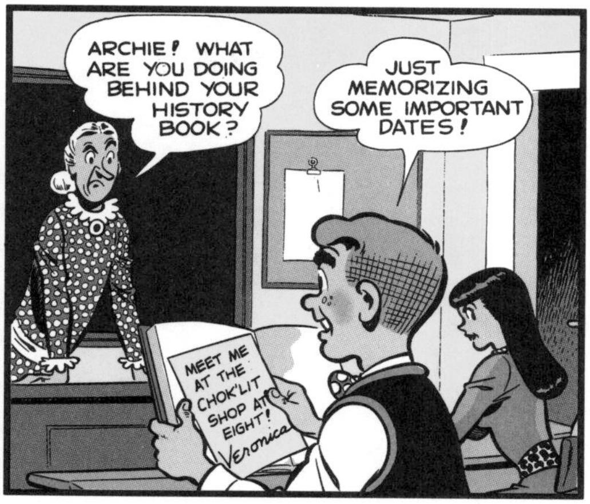
ARCHIE! WHAT ARE YOU DOING BEHIND YOUR HISTORY BOOK?
JUST MEMORIZING SOME IMPORTANT DATES!
MEET ME AT THE CHOK'LIT SHOP AT EIGHT! Veronica

PEP COMICS #83,
January, 1951.

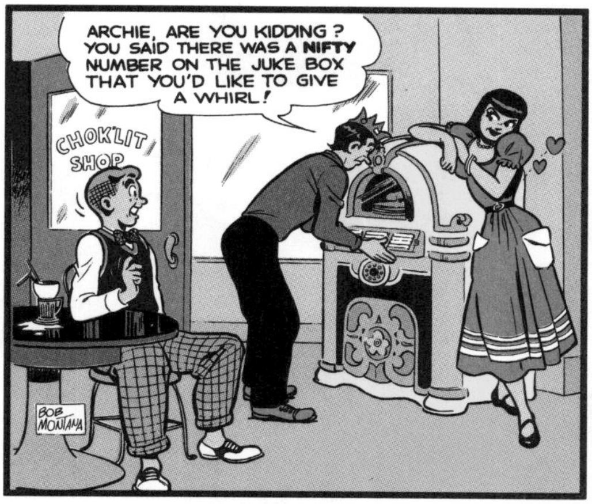
ARCHIE, ARE YOU KIDDING? YOU SAID THERE WAS A NIFTY NUMBER ON THE JUKE BOX THAT YOU'D LIKE TO GIVE A WHIRL!
CHOK'LIT SHOP
BOB MONTANA

LAUGH COMICS #43,
February, 1951.

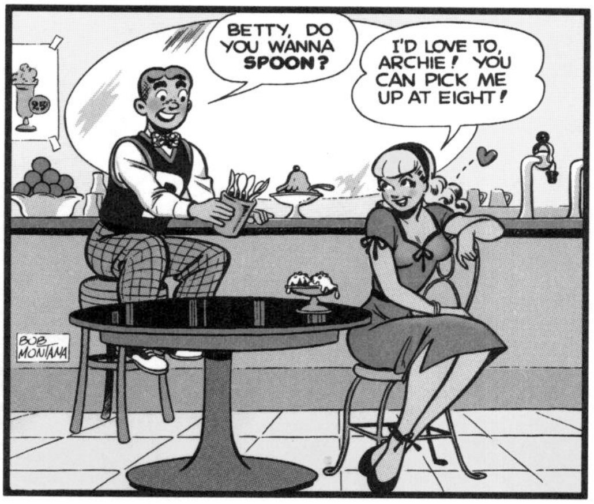
BETTY, DO YOU WANNA SPOON?
I'D LOVE TO, ARCHIE! YOU CAN PICK ME UP AT EIGHT!
BOB MONTANA

ARCHIE COMICS #48,
January-February, 1951.

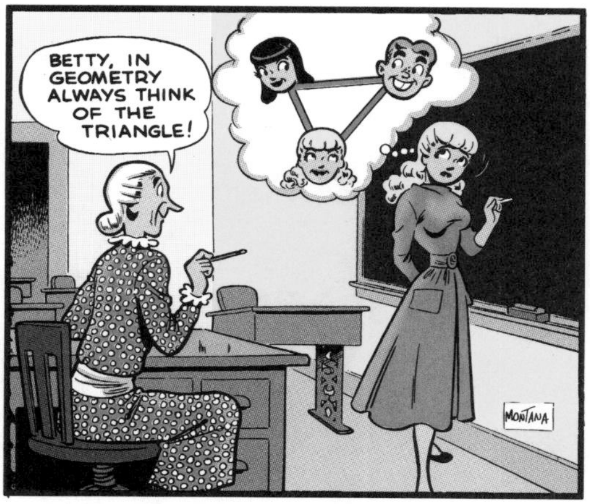
BETTY, IN GEOMETRY ALWAYS THINK OF THE TRIANGLE!
MONTANA

PEP COMICS #78,
March, 1950.

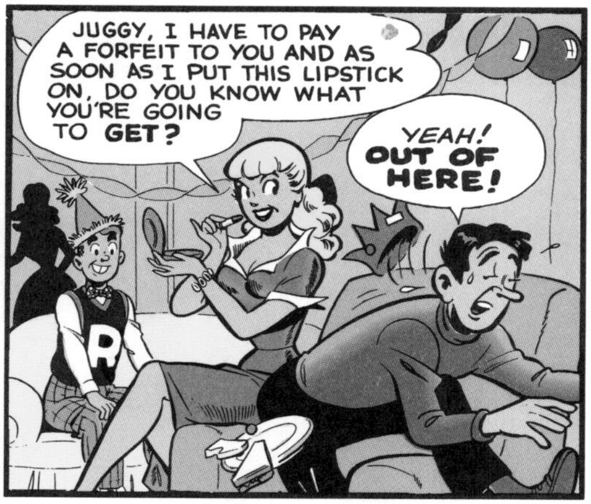
JUGGY, I HAVE TO PAY A FORFEIT TO YOU AND AS SOON AS I PUT THIS LIPSTICK ON, DO YOU KNOW WHAT YOU'RE GOING TO GET?
YEAH! OUT OF HERE!

JUGHEAD COMICS #5,
April, 1951.

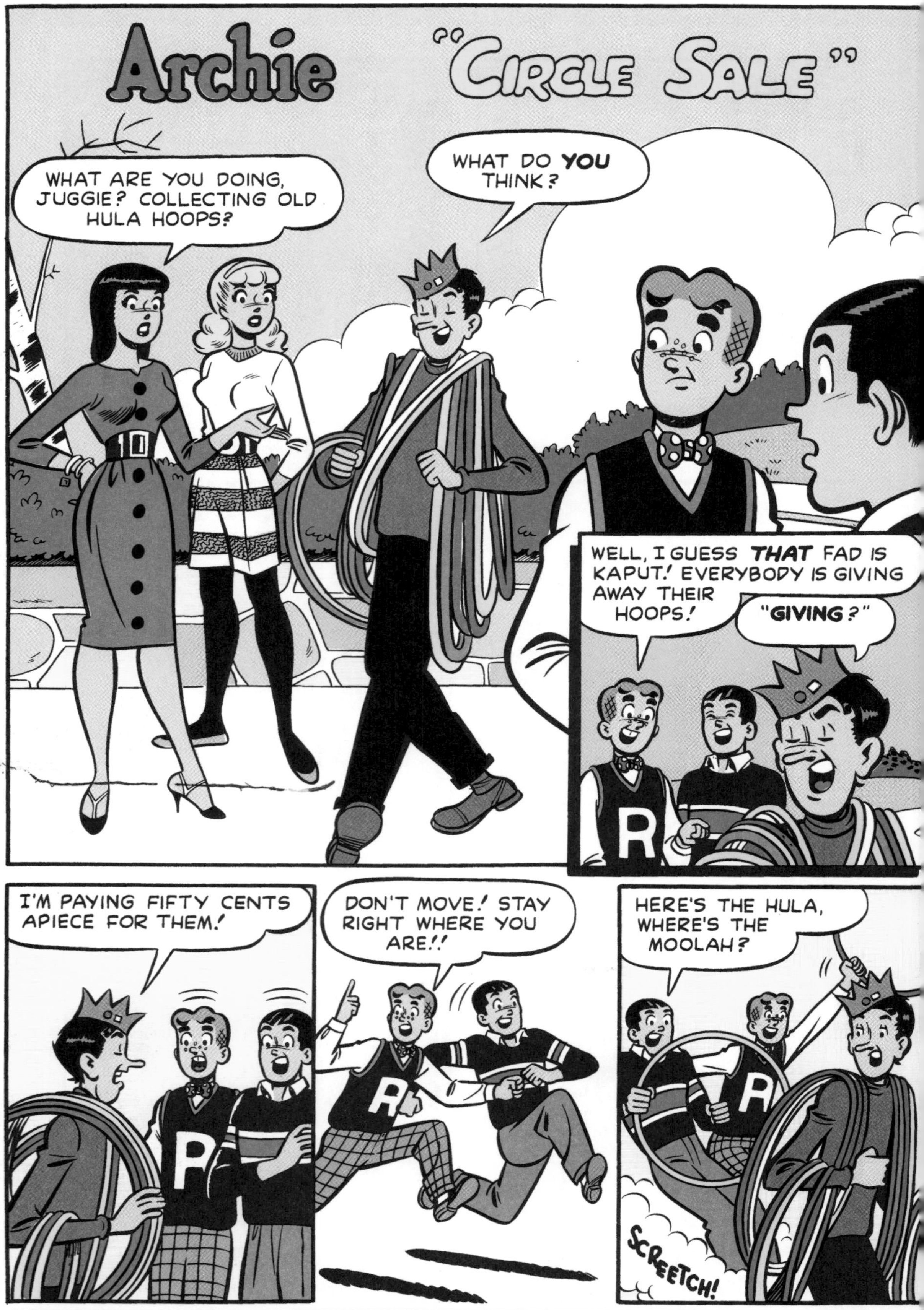
Archie
"CIRCLE SALE"
WHAT ARE YOU DOING, JUGGIE? COLLECTING OLD HULA HOOPS?
WHAT DO YOU THINK?
WELL, I GUESS THAT FAD IS KAPUT! EVERYBODY IS GIVING AWAY THEIR HOOPS!
"GIVING?"
I'M PAYING FIFTY CENTS APIECE FOR THEM!
DON'T MOVE! STAY RIGHT WHERE YOU ARE!!
HERE'S THE HULA, WHERE'S THE MOOLAH?
SCREETCH!

ORIGINALLY PRESENTED IN **ARCHIE COMICS #102**, JULY 1959.

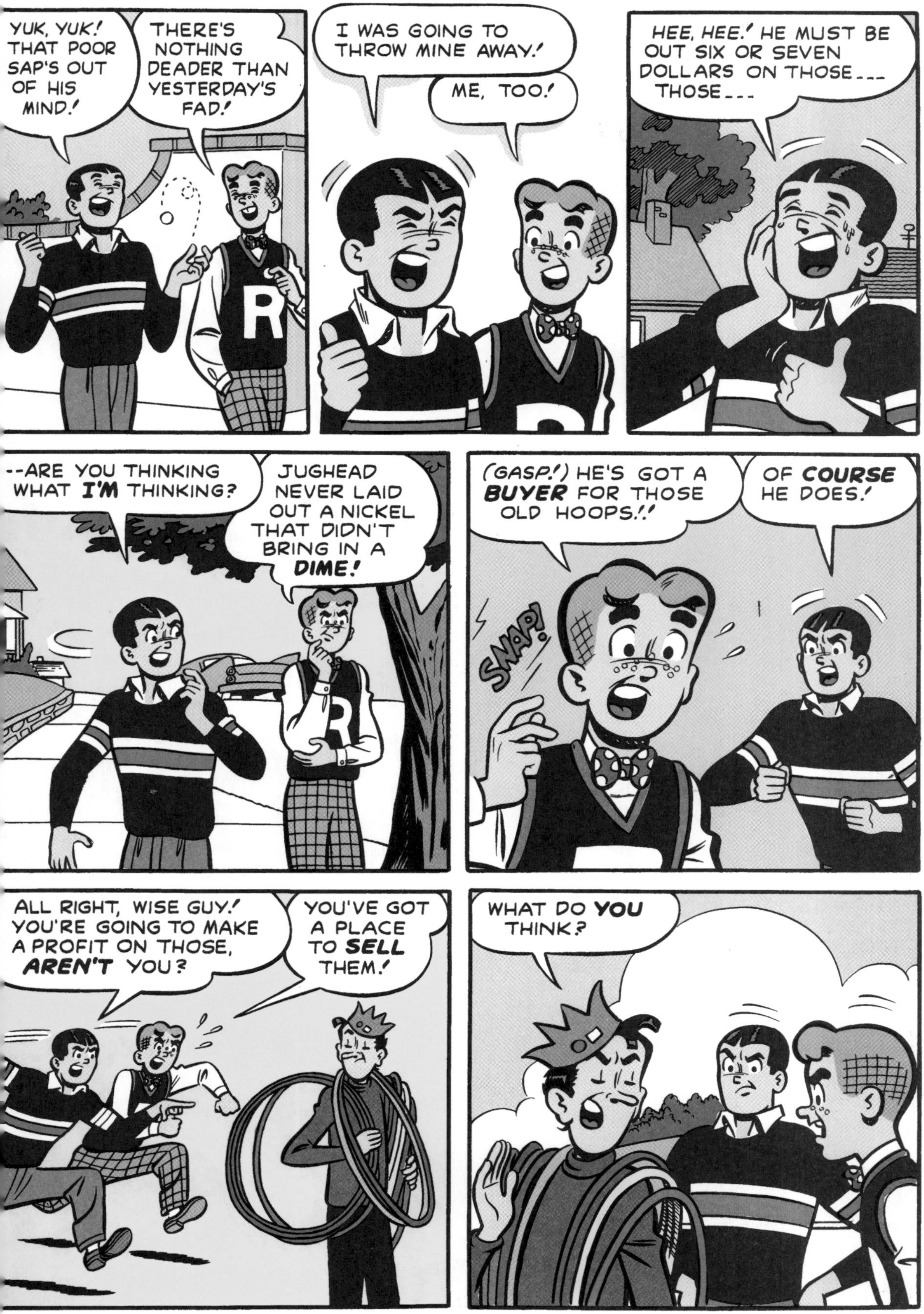
YUK, YUK! THAT POOR SAP'S OUT OF HIS MIND!
THERE'S NOTHING DEADER THAN YESTERDAY'S FAD!
I WAS GOING TO THROW MINE AWAY!
ME, TOO!
HEE, HEE! HE MUST BE OUT SIX OR SEVEN DOLLARS ON THOSE--- THOSE---
--ARE YOU THINKING WHAT **I'M** THINKING?
JUGHEAD NEVER LAID OUT A NICKEL THAT DIDN'T BRING IN A **DIME!**
(GASP!) HE'S GOT A **BUYER** FOR THOSE OLD HOOPS!!
SNAP!
OF **COURSE** HE DOES!
ALL RIGHT, WISE GUY! YOU'RE GOING TO MAKE A PROFIT ON THOSE, **AREN'T** YOU?
YOU'VE GOT A PLACE TO **SELL** THEM!
WHAT DO **YOU** THINK?

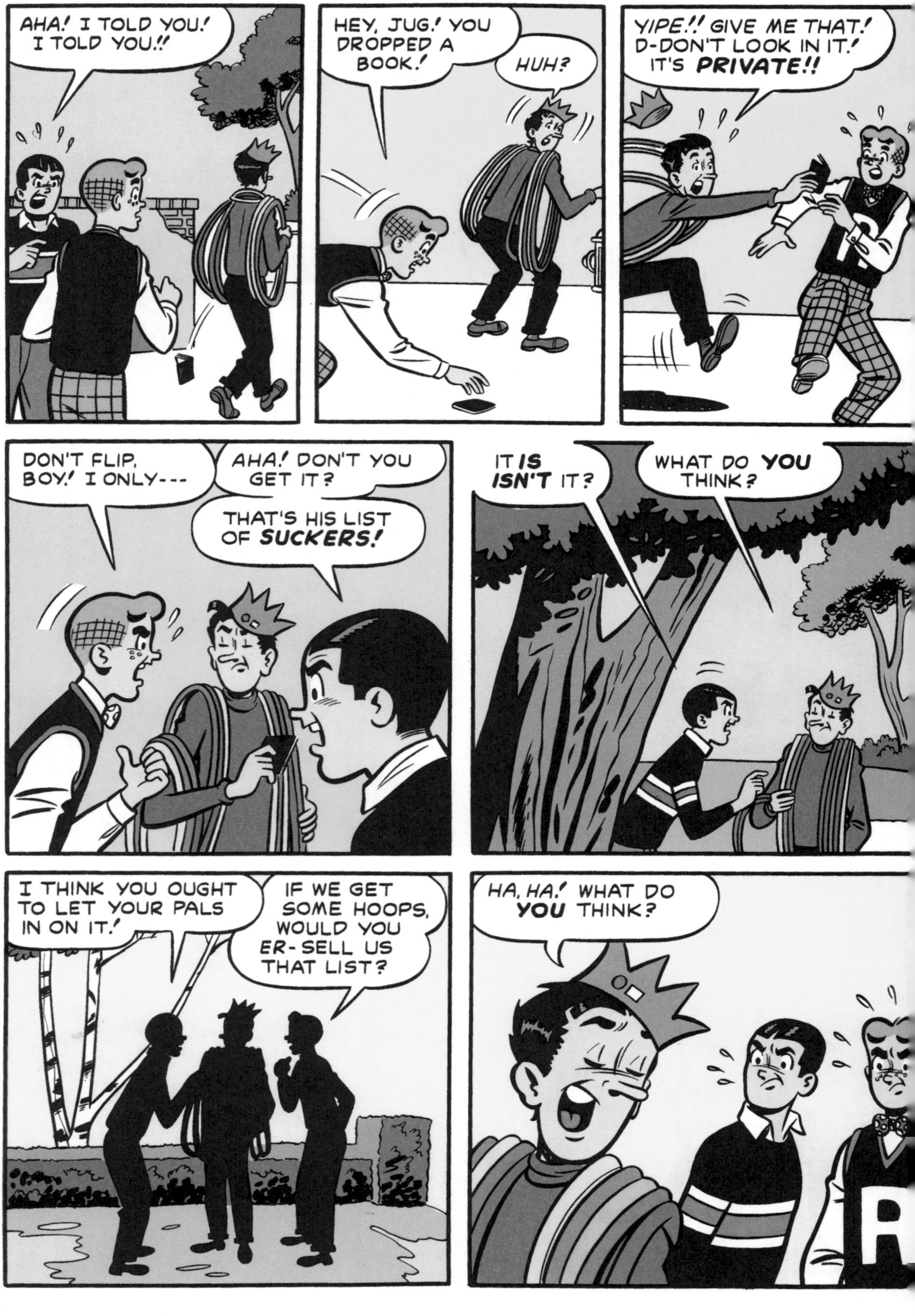
AHA! I TOLD YOU! I TOLD YOU!!
HEY, JUG! YOU DROPPED A BOOK!
HUH?
YIPE!! GIVE ME THAT! D-DON'T LOOK IN IT! IT'S PRIVATE!!
DON'T FLIP, BOY! I ONLY---
AHA! DON'T YOU GET IT?
THAT'S HIS LIST OF SUCKERS!
IT IS ISN'T IT?
WHAT DO YOU THINK?
I THINK YOU OUGHT TO LET YOUR PALS IN ON IT!
IF WE GET SOME HOOPS, WOULD YOU ER-SELL US THAT LIST?
HA, HA! WHAT DO YOU THINK?

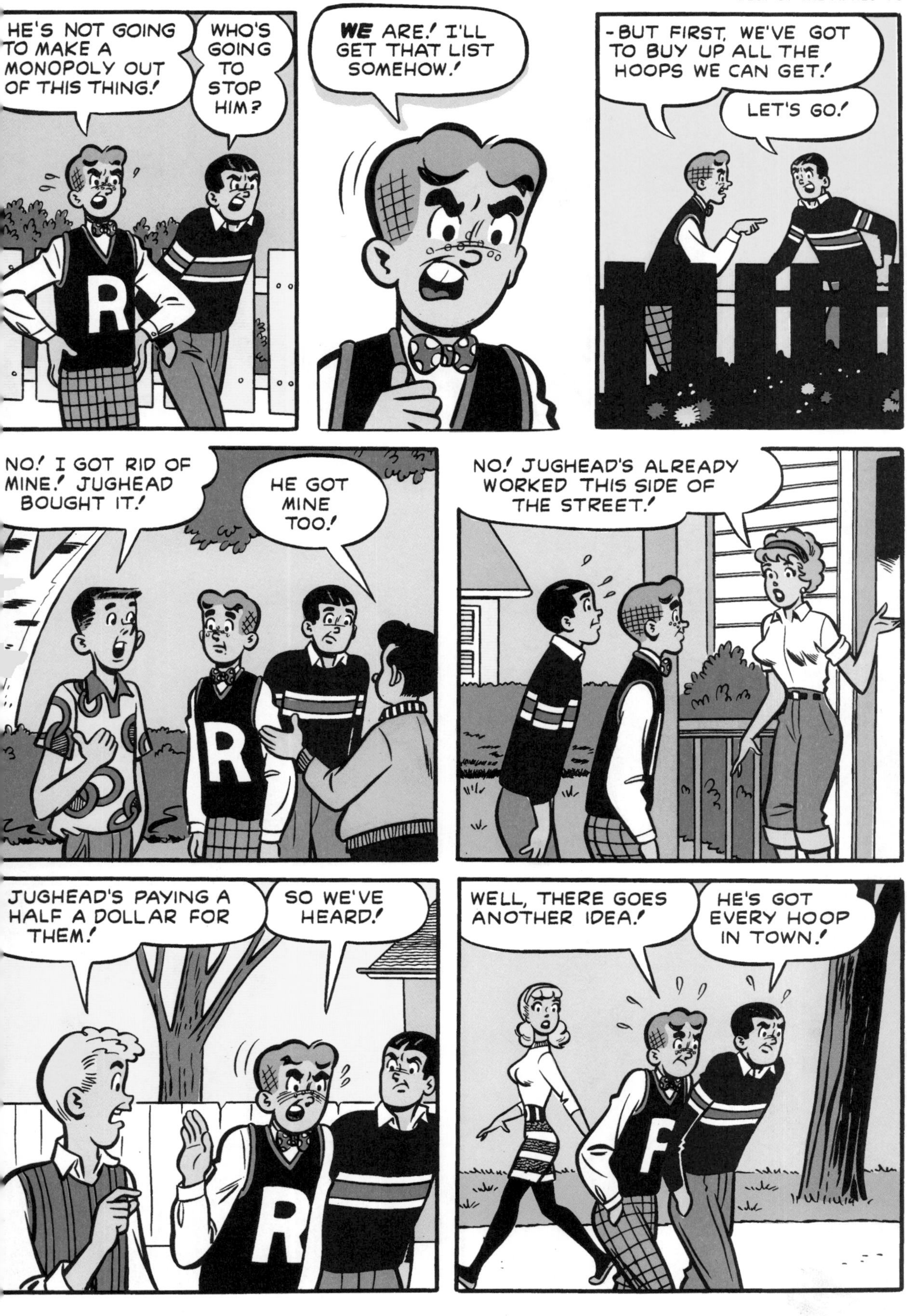
HE'S NOT GOING TO MAKE A MONOPOLY OUT OF THIS THING!
WHO'S GOING TO STOP HIM?
WE ARE! I'LL GET THAT LIST SOMEHOW!
-BUT FIRST, WE'VE GOT TO BUY UP ALL THE HOOPS WE CAN GET!
LET'S GO!
NO! I GOT RID OF MINE! JUGHEAD BOUGHT IT!
HE GOT MINE TOO!
NO! JUGHEAD'S ALREADY WORKED THIS SIDE OF THE STREET!
JUGHEAD'S PAYING A HALF A DOLLAR FOR THEM!
SO WE'VE HEARD!
WELL, THERE GOES ANOTHER IDEA!
HE'S GOT EVERY HOOP IN TOWN!

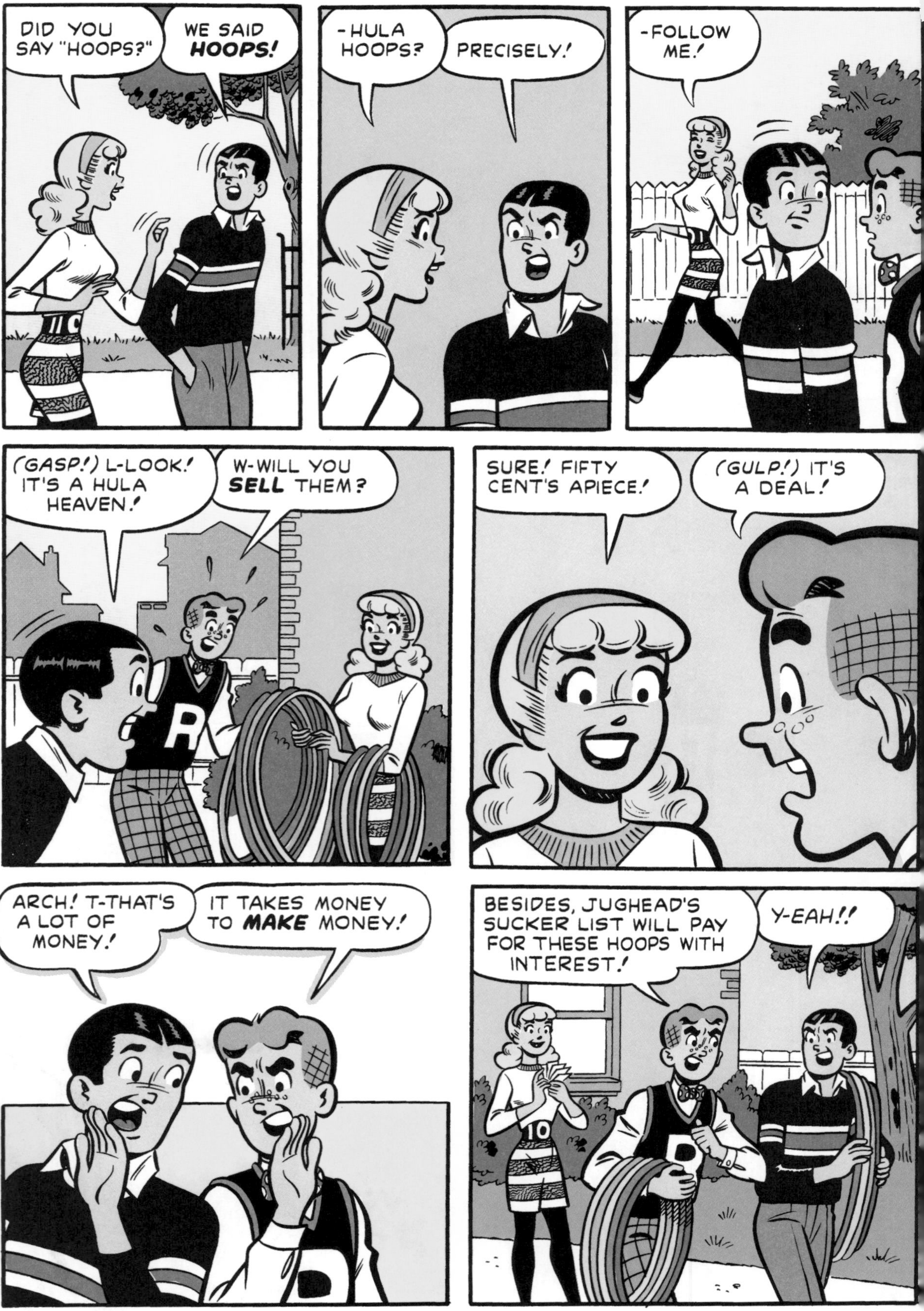
DID YOU SAY "HOOPS?"
WE SAID **HOOPS!**
-HULA HOOPS?
PRECISELY!
-FOLLOW ME!
(GASP!) L-LOOK! IT'S A HULA HEAVEN!
W-WILL YOU **SELL** THEM?
SURE! FIFTY CENT'S APIECE!
(GULP!) IT'S A DEAL!
ARCH! T-THAT'S A LOT OF MONEY!
IT TAKES MONEY TO **MAKE** MONEY!
BESIDES, JUGHEAD'S SUCKER LIST WILL PAY FOR THESE HOOPS WITH INTEREST!
Y-EAH!!

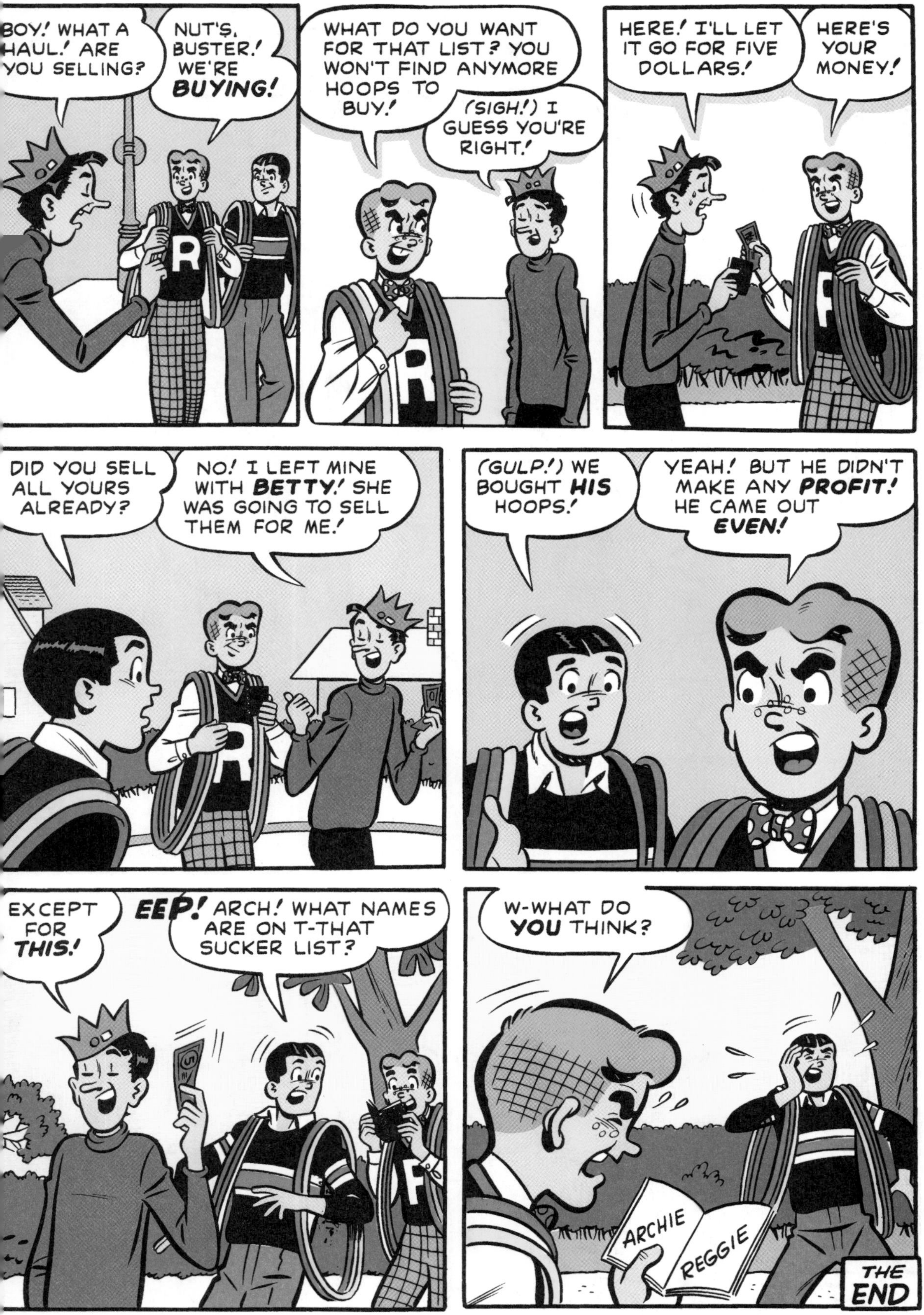
BOY! WHAT A HAUL! ARE YOU SELLING?
NUT'S, BUSTER! WE'RE BUYING!
WHAT DO YOU WANT FOR THAT LIST? YOU WON'T FIND ANYMORE HOOPS TO BUY!
(SIGH!) I GUESS YOU'RE RIGHT!
HERE! I'LL LET IT GO FOR FIVE DOLLARS!
HERE'S YOUR MONEY!
DID YOU SELL ALL YOURS ALREADY?
NO! I LEFT MINE WITH BETTY! SHE WAS GOING TO SELL THEM FOR ME!
(GULP!) WE BOUGHT HIS HOOPS!
YEAH! BUT HE DIDN'T MAKE ANY PROFIT! HE CAME OUT EVEN!
EXCEPT FOR THIS!
EEP! ARCH! WHAT NAMES ARE ON T-THAT SUCKER LIST?
W-WHAT DO YOU THINK?
ARCHIE
REGGIE
THE END

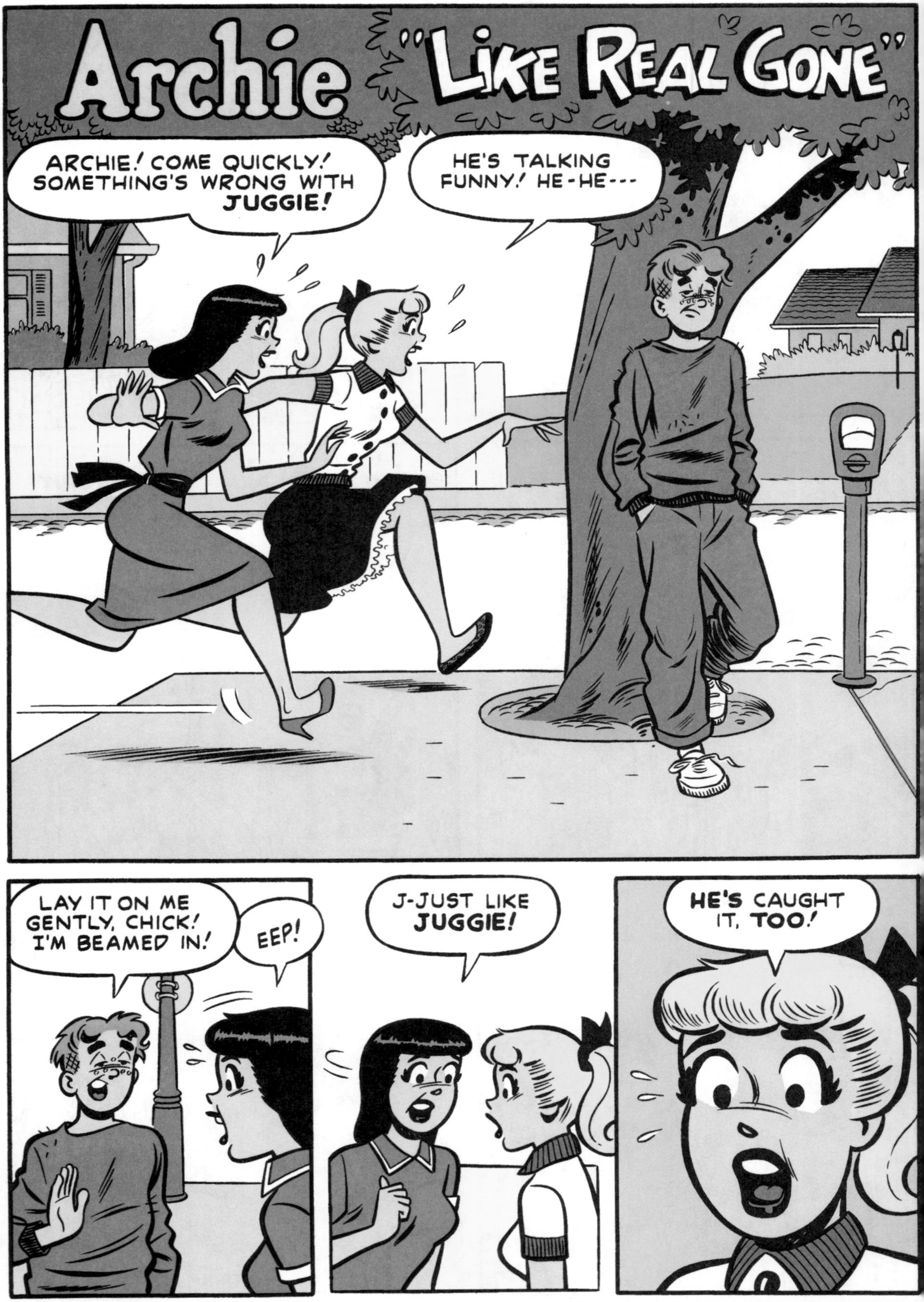
Archie
"LIKE REAL GONE"
ARCHIE! COME QUICKLY! SOMETHING'S WRONG WITH **JUGGIE!**
HE'S TALKING FUNNY! HE-HE---
LAY IT ON ME GENTLY, CHICK! I'M BEAMED IN!
EEP!
J-JUST LIKE **JUGGIE!**
HE'S CAUGHT IT, **TOO!**

ORIGINALLY PRESENTED IN **LAUGH COMICS #104**, NOVEMBER, 1959.

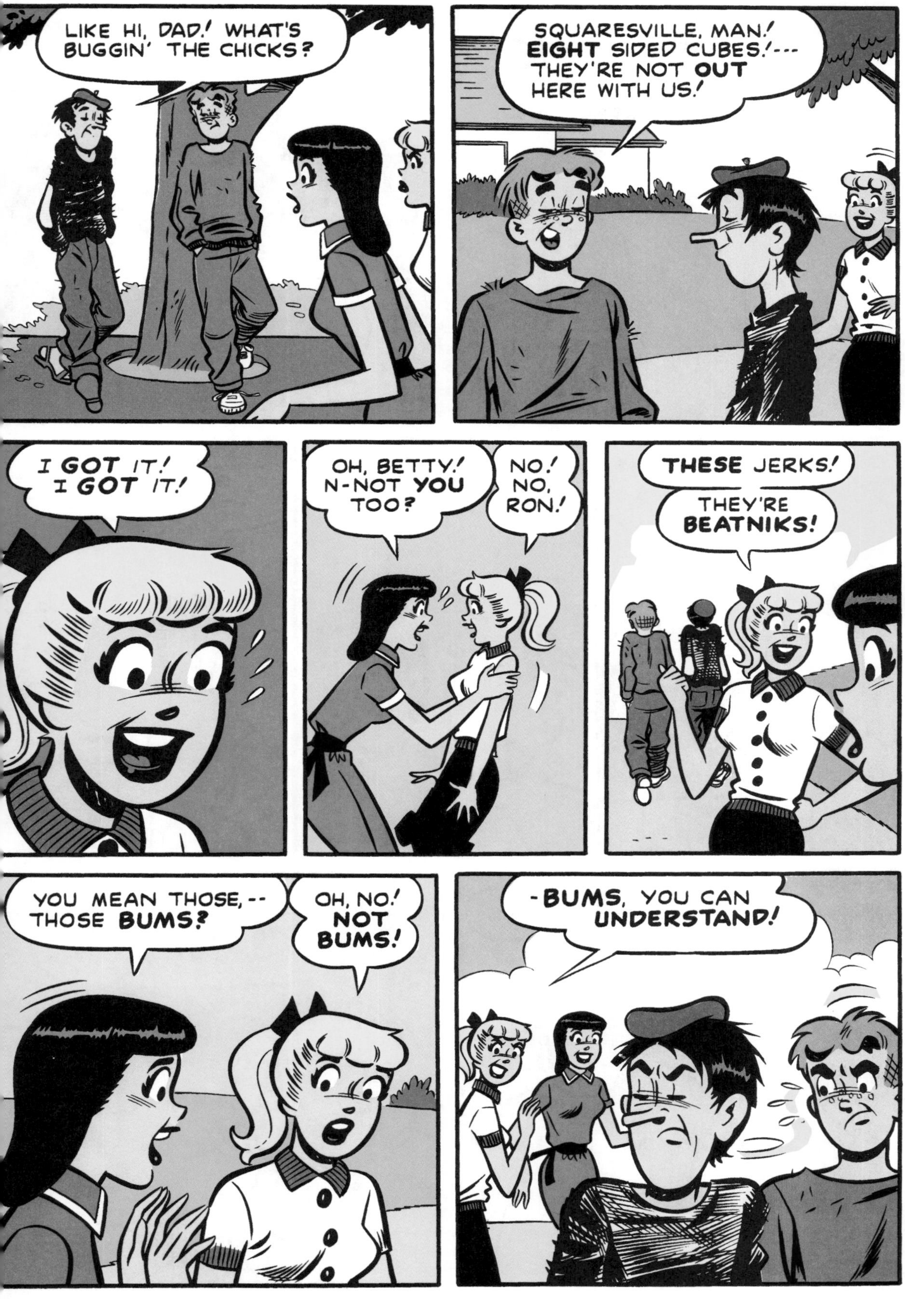
LIKE HI, DAD! WHAT'S BUGGIN' THE CHICKS?
SQUARESVILLE, MAN! EIGHT SIDED CUBES!--- THEY'RE NOT OUT HERE WITH US!
I GOT IT! I GOT IT!
OH, BETTY! N-NOT YOU TOO?
NO! NO, RON!
THESE JERKS!
THEY'RE BEATNIKS!
YOU MEAN THOSE,-- THOSE BUMS?
OH, NO! NOT BUMS!
-BUMS, YOU CAN UNDERSTAND!

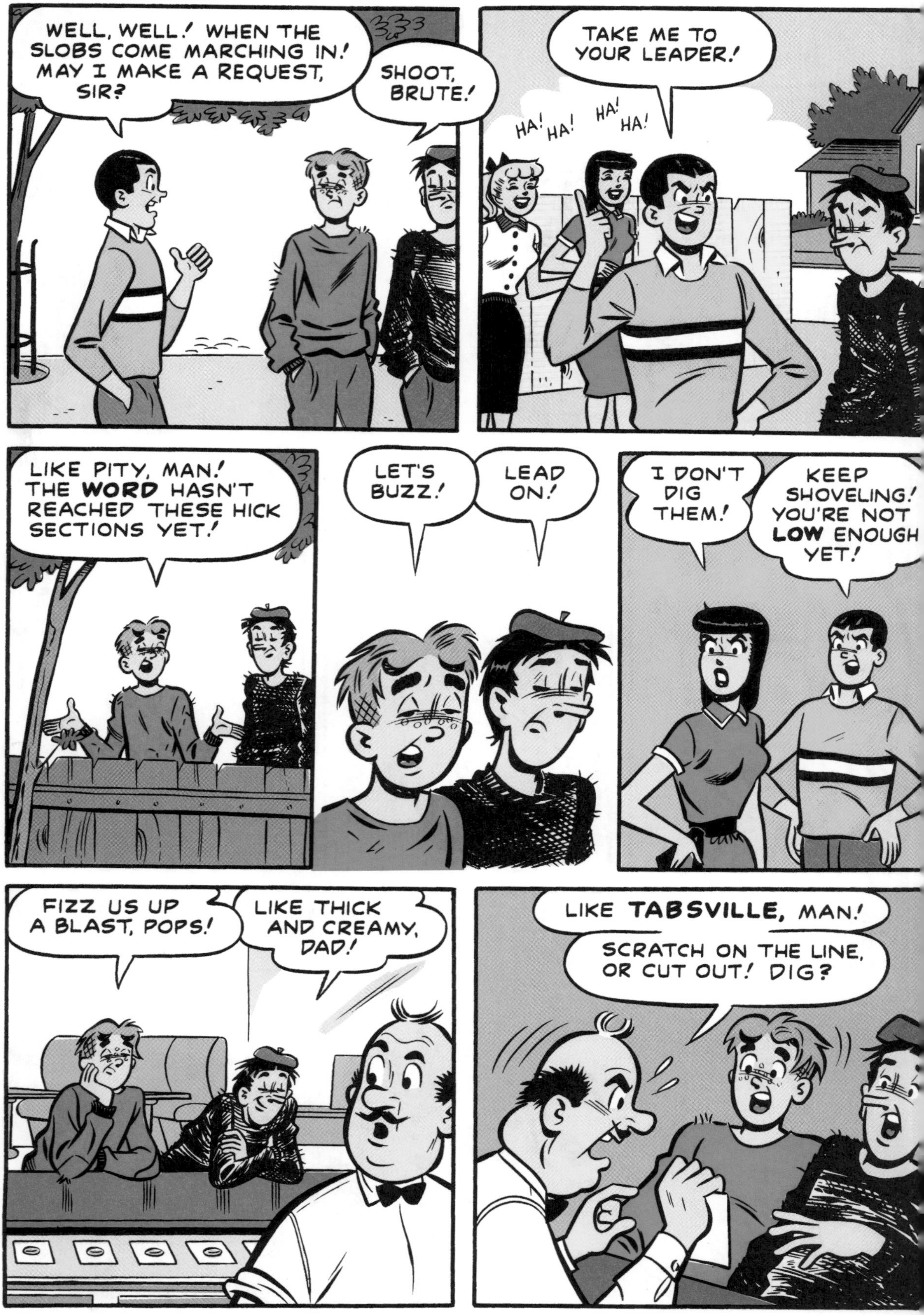
WELL, WELL! WHEN THE SLOBS COME MARCHING IN! MAY I MAKE A REQUEST, SIR?
SHOOT, BRUTE!
TAKE ME TO YOUR LEADER!
HA! HA! HA! HA!
LIKE PITY, MAN! THE WORD HASN'T REACHED THESE HICK SECTIONS YET!
LET'S BUZZ!
LEAD ON!
I DON'T DIG THEM!
KEEP SHOVELING! YOU'RE NOT LOW ENOUGH YET!
FIZZ US UP A BLAST, POPS!
LIKE THICK AND CREAMY, DAD!
LIKE TABSVILLE, MAN!
SCRATCH ON THE LINE, OR CUT OUT! DIG?

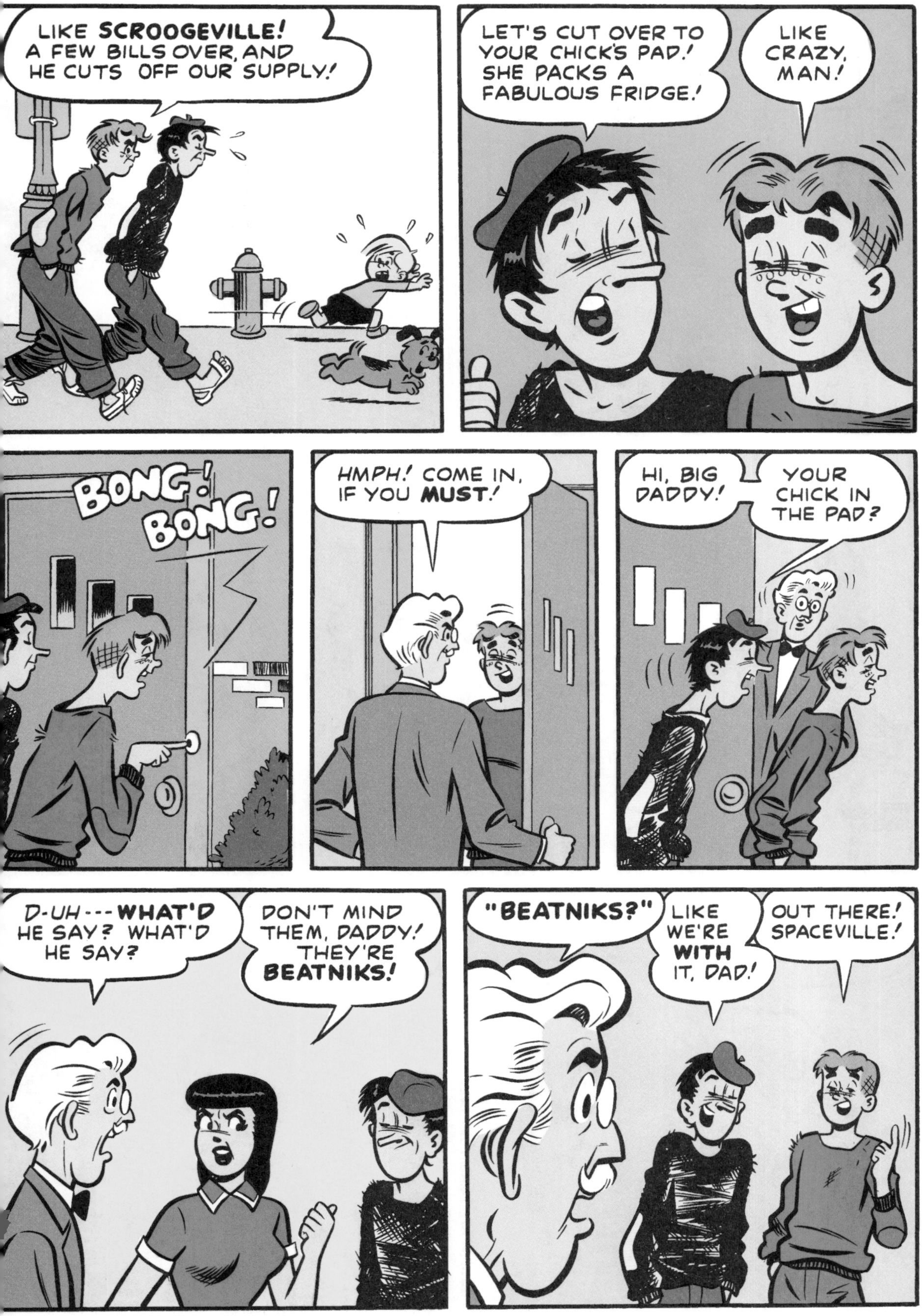
LIKE SCROOGEVILLE! A FEW BILLS OVER, AND HE CUTS OFF OUR SUPPLY!
LET'S CUT OVER TO YOUR CHICK'S PAD! SHE PACKS A FABULOUS FRIDGE!
LIKE CRAZY, MAN!
BONG! BONG!
HMPH! COME IN, IF YOU MUST!
HI, BIG DADDY!
YOUR CHICK IN THE PAD?
D-UH---WHAT'D HE SAY? WHAT'D HE SAY?
DON'T MIND THEM, DADDY! THEY'RE BEATNIKS!
"BEATNIKS?"
LIKE WE'RE WITH IT, DAD!
OUT THERE! SPACEVILLE!

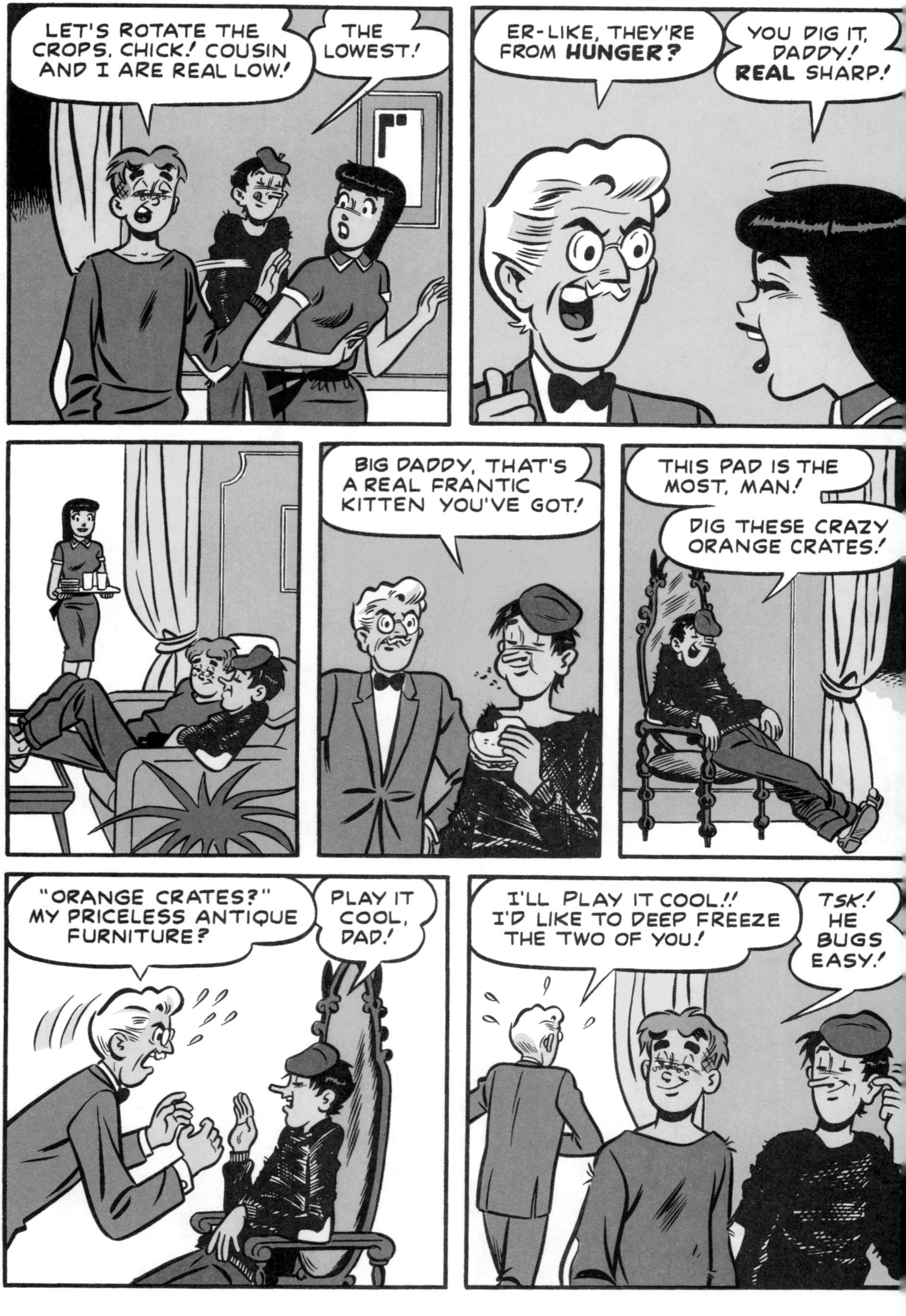
LET'S ROTATE THE CROPS, CHICK! COUSIN AND I ARE REAL LOW!
THE LOWEST!
ER-LIKE, THEY'RE FROM HUNGER?
YOU DIG IT, DADDY! REAL SHARP!
BIG DADDY, THAT'S A REAL FRANTIC KITTEN YOU'VE GOT!
THIS PAD IS THE MOST, MAN!
DIG THESE CRAZY ORANGE CRATES!
"ORANGE CRATES?" MY PRICELESS ANTIQUE FURNITURE?
PLAY IT COOL, DAD!
I'LL PLAY IT COOL!! I'D LIKE TO DEEP FREEZE THE TWO OF YOU!
TSK! HE BUGS EASY!

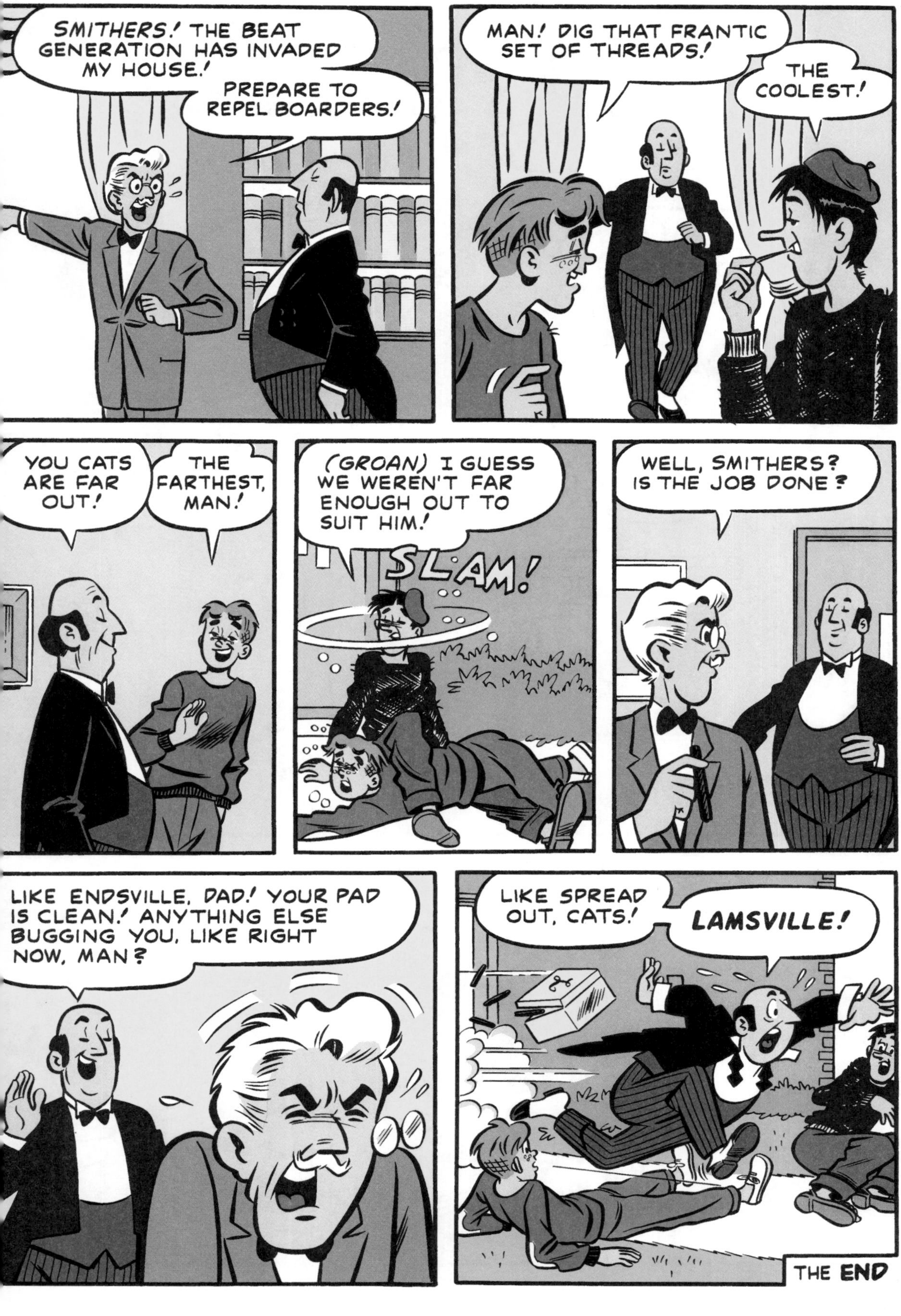
SMITHERS! THE BEAT GENERATION HAS INVADED MY HOUSE!
PREPARE TO REPEL BOARDERS!
MAN! DIG THAT FRANTIC SET OF THREADS!
THE COOLEST!
YOU CATS ARE FAR OUT!
THE FARTHEST, MAN!
(GROAN) I GUESS WE WEREN'T FAR ENOUGH OUT TO SUIT HIM!
SLAM!
WELL, SMITHERS? IS THE JOB DONE?
LIKE ENDSVILLE, DAD! YOUR PAD IS CLEAN! ANYTHING ELSE BUGGING YOU, LIKE RIGHT NOW, MAN?
LIKE SPREAD OUT, CATS!
LAMSVILLE!
THE END

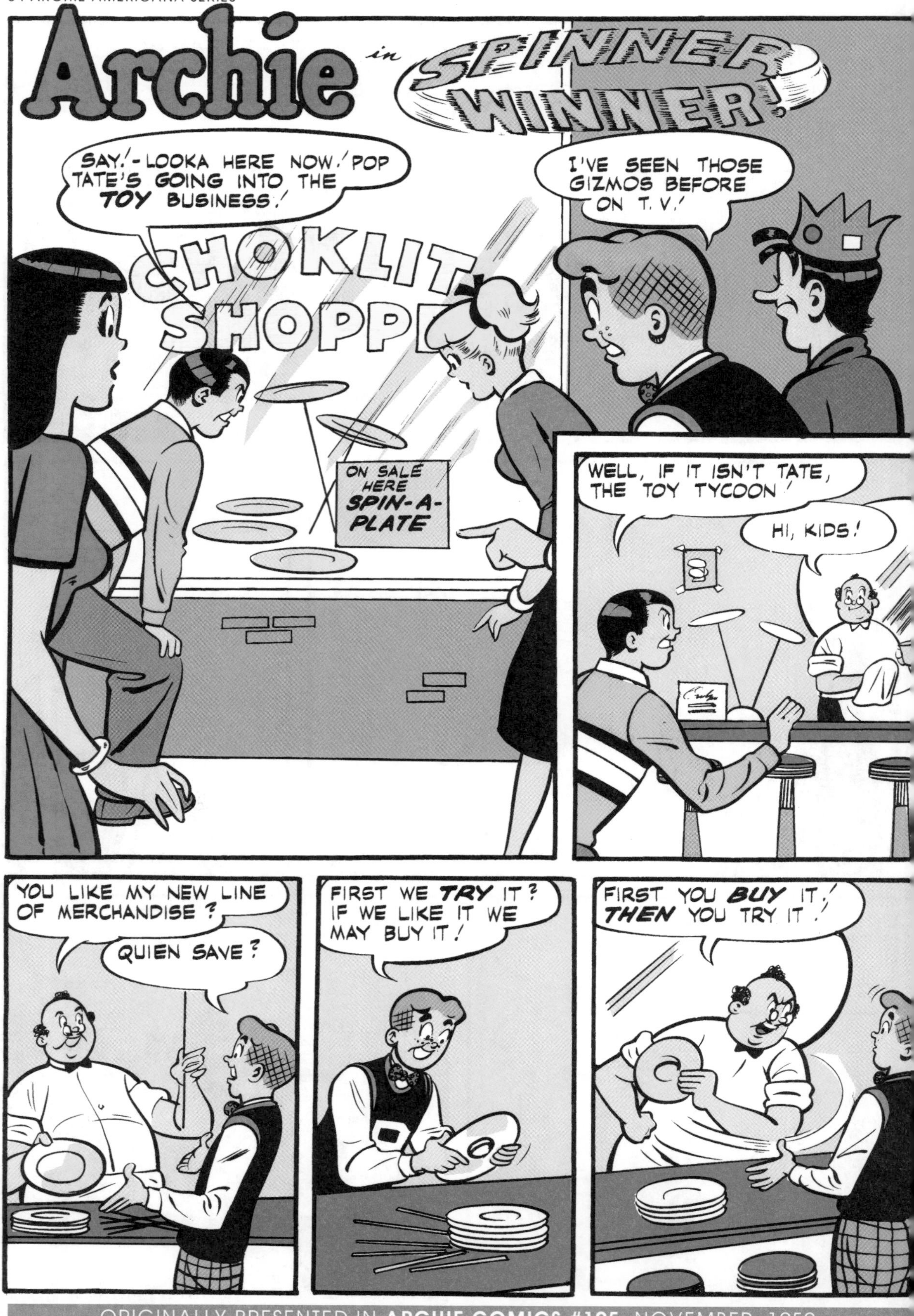
Archie in SPINNER WINNER!
SAY! - LOOKA HERE NOW! POP TATE'S GOING INTO THE TOY BUSINESS!
I'VE SEEN THOSE GIZMOS BEFORE ON T.V.!
CHOKLIT SHOPPE
ON SALE HERE SPIN-A-PLATE
WELL, IF IT ISN'T TATE, THE TOY TYCOON!
HI, KIDS!
YOU LIKE MY NEW LINE OF MERCHANDISE?
QUIEN SAVE?
FIRST WE TRY IT? IF WE LIKE IT WE MAY BUY IT!
FIRST YOU BUY IT! THEN YOU TRY IT!

ORIGINALLY PRESENTED IN **ARCHIE COMICS #105**, NOVEMBER, 1959.

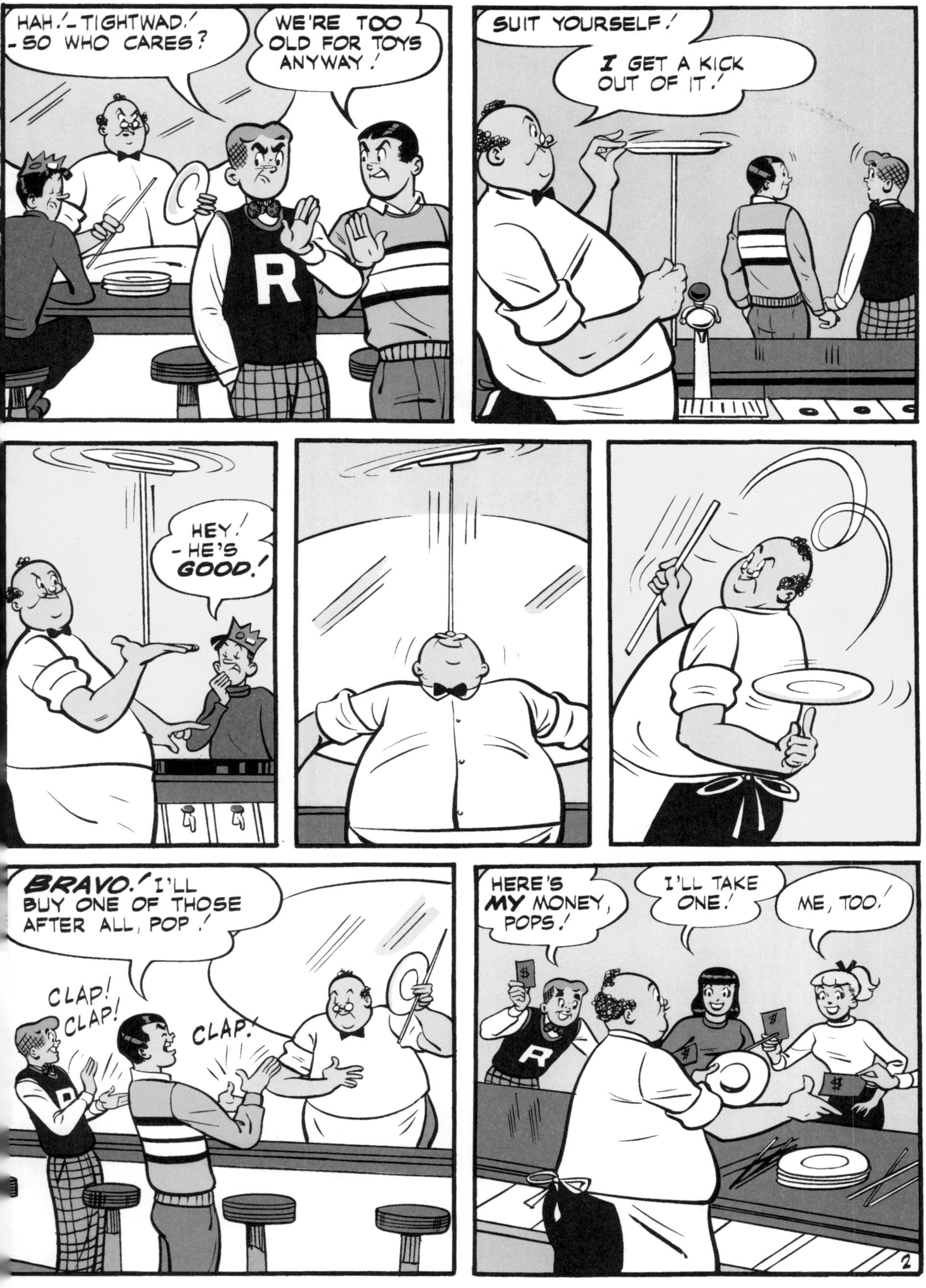
HAH!-TIGHTWAD! -SO WHO CARES?
WE'RE TOO OLD FOR TOYS ANYWAY!
SUIT YOURSELF!
I GET A KICK OUT OF IT!
HEY! -HE'S GOOD!
BRAVO! I'LL BUY ONE OF THOSE AFTER ALL, POP!
CLAP! CLAP!
CLAP!
HERE'S MY MONEY, POPS!
I'LL TAKE ONE!
ME, TOO!
2

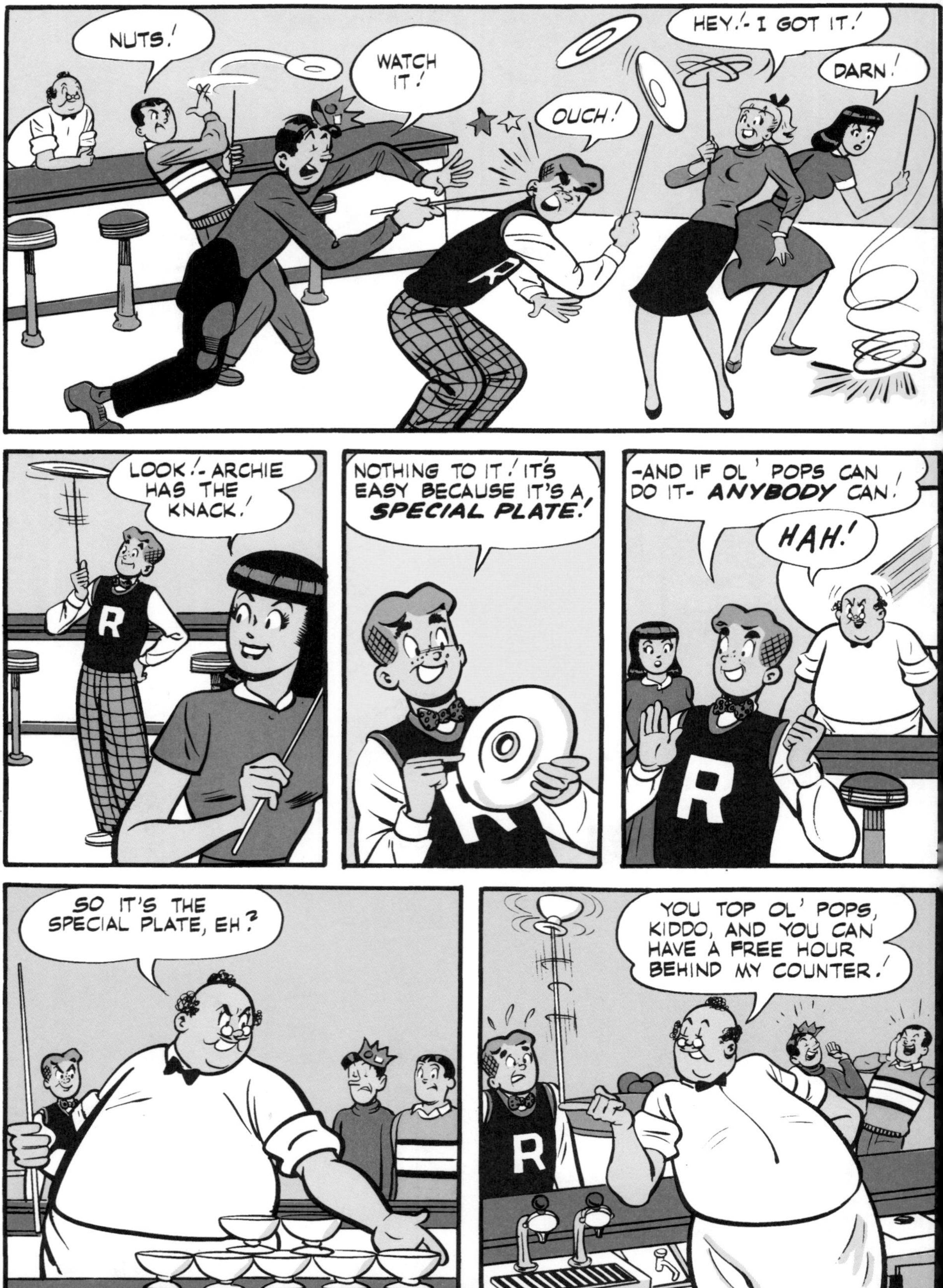
NUTS!
WATCH IT!
OUCH!
HEY!- I GOT IT!
DARN!
LOOK!- ARCHIE HAS THE KNACK!
NOTHING TO IT! IT'S EASY BECAUSE IT'S A *SPECIAL PLATE!*
-AND IF OL' POPS CAN DO IT- *ANYBODY* CAN!
HAH!
SO IT'S THE SPECIAL PLATE, EH?
YOU TOP OL' POPS, KIDDO, AND YOU CAN HAVE A FREE HOUR BEHIND MY COUNTER!

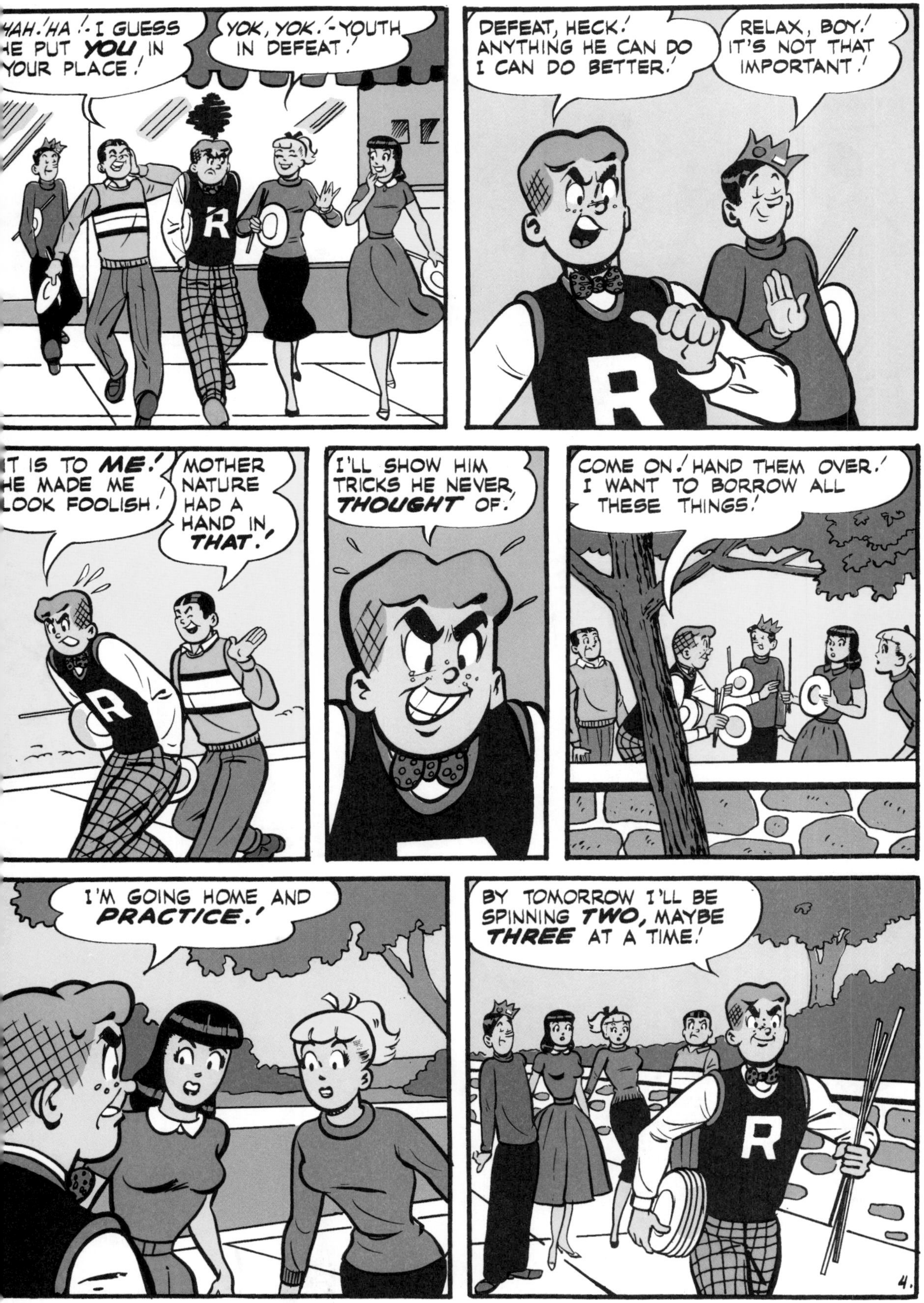
HAH! HA! - I GUESS HE PUT YOU IN YOUR PLACE!
YOK, YOK! - YOUTH IN DEFEAT!
DEFEAT, HECK! ANYTHING HE CAN DO I CAN DO BETTER!
RELAX, BOY! IT'S NOT THAT IMPORTANT!
IT IS TO ME! HE MADE ME LOOK FOOLISH!
MOTHER NATURE HAD A HAND IN THAT!
I'LL SHOW HIM TRICKS HE NEVER THOUGHT OF!
COME ON! HAND THEM OVER! I WANT TO BORROW ALL THESE THINGS!
I'M GOING HOME AND PRACTICE!
BY TOMORROW I'LL BE SPINNING TWO, MAYBE THREE AT A TIME!
4.

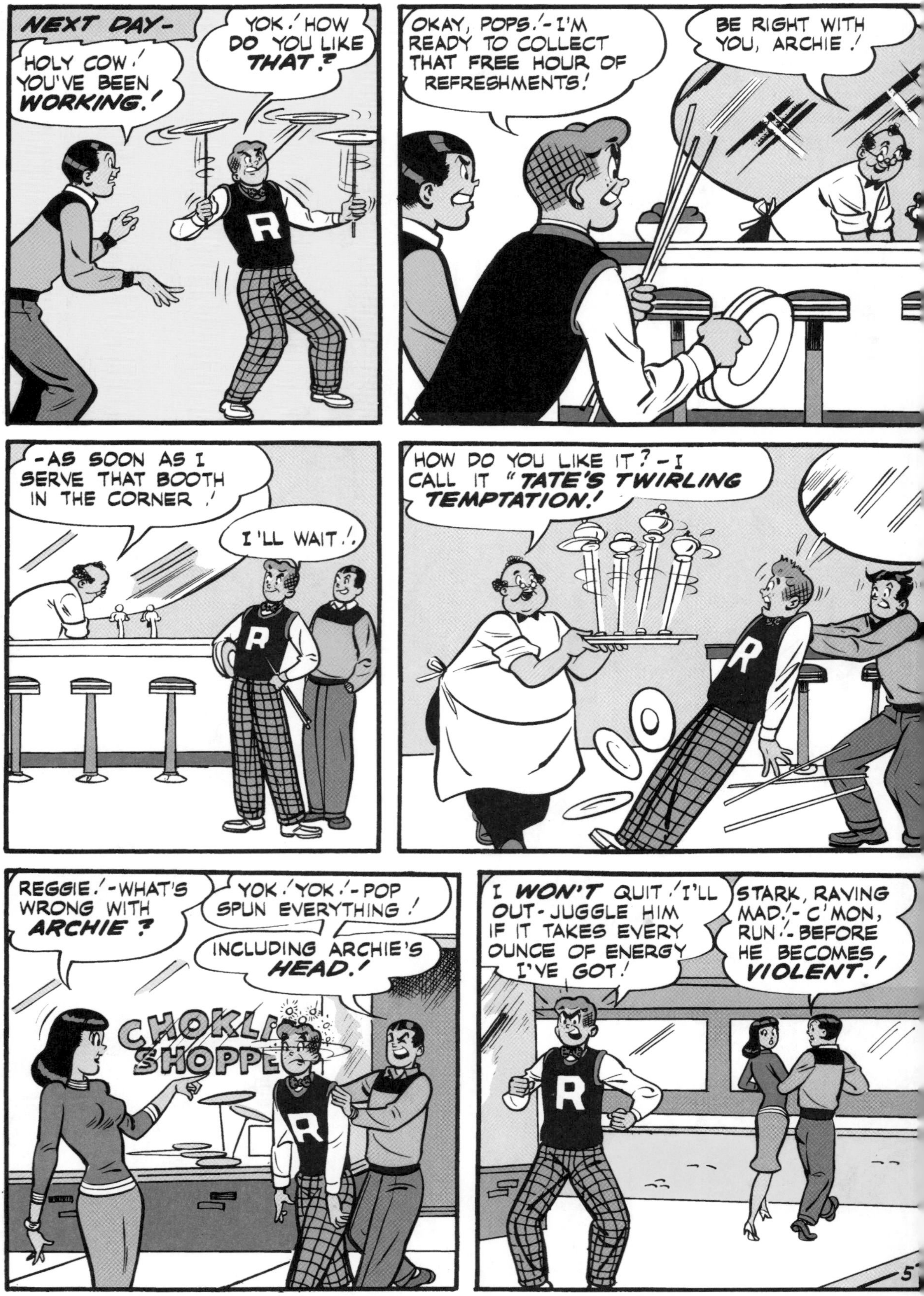
NEXT DAY-
HOLY COW! YOU'VE BEEN WORKING!
YOK! HOW DO YOU LIKE THAT?
OKAY, POPS!- I'M READY TO COLLECT THAT FREE HOUR OF REFRESHMENTS!
BE RIGHT WITH YOU, ARCHIE!
-AS SOON AS I SERVE THAT BOOTH IN THE CORNER!
I'LL WAIT!
HOW DO YOU LIKE IT? - I CALL IT "TATE'S TWIRLING TEMPTATION!"
REGGIE!-WHAT'S WRONG WITH ARCHIE?
YOK! YOK!- POP SPUN EVERYTHING!
INCLUDING ARCHIE'S HEAD!
I WON'T QUIT! I'LL OUT-JUGGLE HIM IF IT TAKES EVERY OUNCE OF ENERGY I'VE GOT!
STARK, RAVING MAD!- C'MON, RUN!- BEFORE HE BECOMES VIOLENT!
5

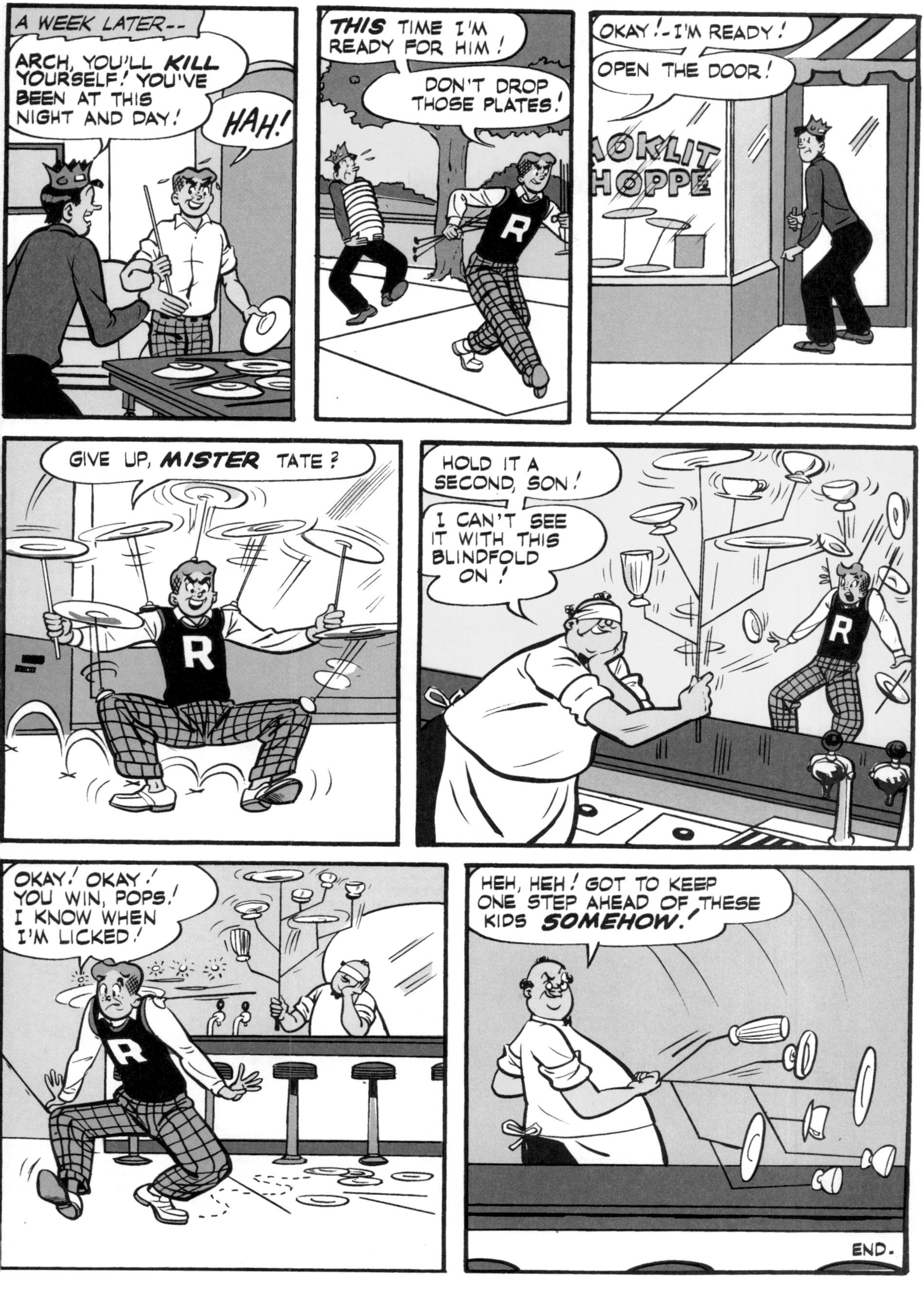
A WEEK LATER--
ARCH, YOU'LL KILL YOURSELF! YOU'VE BEEN AT THIS NIGHT AND DAY!
HAH!
THIS TIME I'M READY FOR HIM!
DON'T DROP THOSE PLATES!
OKAY!-I'M READY!
OPEN THE DOOR!
GIVE UP, MISTER TATE?
HOLD IT A SECOND, SON!
I CAN'T SEE IT WITH THIS BLINDFOLD ON!
OKAY! OKAY! YOU WIN, POPS! I KNOW WHEN I'M LICKED!
HEH, HEH! GOT TO KEEP ONE STEP AHEAD OF THESE KIDS SOMEHOW!
END.

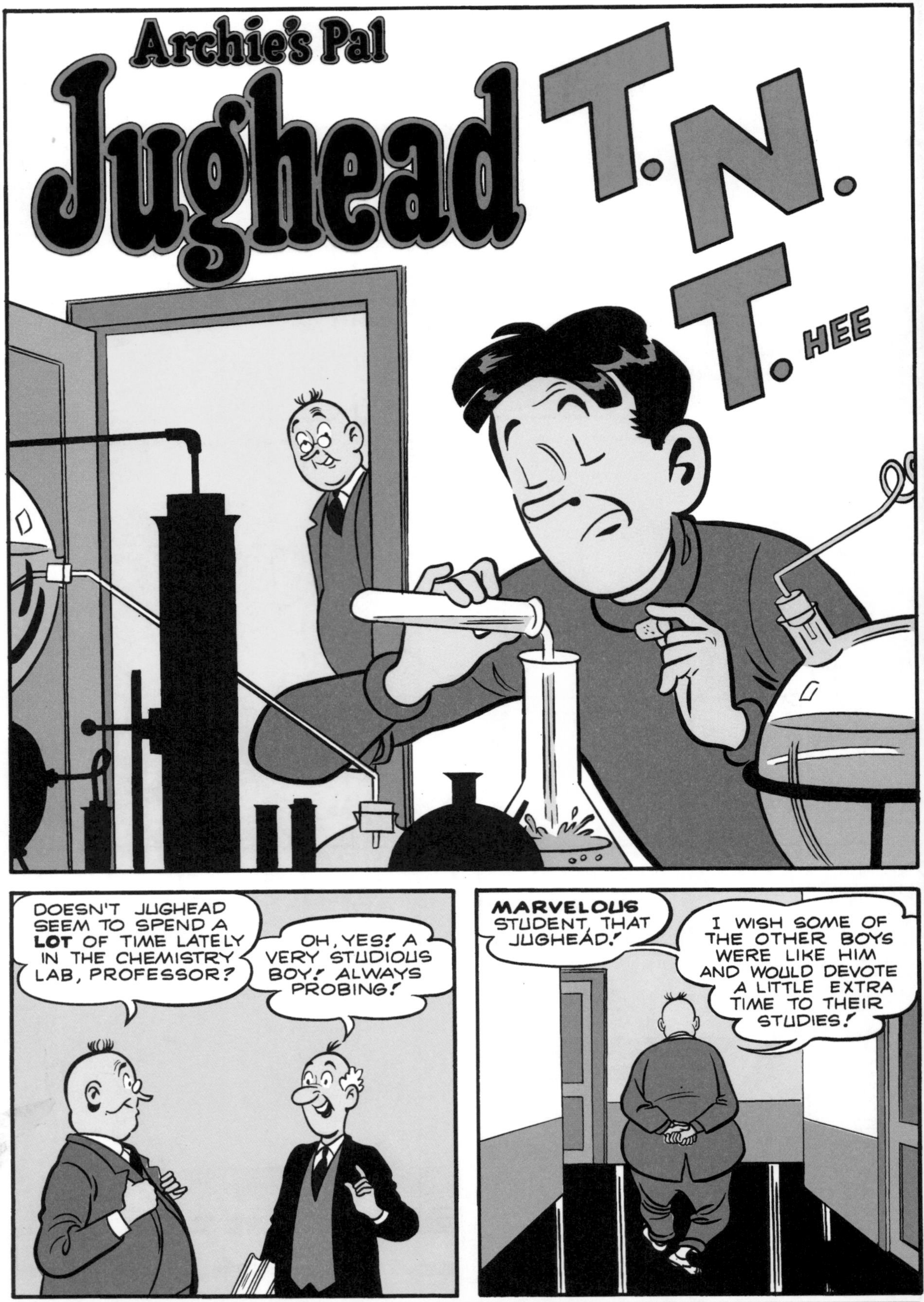
Archie's Pal
Jughead
T.N.T. HEE
DOESN'T JUGHEAD SEEM TO SPEND A **LOT** OF TIME LATELY IN THE CHEMISTRY LAB, PROFESSOR?
OH, YES! A VERY STUDIOUS BOY! ALWAYS PROBING!
MARVELOUS STUDENT, THAT JUGHEAD!
I WISH SOME OF THE OTHER BOYS WERE LIKE HIM AND WOULD DEVOTE A LITTLE EXTRA TIME TO THEIR STUDIES!

ORIGINALLY PRESENTED IN **ARCHIE COMICS #106**, DECEMBER, 1959.

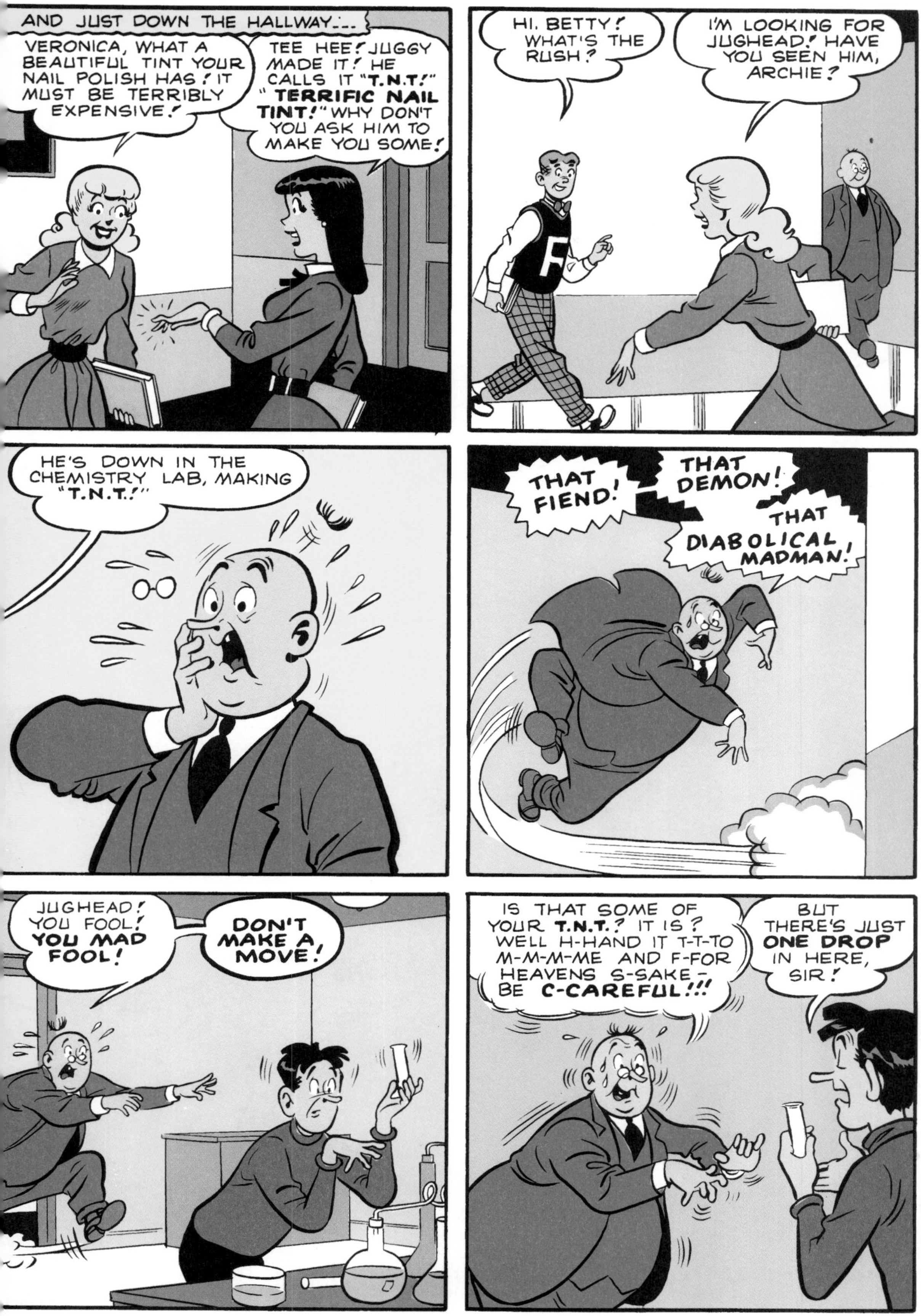
AND JUST DOWN THE HALLWAY...
VERONICA, WHAT A BEAUTIFUL TINT YOUR NAIL POLISH HAS! IT MUST BE TERRIBLY EXPENSIVE!
TEE HEE! JUGGY MADE IT! HE CALLS IT "T.N.T.!" "TERRIFIC NAIL TINT!" WHY DON'T YOU ASK HIM TO MAKE YOU SOME!
HI, BETTY! WHAT'S THE RUSH?
I'M LOOKING FOR JUGHEAD! HAVE YOU SEEN HIM, ARCHIE?
HE'S DOWN IN THE CHEMISTRY LAB, MAKING "T.N.T.!"
THAT FIEND!
THAT DEMON!
THAT DIABOLICAL MADMAN!
JUGHEAD! YOU FOOL! YOU MAD FOOL!
DON'T MAKE A MOVE!
IS THAT SOME OF YOUR T.N.T.? IT IS? WELL H-HAND IT T-T-TO M-M-ME AND F-FOR HEAVENS S-SAKE - BE C-CAREFUL!!!
BUT THERE'S JUST ONE DROP IN HERE, SIR!

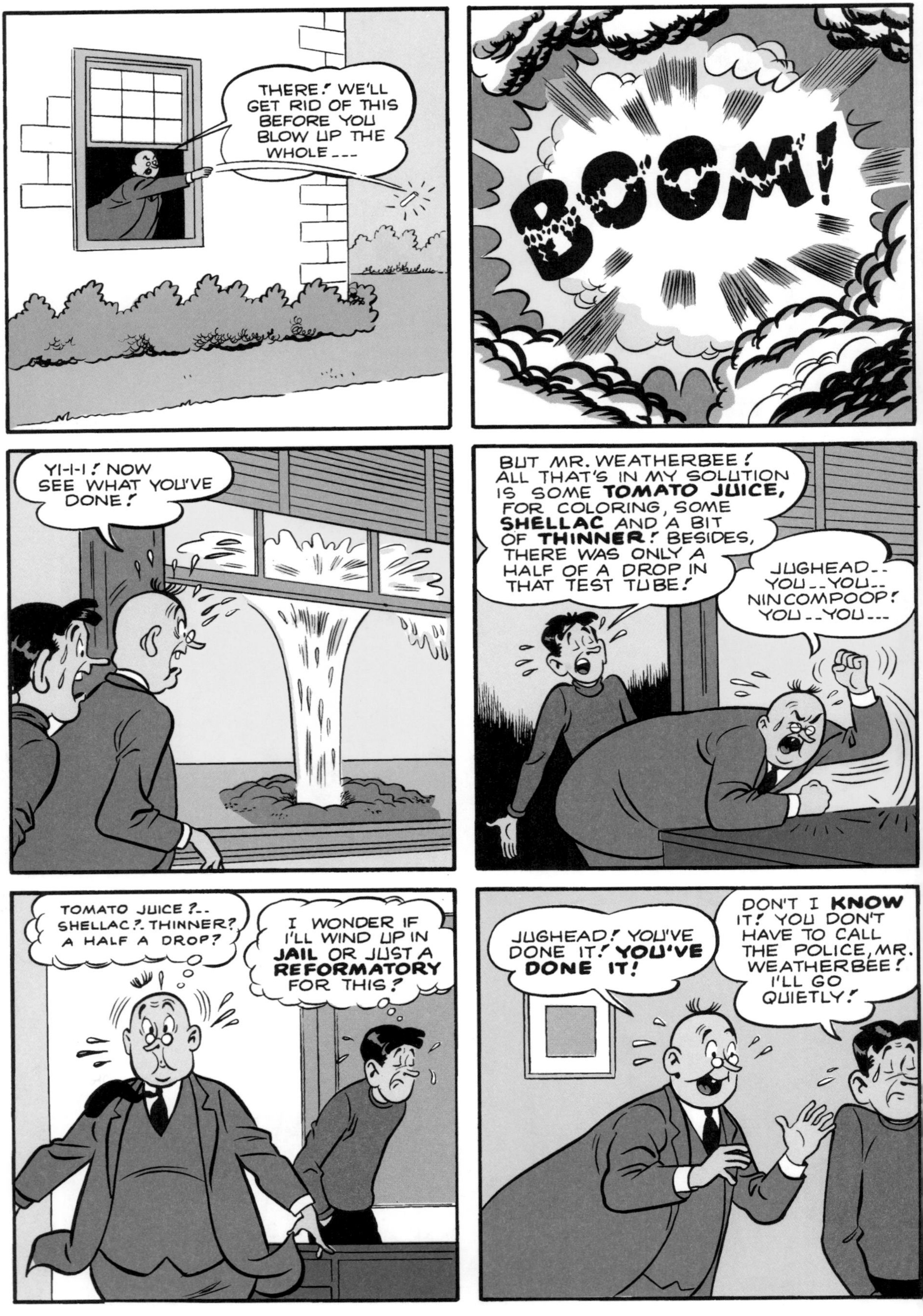
THERE! WE'LL GET RID OF THIS BEFORE YOU BLOW UP THE WHOLE---
BOOM!
YI-I-I! NOW SEE WHAT YOU'VE DONE!
BUT MR. WEATHERBEE! ALL THAT'S IN MY SOLUTION IS SOME TOMATO JUICE, FOR COLORING, SOME SHELLAC AND A BIT OF THINNER! BESIDES, THERE WAS ONLY A HALF OF A DROP IN THAT TEST TUBE!
JUGHEAD-- YOU--YOU-- NINCOMPOOP! YOU--YOU---
TOMATO JUICE?-- SHELLAC?-THINNER? A HALF A DROP?
I WONDER IF I'LL WIND UP IN JAIL OR JUST A REFORMATORY FOR THIS?
JUGHEAD! YOU'VE DONE IT! YOU'VE DONE IT!
DON'T I KNOW IT! YOU DON'T HAVE TO CALL THE POLICE, MR. WEATHERBEE! I'LL GO QUIETLY!

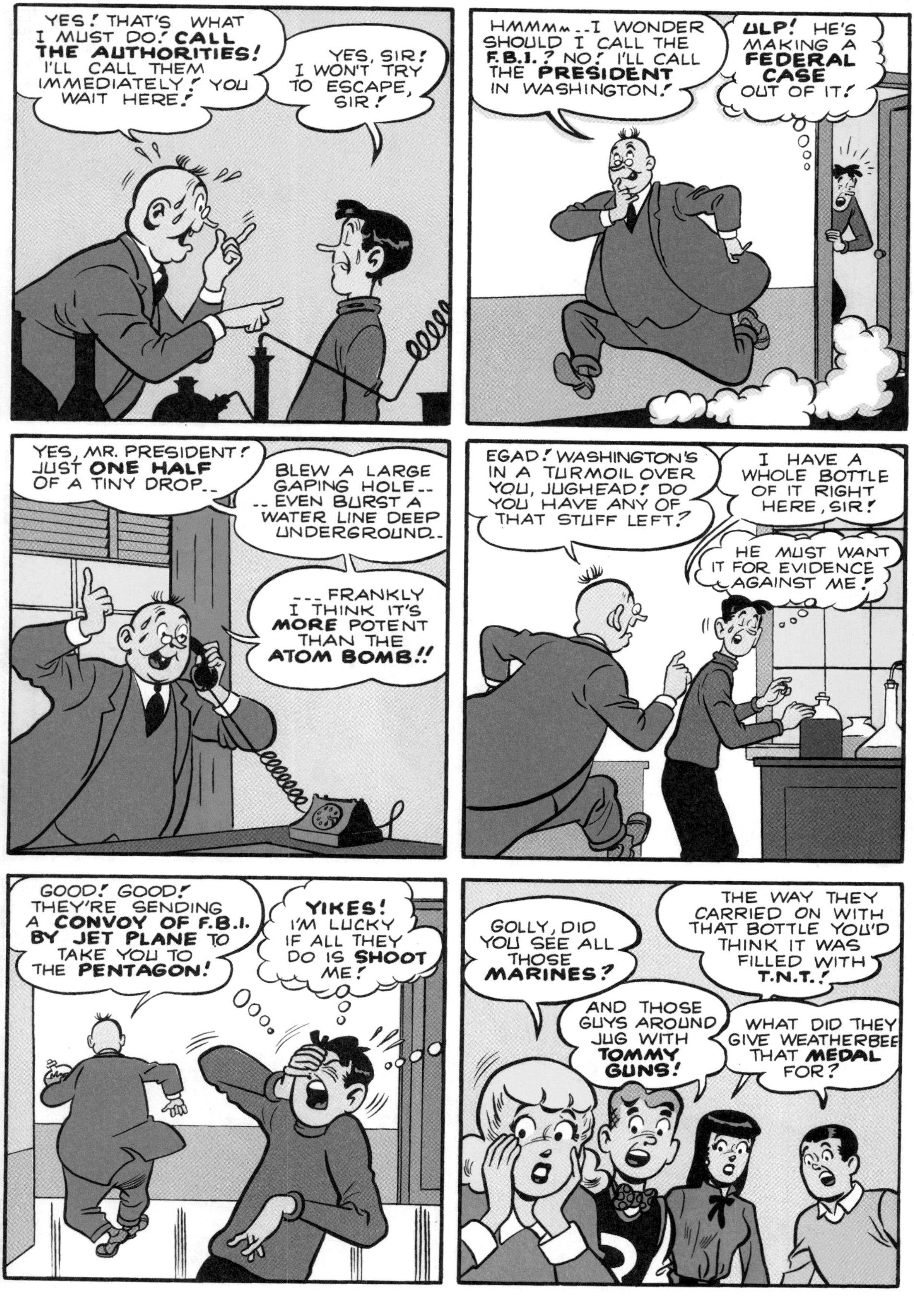
YES! THAT'S WHAT I MUST DO! CALL THE AUTHORITIES! I'LL CALL THEM IMMEDIATELY! YOU WAIT HERE!
YES, SIR! I WON'T TRY TO ESCAPE, SIR!
HMMMM..I WONDER SHOULD I CALL THE F.B.I.? NO! I'LL CALL THE PRESIDENT IN WASHINGTON!
ULP! HE'S MAKING A FEDERAL CASE OUT OF IT!
YES, MR. PRESIDENT! JUST ONE HALF OF A TINY DROP..
BLEW A LARGE GAPING HOLE.. ..EVEN BURST A WATER LINE DEEP UNDERGROUND..
...FRANKLY I THINK IT'S MORE POTENT THAN THE ATOM BOMB!!
EGAD! WASHINGTON'S IN A TURMOIL OVER YOU, JUGHEAD! DO YOU HAVE ANY OF THAT STUFF LEFT?
I HAVE A WHOLE BOTTLE OF IT RIGHT HERE, SIR!
HE MUST WANT IT FOR EVIDENCE AGAINST ME!
GOOD! GOOD! THEY'RE SENDING A CONVOY OF F.B.I. BY JET PLANE TO TAKE YOU TO THE PENTAGON!
YIKES! I'M LUCKY IF ALL THEY DO IS SHOOT ME!
GOLLY, DID YOU SEE ALL THOSE MARINES?
THE WAY THEY CARRIED ON WITH THAT BOTTLE YOU'D THINK IT WAS FILLED WITH T.N.T.!
AND THOSE GUYS AROUND JUG WITH TOMMY GUNS!
WHAT DID THEY GIVE WEATHERBEE THAT MEDAL FOR?

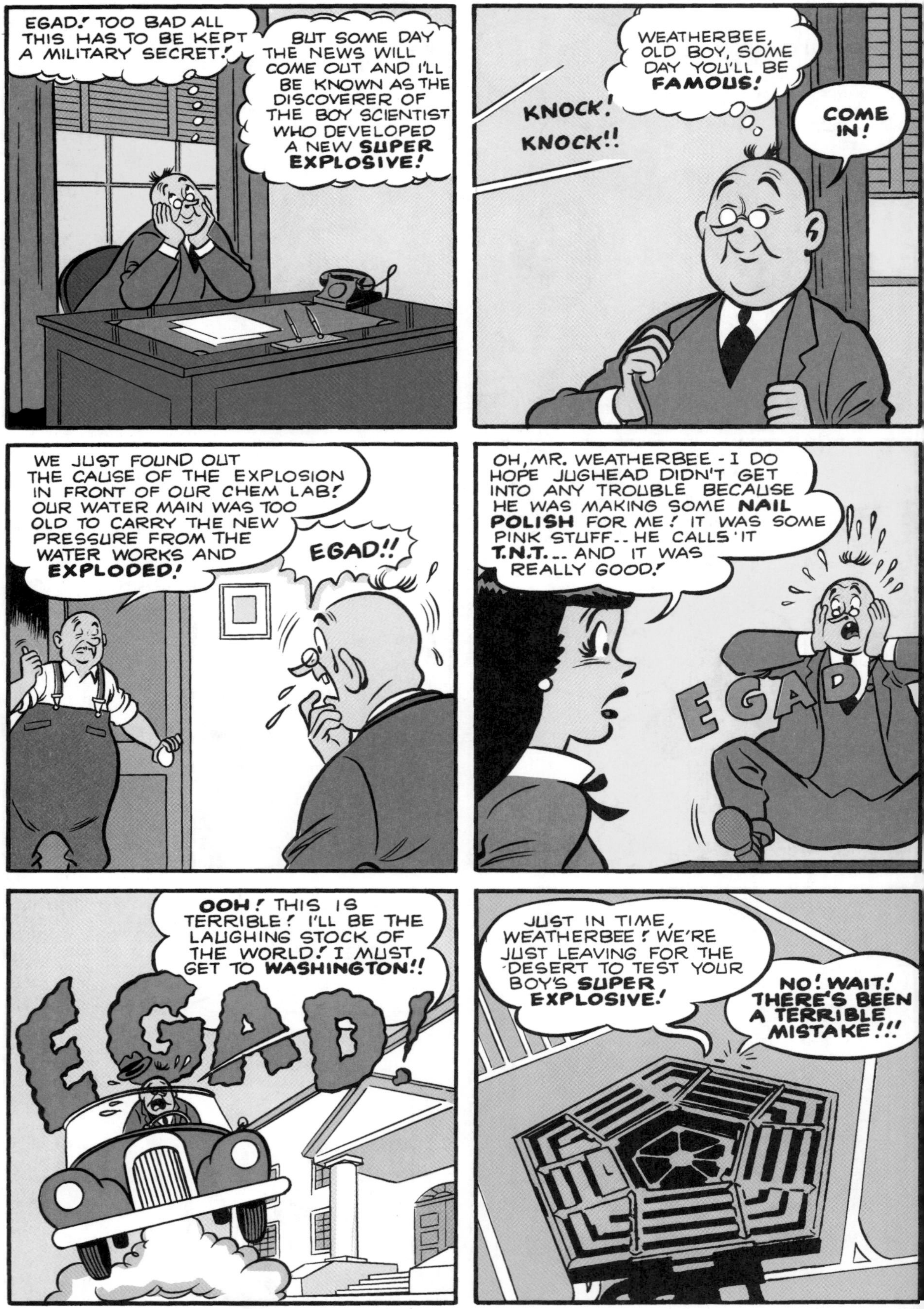
EGAD! TOO BAD ALL THIS HAS TO BE KEPT A MILITARY SECRET!
BUT SOME DAY THE NEWS WILL COME OUT AND I'LL BE KNOWN AS THE DISCOVERER OF THE BOY SCIENTIST WHO DEVELOPED A NEW **SUPER EXPLOSIVE!**
WEATHERBEE, OLD BOY, SOME DAY YOU'LL BE **FAMOUS!**
KNOCK! KNOCK!!
COME IN!
WE JUST FOUND OUT THE CAUSE OF THE EXPLOSION IN FRONT OF OUR CHEM LAB! OUR WATER MAIN WAS TOO OLD TO CARRY THE NEW PRESSURE FROM THE WATER WORKS AND **EXPLODED!**
EGAD!!
OH, MR. WEATHERBEE - I DO HOPE JUGHEAD DIDN'T GET INTO ANY TROUBLE BECAUSE HE WAS MAKING SOME **NAIL POLISH** FOR ME! IT WAS SOME PINK STUFF.. HE CALLS IT **T.N.T.** .. AND IT WAS REALLY GOOD!
EGAD
OOH! THIS IS TERRIBLE! I'LL BE THE LAUGHING STOCK OF THE WORLD! I MUST GET TO **WASHINGTON!!**
EGAD!
JUST IN TIME, WEATHERBEE! WE'RE JUST LEAVING FOR THE DESERT TO TEST YOUR BOY'S **SUPER EXPLOSIVE!**
NO! WAIT! THERE'S BEEN A TERRIBLE MISTAKE!!!

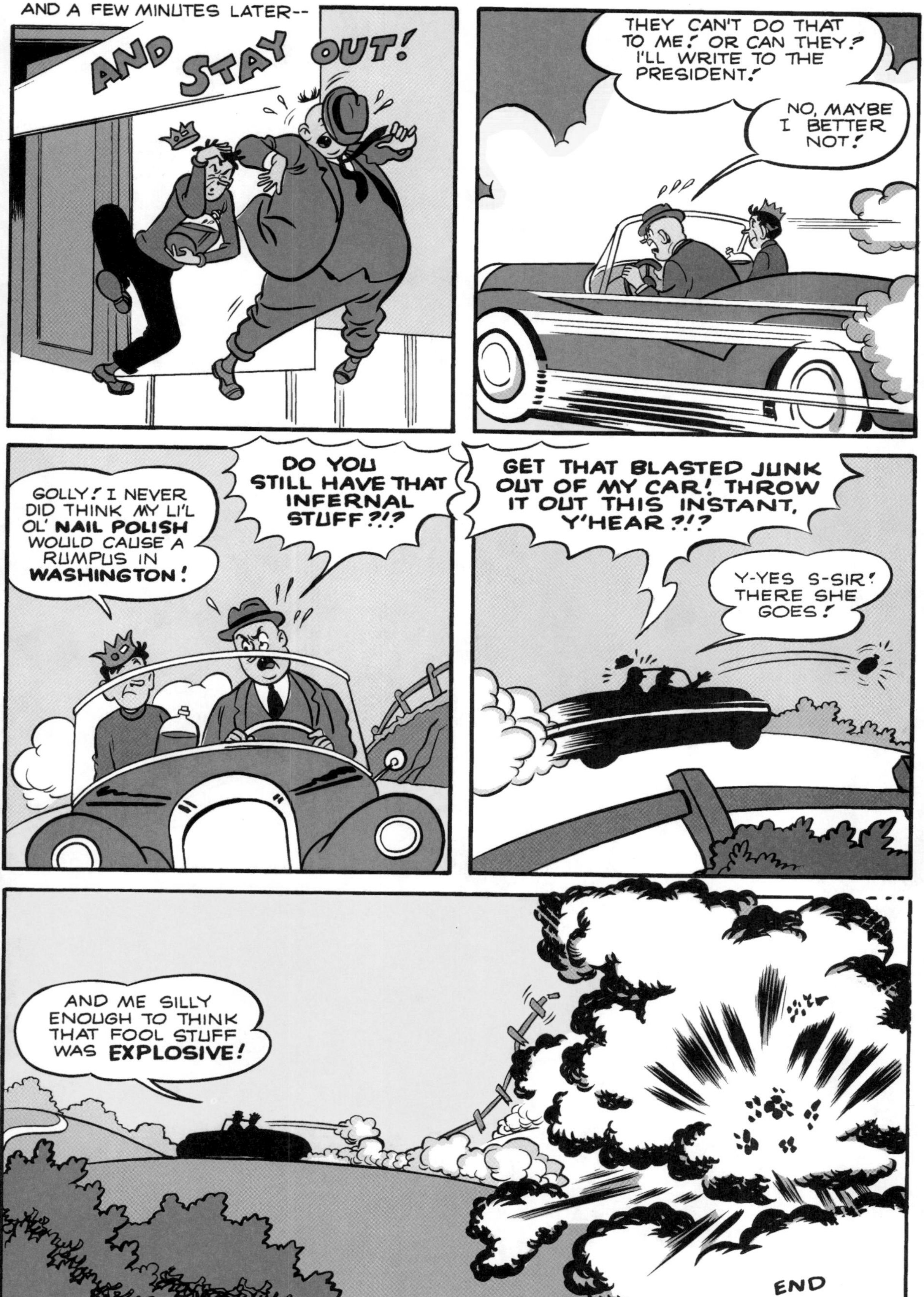
AND A FEW MINUTES LATER--
AND STAY OUT!
THEY CAN'T DO THAT TO ME! OR CAN THEY? I'LL WRITE TO THE PRESIDENT!
NO, MAYBE I BETTER NOT!
GOLLY! I NEVER DID THINK MY LI'L OL' NAIL POLISH WOULD CAUSE A RUMPUS IN WASHINGTON!
DO YOU STILL HAVE THAT INFERNAL STUFF?!?
GET THAT BLASTED JUNK OUT OF MY CAR! THROW IT OUT THIS INSTANT, Y'HEAR?!?
Y-YES S-SIR! THERE SHE GOES!
AND ME SILLY ENOUGH TO THINK THAT FOOL STUFF WAS EXPLOSIVE!
END

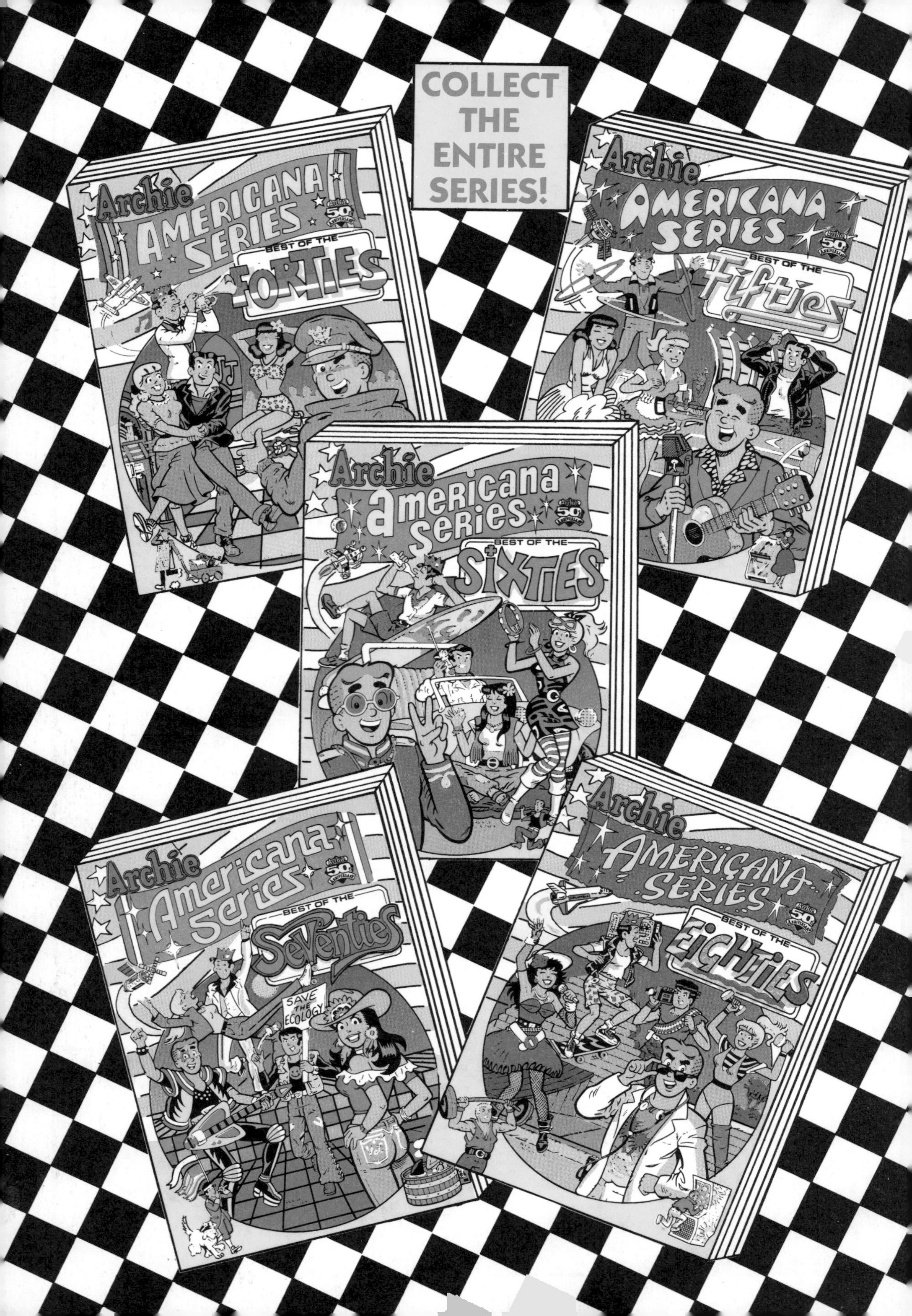

COLLECT THE ENTIRE SERIES!
Archie Americana Series
Best of the Forties
Archie Americana Series
Best of the Fifties
Archie Americana Series
Best of the Sixties
Archie Americana Series
Best of the Seventies
SAVE THE ECOLOGY
Archie Americana Series
Best of the Eighties